EXPLORING
THE TAROT

EXPLORING THE TAROT

by Carl Japikse

ARIEL PRESS

Columbus, Ohio

This book is made possible by a gift
to the Publications Fund of Light
by Marilyn and Richard McCraney

ISBN 0-89804-043-4

Table of Contents

EXPLORING THE TAROT

TO
THE FOOL

CHAPTER ONE

Questions and Answers

This is a book about questions and answers. There are many things that differentiate human beings from advanced animals—the ability to make and use tools, the capacity to think, and the ability to be aware of our own selfhood, to name a few. Another important difference is the ability to formulate questions and seek the answers. Dogs and cats have the capacity to know when it is time to be fed, but they lack the ability to ask us: "Are you going to be home tonight when I am hungry?" They just assume that we will be. With people, it is different. The ability to ask questions gives us the capacity to probe our universe and to explore its unseen dimensions, whether we are a small child or a mature adult. Tell a child not to cross the street and the child will wonder why he or she should not do exactly that. Is the danger in the street itself? Or does it lurk in the shadows of the homes which sit on the other side? These are questions that require answers, and if we are unwilling to provide them, the child will eventually resort to his or her own means of exploration to find them.

As adults, our questions turn to other issues. Why can't I find happiness? Why have I been passed over for a promotion at work? Why don't my kids respect me? What am I doing with my life, anyway? Many of us ignore these questions, and never pursue the answers—at least until life forces us to pay more serious attention. A crisis occurs—a loved one dies, we lose our job, or our spouse leaves—and at last we tackle the questions we should have been asking. More often than not, however, we do not come up with satisfactory answers. Why? It is not because the answers do not exist. It is primarily because we do not know how to go about finding them. We lack the tools to explore life mentally and find the hidden secrets we long to discover.

It is not that the tools do not exist, but that the average person is unfamiliar with them. We are not taught about these tools in public school—or even at college. If we find them and learn to use them, we have to do so on our own. They are not tools that give us ready-made answers, like a textbook, or do our thinking for us. They are tools that train the mind to understand our circumstances and experiences. They enable us to find the answers to our questions about life. The I Ching, the Chinese Book of Changes, is one such tool. Intelligently used, astrology can be another. The Nordic Runes are also an excellent tool for understanding life.

At the top of the list, however, is the Tarot. It is one of the most complete and versatile systems for exploring life, in both its inner and outer dimensions, ever devised.

The Tarot is a set of seventy-eight cards. Twenty-two of the cards form what is known as the major arcana. They are numbered zero through twenty-one and each has a title and a symbolic illustration to go with it, such as The Fool, The World, The Star, or The High Priestess. Fifty-six of the cards form what is known as the minor arcana. This arcana is subdivided into four suits of fourteen cards each, numbered ace through ten, Page, Knight, Queen, and King. The four suits are Pentacles, Cups, Rods, and Swords. It is from this minor arcana of the Tarot that our modern deck of playing cards was derived. The Pentacles have become Diamonds, the Cups have become Hearts, the Rods have become Clubs, and the Swords have become Spades. In addition, the Page and Knight cards have been compressed into a single card, the Jack or Knave.

In response to a specific question, a number of cards from the

4

Tarot deck are laid out in a pattern. The symbols on each card are then interpreted, and the combination of insights gained from this interpretation generates a deeper understanding of the basic issues and forces at work.

The origins of the Tarot are lost in time. Extant decks can be traced back as far as the fourteenth century in Europe, but references to the Tarot can be found in even earlier records. Many experts believe the modern Tarot descended from Egyptian sources. According to one source, for example, the twenty-two cards in the major arcana correspond to hieroglyphic paintings found in Egyptian temples used for initiation. They were arranged by pairs, each part representing half of a needed lesson. It is thought, therefore, that our modern Tarot has its roots at least in part in the mystery schools of ancient Egypt. The actual genealogy of the Tarot is relatively unimportant, however. We can deduce its origins simply by studying the nature of its symbolism. The Tarot clearly owes an enormous debt to the Kabalah, the great philosophical system of Jewish mysticism. It is also heavily steeped in alchemical, astrological, and numerological symbolism.

The one thing that can be stated for certain is that it was not developed by gypsy fortune tellers, even though for many long centuries it seemed to be used primarily by such demi-monde characters. The Tarot is a remarkable, complex system of esoteric symbols that was developed originally by initiates of the Western mystery schools for the purpose of training the mind to recognize and interact with specific forces of the Higher Self and the invisible dimensions of life. The symbols eventually took the form of a deck of cards, making the symbols easier to use. The deck also gives the symbols a form of protection. The average person, picking up a Tarot deck, will misconstrue the cards for a simple game (or reject them as "the devil's plaything") instead of recognizing them as a powerful tool of inquiry.

In dealing with the Tarot, it is important to understand the full meaning of this last statement. There are many levels within the Tarot. There are the physical, tangible cards themselves. There is the "fortune telling" Tarot and the intellectual Tarot. And there is the Tarot of the initiates—the Real Tarot, if it may be called that.

The physical Tarot is the most varied and the least important. There have always been a wide range of Tarot decks; many of them are similar, some are unique, even bizarre. With the recent surge of interest in the Tarot, there has been a sudden influx in the appearance of new Tarot decks. Now, in addition to such standard decks as the Rider deck and the Aquarian Tarot, there are feminist Tarot decks, witchcraft Tarot decks, Tantric Yoga Tarot decks, and American Indian Tarot decks. About the only kind of Tarot deck that has not yet been developed is an "aliens from the third moon of Jupiter" deck!

Some of these decks are nicely illustrated; many of them are crudely drawn and even more crudely printed. But it must be understood that the physical cards are not the actual Tarot—they are just symbols. They have no inherent value in and of themselves; their only function is to help the user to discern the Real Tarot behind the symbols. Some Tarot decks do not do this at all; others do it very effectively.

The "fortune telling" Tarot is the first subtle level beyond the physical cards. It is the collective thought-form that has been built up around the use of the Tarot by gypsy fortune tellers and "readers." It sees the Tarot only as a guide to the most banal kinds of questions—the kind that are typically associated with fortune telling. The standard interpretations given the cards are also part of this fortune telling Tarot. If the Ten of Swords appears in a spread, for example, the usual practitioner of the Tarot will interpret it as a sign of suffering and ruin. If it appears upside down, the reader will generally ascribe a meaning of profit and power. It is a highly simplistic, almost childish approach to a profound system. None-theless, a great many of the people using the Tarot never go beyond this fortune telling level. Most books and guides to interpreting the Tarot are entrenched in this level of the Tarot as well.

The intellectual Tarot is discovered by fewer people, but it is not much more profound than the fortune telling Tarot, even though it seems to be. This is the level of the Tarot tapped by esoteric students who love to pore over dusty documents and research arcane truths as though they were a complex cake recipe. They will diligently study the parallels between the Tarot and the Kabalah; they will cross reference aspects of the Tarot with elements of the I Ching or astrology; and they will become quite learned in the ins and outs of the Tarot. But they are still not tapping the power and vitality of the Tarot—the life essence of this remarkable system. They still do not know how to use the Tarot as a tool to explore life. Instead, they get caught in the trap of examining and dissecting the Tarot itself.

The Real Tarot is much more sublime than these outer levels. It is a system of archetypal forces which exists within the mind of God, and can be readily known by human intelligence, if we apply ourselves correctly. The purpose of the physical Tarot is to codify a set of symbols which, when correctly used, leads us reliably to a deeper understanding of these inner forces and how they affect human life. The Tarot, therefore, is a system which is designed to unveil to us the inner workings of life. It is a tool for exploring the mind of God and how It relates to the average human being.

For this reason, we need to approach the Tarot with the intent of learning to use it to harness the Real Tarot to answer our questions about life. We can set our sights lower, of course, and use it for fortune telling or as an intellectual exercise, but we will get exactly what we invest, no more, no less. Fortune telling systems for using the Tarot may seem simpler to learn, but they are just pale imitations of the Real Tarot. We do not need to settle for anything less than the highest!

This is good advice in the very first step of using the Tarot—picking a deck. With so many decks to choose from, it may seem bewildering to have to make a selection. But it is not nearly as difficult as it seems. Most decks are steeped in the fortune telling level of the Tarot, and are so tainted by them that they are impossible to use in any more serious endeavor. A deck which actually has words like "misfortune" or "gain" printed right on the cards of the minor arcana should be disqualified immediately. Just so, a deck that seeks to present a specialized point of view is equally unsuitable. A deck which includes only female figures may appeal to someone with a goddess complex, for instance, but it is incapable of producing balanced answers to serious questions about life. Both male and female forces are active in life, and any system which unilaterally excludes one or the other will be unworkable.

In my experience, the two best decks are the Rider deck, which was developed a century ago by A.E. Waite and is traditionally recognized as the esoteric standard, and the Aquarian deck, a more recent upstart designed by artist David Palladini. I have used them both extensively, but have come to favor the Aquarian deck. For one thing, the artwork is much superior, but this is just a minor consideration. The major reason is that it never ceases to reveal to me ever more profound levels of insight and understanding. And because it has been in print for only a relatively few years, it is not as polluted by worn-out traditions as other, older decks are. So it is easier to use.

Throughout this book, I will refer to the Aquarian deck as my standard reference. All illustrations are taken from the Aquarian Tarot as well. This is not to say that you should not use other Tarot decks. For one thing, a new deck may come along someday that will surpass the Aquarian Tarot. For another, you may respond more favorably to another deck, for some good reason of your own. I own many Tarot decks myself, and frequently compare them with each other, as a means of enriching the interpretations of the deck I use. What is not included on each card, after all, may be just as significant as what is.

Do not limit yourself in your explorations of the inner life. But when you make choices, such as the choice of a Tarot deck, be sure to choose wisely, intelligently. Do not just succumb to the lure of simplistic interpretations. Set your sights higher. Take the time to choose a deck that will lead you to the Real Tarot, reliably, time after time.

The purpose of working with the Tarot, after all, is that it is an outstanding tool for exploring life mentally—for answering our questions. Occasionally we may want to know the specific outcome of a specific question. But life is going to reveal these answers to us soon enough anyway, if we just wait for them. The far more important questions are the ones about our selfhood. How can I increase my enjoyment of the work I do? What steps can I take to improve my marriage? What is the meaning of a specific event that has happened? How can I learn to get along better with friends and associates? What lesson in growth do I need to concentrate on most at this stage of my life?

The Tarot is the perfect tool for answering these questions. With skill, each of us can learn to use the Tarot to explore the hidden dimensions of our own life—and perhaps the lives of others as well. It is an important asset in pursuing an examined life. Properly used, it can help us become truly wise.

CHAPTER TWO

Divine Archetypes

In order to understand and use the Tarot properly, it is important to understand the system of divine archetypes it is meant to reveal. The Tarot, after all, is a tool of divination, which means that it is designed to reveal the presence of the divine in our life. Divination perceives the divine and makes It accessible to us.

The divine archetypes are the basic blueprints or patterns from which life as we know it has been created. As such, they should not be confused with Jungian archetypes. The great psychologist Carl Jung used the term archetype to refer to commonly recurring, manmade symbols. In his terminology, for example, the cross would be an archetype for suffering. Obviously, divine archetypes differ from Jungian archetypes in many important ways. For one thing, they are made by God, not man. Second, they exist within the mind of God, not within the mind of mankind, although they can be known and used by men and women. Third, they are pure abstract patterns, not images or symbols.

Plato was describing divine archetypes when he coined the word "Idea." To him, an idea was not something that occurs in the mind of a man or a woman, but a universal truth or pattern existing at the level of timeless essence. Thinking, therefore—to Plato—was a process of attuning the mind to interact with these timeless, abstract Ideas. It had absolutely nothing to do with the ordinary process of analysis and speculation that we normally refer to as "thinking" today. It was a dynamic process that penetrated to the

11

core of the divine archetypes or timeless "Ideas," not just to comprehend them but also to harness their immense power for practical application. Obviously, both the words "idea" and "thinking" have been severely devalued since Plato's time.

It is not just Plato who recognized and wrote about divine archetypes. In the seventh book of her great poem, *Aurora Leigh*, Elizabeth Barrett Browning states:

> We stand here, we,
> If genuine artists, witnessing for God's
> Complete, consummate, undivided work;
> That every natural flower which grows on earth
> Implies a flower upon the spiritual side,
> Substantial, archetypal, all aglow
> With blossoming causes.

To Browning, it was the work of the artist to discern the beauty, design, and force of the archetype and so embody it in his or her work that God's glory would stand unveiled for all less artistic people to see. She understood that the world of archetypes was "all aglow with blossoming causes," and therefore the substance from which everything on earth has been generated. "Art's the witness of what Is behind this show," she declares, adding:

> We, whose spirit-sense is somewhat cleared,
> May catch at something of the bloom and breath—
> Too vaguely apprehended, though indeed
> Still apprehended, consciously or not,
> And still transferred to picture, music, verse,
> For thrilling audient and beholding souls
> By signs and touches which are known to souls.
> How known, they know not—why, they cannot find,

So straight call out on genius, say, "A man
Produced this," when much rather they should say,
"Tis insight and he saw this." Thus is Art
Self-magnified in magnifying a truth
Which, fully recognized, would change the world.

Divine archetypes are the patterns from which all life springs, the truths which we are meant to magnify in our own lives and thereby change our personal worlds, and by extension, the world about us. As such, they are the heart of the inspiration that the genius taps when he or she creates a work of art, builds a new machine, or discovers a new scientific principle. They are the soul of the revelation that the saint or visionary taps when he or she "hears the word of God." They are the essence of divine vitality that the true leader taps as he or she guides others to new achievements. But they are more than just patterns of creation, sources of inspiration. They are living forces, filled with the highest quality of power and energy. The person who learns to tap divine archetypes is able to act dynamically in life and achieve seemingly impossible goals, because he or she is driven by the impetus of archetypal life.

It is not always easy to conceive of archetypes as living forces, but it is crucial to an understanding of the Tarot. The symbols of the Tarot each represent an archetypal force as it affects humanity. They seem static, because the pictorial images of these symbols are frozen in time on a two-dimensional card. But these archetypes that have been portrayed as symbols are nevertheless moving, living forces, and we must adjust our thinking so that we always regard them in this way. Otherwise, we will fall short of tapping into the dynamic power of the Tarot.

This point can best be illustrated in specific examples. Truth, for example, is an archetypal force. We tend to think of truth as something static, defined by facts. Before testifying in court, we are asked to "tell the truth, the whole truth, and nothing but the truth," as if the truth were something that came in a box and could be measured, weighed, photographed, and catalogued. But the archetypal reality that is Truth is abstract, formless. It has no beginning nor end. The truth does not stand still for our convenience, nor the niceties of jurisprudence. Facts that are true today are often false tomorrow. But just because they are going to become false tomorrow does not make them any less true today. To understand the archetypal force of Truth, we must stop defining truth in terms of facts. Facts may at times embody portions of truth, but they can never embody the whole of it. This is why it is so easy to distort the truth with statistics, and why the Bible can be quoted to prove two contradictory points of view. The literal facts and words are being used to obscure truth, not reveal it.

In order to understand Truth, we must view it as an archetypal force. Facts, words, and statistics which reveal archetypal Truth can be labeled "true," although we must always keep in mind that they may only be true temporarily. Tomorrow, a new set of facts, words, or statistics may do a better job. By the same token, facts, words, and statistics that do not serve the spirit of Truth should be labeled false, even though they may occasionally seem to be true literally. Being out of step with the living force of archetypal reality, they are therefore false, not to be trusted.

Peace is another archetypal force. The average person thinks of peace as a state of rest, a state of inactivity. But inactivity is actually alien to the archetypal reality of peace. Divine peace is a most dynamic energy, which courses throughout the planet like a mighty river. (Indeed, the Bible describes it in precisely these terms.) As it sweeps into our life, this river stirs up inconsistencies, resistance, and conflict. But as we face the resulting chaos and strive to deal with it, the living force of peace helps us impose order, purpose, and design, until we have harnessed the raw forces of disorder and created peace. The ideal demonstration of peace, indeed, would be the capacity of a leader to remain poised, wise, and active in the face of chaos or disaster—and to impose his or her sense of poioo and self control upon the situation itself, thereby bringing it to a peaceful conclusion.

The measure of our maturity and enlightenment as a human being is the degree to which we express these and other archetypal forces in our own lives. An intellectual understanding of these divine forces is not enough, nor is pious devotion; we must have the skill and ability to translate the power and benevolence of these abstract qualities into our own self-expression. We must learn not just to tap the archetypes of life, but also to become a conduit through which they can pour with full force and vigor.

Many people know the value of goodwill, for instance. They may honor it, pray for it, and proclaim the necessity of it. Yet their contact with the *archetypal reality* of goodwill may be more imaginary than real, unless they reveal the force of goodwill daily through the way they treat others, the service they perform, and their reverence for life.

Once we comprehend this basic characteristic of divine archetypes, we have set the stage for transforming our lives. It is no longer necessary to fear impoverishment, because we are in touch with the divine force of abundance and can pour it into the work we do. It is no longer necessary to fear loneliness, because we are in touch with the divine force of community and can saturate our relationships with it. It is no longer necessary to be embarrassed by failures or gaffes, because we are in touch with the divine force of grace and can fill our awareness with it whenever needed. It is no longer necessary to fear a loss of inspiration or guidance, because our talents are nourished by the divine forces of wisdom and genius.

We are meant to live in the light of these divine archetypes, not in the shadows of our personal confusion, depression, separativeness, and self-centeredness. There are times we must struggle with life, of course, and wonder why we have taken on certain responsibilities, been plagued by certain restrictions, and so on. When life challenges us, it is good to question the meaning of events and the purpose of our struggles. But the questions do have answers—the questions are designed to lead us into a greater recognition of the joy, wisdom, and love of the divine archetypes, and to inspire us to learn to harness them and express them in our own work and private life.

This is why the Tarot can be such a remarkable tool. Being a system of symbols that reveal archetypal life, when correctly used, the Tarot can help us not only become familiar with these archetypal forces but also learn to interact with them more effectively. In addition, it can give us detailed answers to the kinds of questions we typically ask when confronted by the confusing elements of life.

Other than the writings of Dr. Robert R. Leichtman and myself (primarily in *The Art of Living* and *The Life of Spirit* essay series), very little has been written about the divine archetypes and their nature. It is nice to know that peace or love is an archetypal reality, but the common assumptions that most people make about peace and love have little to do with the genuine archetypal force. There are a few passages here and there in the great writings of the world that point us in the right direction, but for the most part there are few authoritative sources to turn to. Even the Bible provides only brief snippets, rather than full-blown descriptions. So we must be prepared to do our research on our own. In this regard, the Tarot can be a big help. We can use the Tarot, for example, to ask questions such as:

What is the nature of divine goodwill? What changes must I make in my character in order to express goodwill? How can I learn to express greater goodwill through my work? How can I learn to treat so-and-so with greater goodwill? What will be the impact of expressing goodwill on my own character?

What are the elements of divine harmony? In what ways can I learn to cooperate with divine harmony? How can I express harmony to others? What is the impact of harmony on consciousness?

What is the divine essence of brotherhood? What does it mean to act in harmony with the force of brotherhood? What can I do to contribute to the unfoldment of brotherhood?

As we use the Tarot to ask these and similar questions, we are embarking on a wonderful adventure—an exploration of the inner side of life. We are setting sail toward the realm of spiritual archetypes, with the wind at our back. Of course, we are not just limited to inquiring about archetypes. There are many other kinds of questions we can ask in our exploration of the inner life:

Why do people fear death? What is the significance of death in the life process? What archetypal forces govern death?

What is the impact of prayer? How are prayers answered?

What are the underlying causes of my problems with ill health?

What is the impact of anger on human consciousness?

What is the best way to instill a desire to learn in a child?

The questions we ask can even be quite specific, tailored to our individual needs:

How can I best express goodwill in dealing with the obnoxious person I have to work with?

What do I need to do in order to enrich my marriage?

What must I emphasize in raising my children?

What subconscious forces do I need to learn to control and direct more constructively?

The actual question is not too important; what counts is knowing that whatever the question is, it has an answer. Whatever mess we happen to find ourself in, there is an archetypal force we are meant to discover and harness. There is an ideal plan, constructed of archetypal reality, that we can invoke, tap, and apply. If we use the Tarot with this understanding, then we will never get bogged down in the superficial levels of the symbols; we will never succumb to the fortune telling thought-forms which pollute it. We will always be plugged into the Real Tarot, the Tarot that exists in the abstract, archetypal realms of essence and cause.

In the beginning, of course, there will be no real assurance that we are, in fact, plugged into the Real Tarot. Using the Tarot will seem awkward, difficult, perhaps even overwhelming—not much different than learning to ride a bike or swim. But as we develop expertise, our confidence will grow. And so will our intuition. Ultimately, this is one of the key purposes of the Tarot. It is a tool that trains us in using the intuition. It helps us develop our awareness of the inner dimensions of life.

There are many levels of intuitive skill. The simplest levels amount to little more than accurate fortune telling—an ability to predict the future and read superficial elements of a person's character. The most profound is the ability to interact directly with archetypal forces and our own spiritual essence. In between, there are many grades and applications. As a general rule, the more spectacular a psychic performance is, the cruder it turns out to be. The more refined and subtle it is, the more meaningful it can be. It is for this reason that we need to train ourselves to work with archetypal forces and spiritual realities, and make this discipline the backdrop for developing our intuition. It safeguards us from going off in tangents that will only lead us into mischief.

When used in this way, the Tarot becomes a teacher as well as an oracle. It encourages us to learn to use our intuition to answer the questions we ask. At first, we can use the guidelines presented in this book or some other source; they let us make a start. But once we get used to the Tarot, we will discover that each card—or rather the Real Tarot it represents—has a life and a vitality of its own. This inner life cannot be tapped by relying on someone else's interpretation of the Tarot. It can only be tapped intuitively, by learning to commune directly with the inner meaning of the card, as it applies to the specific question at hand.

For this reason, I will not give interpretations of the Tarot cards in this book. I will present suggestions and ideas on how to understand and harness *the power behind* each card, as well as construct an overall sense of meaning for the deck as a whole. By the end of the book, you will have a clear sense of how to use the Tarot to explore the most complex questions of life, as well as the simpler ones. But you must be willing to develop your intuition—or at least your creative imagination—to take advantage of this book. If you are looking for literal answers, you will not find them here.

The answers come from the Tarot—the Real Tarot of archetypal life. The seventy-eight cards of the Tarot are the mechanism by which we contact the answers and tap the latent power within them. To some, it may seem impossible that meaningful answers about the nature of life can come from a deck of cards—or that they would be able to understand the answers in any event. But the rule governing this process is a simple one. If you are able to voice the question, you are ready to start the journey of discovery that leads to its answer. Whether the journey is short or long depends upon many factors: your prejudices, the strength of your wish life, and your capacity for self-deception.

The journey, of course, takes you within.

CHAPTER THREE

Examining Life

It is not possible to use the Tarot correctly unless we understand its inner roots in the archetypal realities of life. We must build a strong acquaintance with these inner forces and learn to think in their terms—in terms of causes, motivations, and designs. Nonetheless, we must also understand that there is more to life than the divine design. It is one thing to know the ideal solution for a troubling situation, and quite another to invoke and implement it. Daily life requires more than just an abstract knowledge of the ideal; it requires us to act with common sense, skill, and wisdom in implementing the ideal as much as possible.

We must have a strong awareness of the divine archetypes, in other words, but our primary focus, both in personal growth and in using the Tarot, should be constructive daily living. As Alexander Pope put it in his brilliant *Essay on Man*:

> Know then thyself, presume not God to scan;
> The proper study of Mankind is Man.

This is an excellent motto for our use of the Tarot, too. It is not just divine life that has structure and meaning. Our own character is meant to be our personal structure of wisdom, reflecting, microcosmically, what the divine mind expresses macrocosmically through the archetypes. The fact that most people have invested neither the time nor the energy to mold their character into this kind of structure does not diminish the value of the basic principle. Just so, the fact that most people do not understand the true potential of the Tarot as a tool for exploring human life does not diminish the value of this remarkable tool.

Human character is a marvelous creation. Ideally, our character should be an embodiment of the life plan and purpose of our higher self (the soul). This plan or blueprint for our life consists of a set of choices made by the higher self before we enter this life. As we grow up, we create our character, either as a reflection or embodiment of this inner plan or as a reaction to family conditions, life experiences, social influences, and inherited restrictions. Unfortunately, much of the structure of our character develops when we are quite young and is therefore based on immature, childish likes and dislikes, fears, and anxieties—not the mature, intelligent values of an adult. We view ourselves as adults, of course, but all too often allow immature and undeveloped traits to guide and dictate our behavior, feeling, and thinking.

As character develops, we codify these traits into a set of values from which we determine priorities, goals, and behavior. A value is an intangible assessment of the relative worth to us of any idea, principle, feeling, or tangible object. One person might put great value on property ownership; another might disdain it. One person might value faith in God as his most treasured possession; another might value his individual understanding of life above all else. Values can be based on mental convictions, personal beliefs, or social conditioning. But the strongest, most reliable ones will be those that have been inspired by archetypal realities and have been carefully tested and weighed mentally before being adopted.

It should be understood that most people have several sets of values. There are the values of character, which are ingrained; they will always be acted on. There are the values of our subconscious, which often contradict one another and are the root of most internal conflict. And then there are the values we consciously hold and ascribe to, which have almost no power whatsoever. They are generally just values we believe in to soothe our conscience. Instead of guiding our actions, these values are most commonly used to justify whatever action we have already chosen. How often do we hear someone say, for instance, "I am doing this in order to protect your best interest," when in fact it is clear that he is thinking only of his own selfish interests?

From an intuitive perspective, the values, priorities, traits, and patterns of our character form a definite structure. In the undeveloped person, it will be a confusing, contradictory structure which complicates life rather than simplifies it. In a more advanced person, who spends time examining life, it will be a clean, well-organized structure capable of distributing great power. Such a person will be able to act dynamically in life and accomplish a great deal.

This human character is not a static mechanism. It interacts with life, drawing to us the associates and experiences we need. If our character is harmoniously aligned with the patterns of the higher self, and we spend most of our time engaged in wise, helpful, and constructive activities, we will attract friends and experiences that help us achieve our goals. On the other hand, if our character is a hodge-podge of unresolved disputes, irresponsible actions, and selfishness, we will attract friends and experiences that will thwart our plans and goals and generally make life more difficult.

It is not difficult to upgrade the quality of our character; it simply requires a certain dedication to what is known as "self-examination." This does not mean that we stand nude in front of a mirror and look at ourself; it means we pause daily to reflect on who we are and why we do and say the things that we do. We look beyond the superficial layer of our outer behavior and defense mechanisms and try to chart the interior dimensions of our being. In specific:

• We examine our habits, to see how we acquired them and whether or not they continue to serve our best interests. Where they do not, we work to improve or change them.

• We examine our likes and dislikes, to review how we came to adopt them. Do we control them, or do they control us? Do they reflect the best within us? If not, then we need to revise them.

• We examine our values. As indicated, this is not an easy task, for we must distinguish between consciously-held values, the values that function subconsciously, and the values that determine our actual behavior. We must trace these values back to their origins, determine if they were made intelligently or just imposed on us, and then evaluate their ongoing effectiveness in our life. As necessary, we should redefine our values so that they embody as much of the plan and pattern of the higher self as possible.

It is equally important to look for inconsistencies in the way we apply our values. We may think we value friendship, for example, when in reality we only value what our friends can do for us, not what we can do for them. In point of fact, we value selfishness, not friendship.

• We examine our priorities. When two or more values conflict with one another, are we able to perceive quickly which one is of greatest value, and therefore act on it rather than the others? How have we established these priorities? Do they incorporate the design of the higher self?

• We examine our skills and talents. What gifts do we have for contributing to human life, not just through the work we do but also through our relationships, social life, and personal pursuits? Do we honor these skills and talents fully in our daily life? How can we make better use of our personal resources?

• We examine our duties and obligations. Throughout life, we make commitments—when we marry, when we take on employment, when we conceive children, and so on. What do these commitments mean? How well are we fulfilling them? How do we need to revise our attitudes or priorities to fulfill these duties? Have any of the obligations of a commitment changed since we first took it on?

• We examine our sense of self-esteem and our ability to preserve a strong sense of individuality. Do we like or dislike ourself? Are we able to approve of the good things we do, and manage our disappointments and failures wisely? Do we have the strength of character to think for ourself and stand for what we know is right?

• We examine our basic level of contentment and poise. Are we well-adjusted and reasonably content with our major roles in life? Or do we feel trapped in our marriage, stuck in a dead end job, or imprisoned by commitments we made without understanding their consequences? Discontentment is often a sign that we are seriously out of harmony with the plan and design of the higher self for this life. What steps must we take to restore greater harmony to our life?

• We examine the dark side of our nature. Every human being is dual in nature, a blend of the highest aspirations and goals on the one hand and selfish and unredeemed weaknesses on the other. As we grow, the balance begins to tip more and more in favor of the noble aspirations and qualities, but there is always a dark side we must contend with: prejudices, bigoted ideas, selfish habits, temptations, bad temper, hostilities, fears, worries, superstitions, character flaws, and so on. We need to examine these characteristics, no matter how unpleasant they may be, so that we can work more intelligently to eliminate them. In fact, one of the most important steps in self-examination is establishing a "baseline" of thought and feeling that we know to be our own. This baseline describes the usual content of our character in terms of both healthy and unhealthy thoughts, feelings, values, priorities, and traits. The importance of a clearly-defined baseline is that it lets us quickly determine if a thought or feeling emerging in our awareness is a) our own; b) a stray thought picked up out of mass consciousness; c) a psychic impression of the thoughts and feelings of another person; or d) a thought or feeling being deliberately implanted in our awareness by someone else.

This type of self-examination is the sign of a healthy, enlightened person. It is not something that is done once and then forgotten; self-examination is meant to be an ongoing part of intelligent living. It gives us a way of shaping our self-expression so that it embraces and expresses the very best within us; it encourages us to grow in stature, skill, and enlightenment. But for the process of self-examination to work in these ways, our efforts must be linked to the archetypal design of the higher self.

It is in this regard that the use of the Tarot can be invaluable. We are taught very little, either in school or in church, about the plan of the higher self and how to discern it. In this one all important aspect of life, we have been abandoned to our own devices. As a result, most of us lack the intuitive skills needed to inspect the archetypal plan of the higher self directly, examine the content of our subconscious and character, and compare the two. Even if we are interested in living an examined life, we usually do not know how.

The skillful use of the Tarot can fill this gap. The Tarot is a coherent system or structure of archetypal symbols; the plan of the higher self for our life is likewise a system or structure of archetypal forces. In addition, our character and subconscious are also structures. They are not necessarily as coherent or as well-organized as the plan of the higher self, but they can be. This potential makes it possible to use the Tarot to examine the nature and structure of our own character, weigh it against the inner plan of the higher self, and then determine what changes are necessary to upgrade it.

Indeed, this kind of self-examination should be considered the number one use of the Tarot. In the last chapter, we saw how the Tarot can be used to explore the inner dimensions and archetypal levels of life; in future chapters, we will consider other kinds of uses as well. The Tarot has many potential uses, and should not be limited to just one. But no use of the Tarot is more important than that of conducting the work of self-examination. And no other use reveals to us the versatility and depth of the Tarot. In learning to use the Tarot, therefore, it is the essence of wisdom to practice using it in a program of self-examination.

To be effective, of course, any program of self-examination must be honest. If we are looking for rationalizations or excuses for our errant behavior, we will pervert the whole purpose of self-examina-tion—and abuse the power of the Tarot. It is important to realize how subtle self-deception can be. In a difficult marriage, for instance, each person will tend to focus on the irritating behavior of the other and believe that the only way the marriage can be salvaged is for the other person to change his or her ways. In most cases, however, the real problem is not that the other person's behavior is irritating, but that we allow it to irritate us! If we were more committed to making the marriage work and genuinely cared about the well-being of our spouse, we would not let these petty quirks or character flaws be so troublesome to us.

In such a situation, if we ask the Tarot—"What can be done to improve my marriage?"—we had better be prepared to interpret the answer in terms of what changes and new initiatives we must make, not what our spouse must do. And we must dedicate ourself to the highest, not just the most convenient. In asking for guidance in improving our marriage, for instance, we need to direct the question toward the plan of the higher self—not the gratification of our wish life.

Another way in which many people deceive themselves is to

27

accept the common idea that they are "victims" of life. It is popular in our modern, superficial world to ascribe all problems to victimization—if we grew up in a ghetto we are obviously a victim of poverty and discrimination; if we grew up in a rich suburb we are surely a victim of over-indulgence. If we ever work for anyone else, we are clearly a victim of exploitation; if we are out of work, we are a victim of a sluggish economy. In truth, however, most of us are only victims of ourselves. Our early childhood experiences may have taught us to be greedy and ambitious, thinking only about ourself, but now that we are an adult and have the wisdom to see how destructive such attitudes are, why do we keep on acting in such immature ways? Adults are meant to outgrow the child within them, not be victimized by it. When, as an adult, we blame our misfortunes on being victimized by others, or by society, it is clear that we are not actually an adult. We are still a child running around in an adult body. Adults do not blame others, or life itself, for their problems and hardships. They solve them.

It should be understood that the Tarot, being an intelligent structure developed originally by initiates, has a number of built-in safeguards. If we endeavor to use it to gratify our wish life or indulge in self-deception, our attitude will automatically invoke these safeguards. We will get answers, of course, but they will be designed to limit the damage we can do to ourself. Our higher intelligence, in other words, will use the Tarot in such a way that we will discover our self-deceptions and—it is hoped—mend our ways. Given such results, of course, some people will just blame the Tarot and continue with their self-deceptions. But it should always be remembered that the Tarot itself is just a tool. It is up to us to use the tool responsibly and wisely.

For this reason, it is generally a good idea to take a few moments before using the Tarot to dedicate ourself to the best within us and ask that we may be guided to an understanding of truth. We should try to purge any tendencies toward wish fulfillment or self-deception *before* consulting the Tarot. In addition, if we ever suspect that our use of the Tarot has been clouded by self-deception, we should immediately investigate the possibility. We can do this by asking the Tarot: "What is the value of the guidance I received in my last consultation, and how well did I interpret it?" If the answer indicates that we did engage in a measure of self-deception—for example, just gratifying our wish life—we should then ask a follow-up question: "What are the concepts, attitudes, and values of mine that have fed this self-deception, and how can I eliminate this distortion in the future?"

The goal of self-examination is to peel back all the layers of assumption and social conditioning and discover the inner core of character that actually determines who we are, what we think, and how we behave. We then compare this core of character with the master plan of the higher self for our life. Wherever our character fails to match the plan of the higher self, we endeavor to transform it so that it will. This is high and noble work—the true art of human living.

There are many kinds of questions that can be formulated in using the Tarot to pursue this type of self-examination. Some examples would include:

What are the primary character strengths my higher self would like me to develop at this time? What weaknesses or flaws must be overcome to build these strengths?

What are the origins of my depression (or fear, worry, envy, or anger)? What has been the impact of this problem on my emotions? What has been its impact on my perspective toward life? What has been its impact in my dealings with others? What can I do to heal this problem?

In what ways, if any, do my attitudes and feelings pollute the atmosphere at work? At home? What should I do to eliminate this?

In what areas of my life am I still immature? What does it mean to become mature in these areas?

In what ways do I deceive myself? How can I correct this?

What would it mean to become more caring in my dealings with others?

What are the primary limitations restricting my growth at present? How can these limitations be overcome?

What steps must I take to achieve better integration of my personality? What are the major areas of conflict within my character? What changes must be made to heal the conflict?

In what ways do I lack self-determination? What type of person or group do I allow to dominate or excessively influence me? How do I correct this flaw?

In what ways do I betray my values? How can I eliminate this betrayal?

What qualities do I need in order to become a better parent?

What flaws in my own character are magnified by the character and needs of my children (spouse)?

In pursuing questions of this type, it is important always to strive to answer them as fully as possible. Indeed, one question will often lead to a dozen additional questions to be asked. A full exploration of any one part of our character, subconscious, or health can easily take a year or more to complete and involve dozens of Tarot consultations. It is therefore highly important to exercise patience, restraint, and common sense in investigating the inner dimensions of our being.

The use of the Tarot for self-knowledge can easily be adapted for other applications as well. Throughout life, we are constantly required to make choices and decisions affecting business, our relationships, our personal growth, and our family. These choices and decisions can be made wisely, as an extension of our values and principles, or they can be made whimsically, as an expression of our wish life. The Tarot is the perfect vehicle to use to explore the hidden consequences of important decisions we have to make. We can ask, for example, questions such as:

What would be the long-term outcome of accepting a new job at this time?

What is the best way to discipline my youngest child?

What should be our keynote in marketing for the coming year?

In what ways should we seek to grow as a business?

What common activities will best serve to integrate our family?

What would be the impact of moving to a new home?

How can we as parents best help our child cope with his (or her) special problem?

What would be the problems and benefits of accepting chairmanship of our volunteer group?

As we become comfortable in using the Tarot, we will be amazed at just how versatile it can be in giving us answers to our questions. Divine intelligence is filled with all the answers we will ever need. Moreover, it welcomes our inquiries. But it expects us to act maturely with the insights and answers it gives. If the motive of our questions is cheap gossip, we may as well save our energy. If our motive is to cheat our destiny, we had better understand that it cannot be done. The Tarot is a tool for intelligent inquiry. Correctly used, it can open up the full range of divine wisdom. Foolishly used, it will show you just how foolish human beings can sometimes be.

Until you do indeed "know yourself," at least to some degree, it will be very difficult to learn very much about the Tarot.

A Dialogue with the Tarot

PAGE OF RODS

I had just finished chapter three when I felt something tapping me on the shoulder. I turned around. It was the Page of Rods from the Tarot, sprung to life, six feet tall, water dripping from his cloak, and eager to tell me a thing or two.

"I hope you haven't just bored your readers to tears," he intoned.

"What do you mean?" I asked.

"They thought they were getting a book on the Tarot. You've barely mentioned the word for two whole chapters."

"But they need to understand the value of the Tarot before they can use it," I protested.

"That's true," the Page replied. It sounded as though he were speaking in an echo chamber; I wondered how he created that effect. "But readers are impatient these days. They want their answers, and they want them now."

"Then they shouldn't be using the Tarot," I cried. "It takes a certain amount of self-discipline and patience to develop the skills necessary to use it. It's not a game, after all!"

"Let me show you something you know perfectly well but have chosen to overlook," the Page continued. "Look at me. What do you see?"

"I see a young man treading the straight and narrow path, learning to be led by the mind. I see the principle of discrimination. I should think you would be able to understand my approach to this book!"

"Don't be so damned formal! What you see is a young man sloshing his way out of the swamp. I've been stuck for eons in the reeds and muck of immature thinking, dealing only with the most superficial levels of ideas. I have gone with the flow! I've been trapped in paradigms! I have craved warm fuzzies! I have fallen for every fad and fashion of human thinking, no matter how absurd. I can recite The Prophet forwards and backwards. But I am reaching out with my right arm—you can't see it on the card, but it is there—for someone to help pull me out of the swamp. You could be that someone, but you have to give me something to grab hold of—an arm of your own."

"I think I get your point."

"I hope so," the Page replied. "By the way, do you have a towel? I'd like to clean off some of this muck."

I brought him a towel. "You will be happy to know," I said, as he was cleaning up, "that I have completed my preliminary comments. I am ready to describe the use of the Tarot."

"Good, because I have a lot of questions."

"You have a lot of questions? How can you have questions? You're part of the Tarot. You're supposed to have the answers!"

"Don't be presumptuous!" the Page chided. "Just because you're a human doesn't mean you're the only one smart enough to ask questions. The Tarot constantly asks questions of the people who really know how to use it."

"What do you mean?"

"Just what we've been talking about. The Tarot is a tool for learning to think—especially for learning to think intuitively. Correctly used, it will constantly challenge the assumptions you have made. It will ask you embarrassing questions about your preconceptions and demand that you defend them or change them.

"Look at me again. I've just stepped out of the swamp. You should be asking me questions like: what on earth were you doing in the swamp in the first place? Why is your hat pulled down over your eyes? What do these reeds in the background represent, anyway?

"Because I've been in the swamp, and am just now learning to walk on firm ground, a lot of my thinking is pretty slippery—maybe even slimy. I need to look at my prejudices, superstitions, and false assumptions, and see how they are coloring and distorting my thinking. I need to examine how I am blind to higher truth. I need to learn to distinguish between what is real and what is false.

"I don't need someone to tell me my thinking is biased and distorted—I may just get mad and go back into the swamp. I need someone to take my arm and help me onto dry ground—someone to show me the way, so I can follow."

"How can I do that?" I asked.

"You just have," came the answer. "You've given me the chance to explain myself on my own terms, to come alive in your imagination. Just tell your readers to do that, and they will get the hang of the Tarot. Tell them to take care not to impose their own values and beliefs on something bigger than they are, but to take the time to strike up a dialogue with each card. Let the inner reality or force of the card—you would call it the Real Tarot—speak to them in their imagination and explain its own meaning and significance. That will get them on to dry ground in no time."

"I don't think I could have said it better myself."

"Of course you couldn't!" the Page said. "If you want the truth about the Tarot, you have to go straight to the Tarot."

And with that, he began striding forth, away from the swamp, with such vigor that he soon disappeared from sight. All I was left with was a rather muddy towel—and a lot of new insight.

CHAPTER FOUR

Mapping an Answer

There are many ways the Tarot can be used to examine life. Thinking of a question, you can shuffle the deck and pick a card at random. The card you choose will represent the answer to your question. For example, if your question is—"What should be the major focus of my efforts to grow this coming week?"—and the card you pick is the 3 of Pentacles, the Tarot is telling you to focus on building the internal structures of your character, as described in Chapter 3. The 3 of Pentacles is a card depicting an artisan working in a temple, apparently putting the finishing touches on one of three pillars which hold up a major arch of the temple. The three pillars are highly suggestive of the three pillars of the Tree of Life in the Kabalah, but in most applications it refers to the supporting posts of any structure. The implication therefore is that you should review your values, principles, and priorities, and realign them so that they better support the structure of your character day by day.

One of the unusual features of many of the Pentacles in the Aquarian Tarot is that the drawings have an ethereal overtone. In the 3 of Pentacles, the pillars and arch are solid, yet it is possible to see the blue sky and clouds right through them. This reminds us that although the Pentacles deal with the physical plane and materialistic issues, the real meaning of these cards is always found in the inner, intangible patterns behind the physical appearance. In this case, it is not outer behavior that needs our attention, but rather the inner structure which determines what our outer behavior should be.

Interestingly, this is the card that came up when I asked this question while writing this chapter. Since the next seven days will be spent working on the next few chapters of this book, the advice given me by the Tarot is exceedingly appropriate. My own personal growth during this period should be tied to the work of writing this book; anything else will be a distraction. To do this work properly, I must make sure that my own structure of associations, values, and principles is well ordered and properly polished. The Tarot also appears to be guilty of making a rather atrocious pun, suggesting that I will be working on a "major arch," when of course I will be describing in great detail the major arcana.

The "pick a card, any card" method of using the Tarot is a good way to get a quick answer to a simple question, and is often quite profound. But it should be understood that it is a shortcut method, and thereby limited. The answers obtained by picking a single card will be one-dimensional and fragmentary. Relying on this method exclusively would tend to expose you to a tendency to jump to conclusions.

Some people favor a three-card spread, in which three cards are picked at random in response to a question. The first card defines the issue, the second indicates the action to be taken, and the third suggests the probable outcome. This type of layout will produce excellent results, of course, if the cards are properly interpreted. But I do not use this particular layout in my own work. It is too much a copy of the pattern of hexagrams used in the I Ching. I prefer to leave this layout to the I Ching, where it works marvelously well, instead of grafting it into the Tarot. Each of these tools of divination has its own special value. When I want the type of insight the I Ching provides, I use the I Ching. I see no value in trying to transform the Tarot into something that already exists.

It is for this reason that I favor the ten-card spread that is illustrated on the adjoining page. The unique quality of the Tarot is that it lets us study the inner or archetypal energies at work in any situation, and how they influence us. One or three cards does not capture enough of the movement of these forces. All seventy-eight are far too many. The ten-card layout, however, gives us an ideal map or chart by which we can study these forces and their interaction. This is not to suggest that there are always ten separate forces at work in every situation; there may be more, or there may be fewer. But if there are more, the ten cards we lay out will give us enough clues that we will want to ask additional questions, until we understand the full array of forces in their totality. If there are less, the spread will show which forces are strongest and most dominant through the redundancy of similar or parallel cards. If both the Emperor from the major arcana and the 6 of Rods from the minor arcana appear in the same spread, for instance, it should be clear that one of the major themes of this answer is the need for greater responsibility and nurturing love, since both the Emperor and the 6 of Rods share this common theme.

I regard this layout as a map which will guide me in my exploration of the hidden dimensions of my question. Each step along the way builds on the prior ones and anticipates the ones to come. At the same time, it has its own specific message as to the meaning of the card that occupies its space. These meanings can be listed as follows:

1. The first card is **the starting point.** It defines the basic issue and reveals the major force at work. This card is often blatantly obvious. If you ask a question about coping with the death of a loved one, for instance, the Tarot might well respond with the card "Death" in the starting point. This does not mean you should join your loved one in death; it simply restates and confirms the question, adding that you need to face this issue and not pretend that it did not occur.

41

THE MAP OF THE TAROT

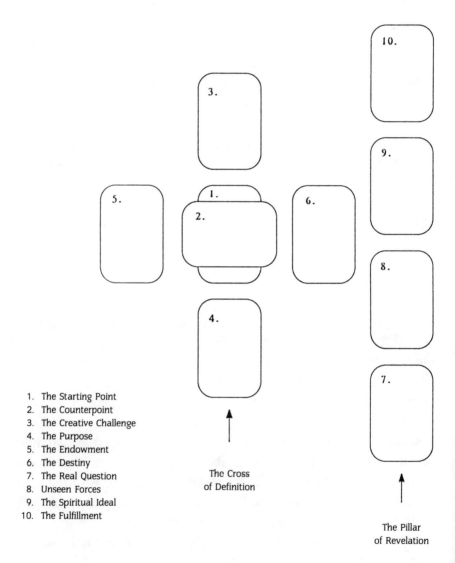

1. The Starting Point
2. The Counterpoint
3. The Creative Challenge
4. The Purpose
5. The Endowment
6. The Destiny
7. The Real Question
8. Unseen Forces
9. The Spiritual Ideal
10. The Fulfillment

The Cross
of Definition

The Pillar
of Revelation

2. The second card is **the counterpoint.** Traditionally, it is laid horizontally across the first card, forming a cross, and is thought to be the force that opposes the first card. Working in this way is a good way to derail the train of the Tarot before leaving the depot, however. It is much better to think of this second card as representing the force that complements the first card—the *yin* that goes with the *yang* to make a complete whole. It often indicates what spiritual quality is lacking in the situation and needs to be added.

3. The third card, stationed just above the first card, is the **creative challenge.** It indicates the lesson you are in the process of learning in this situation, and may also hint at the ideal methodology to use in approaching it. The forces represented by this card are not necessarily at work in the situation—but they are there to be invoked and harnessed, if you choose to do so.

4. The fourth card, placed just below the first card, is **the purpose.** It indicates the perspective of the higher self and reveals something of the content of its plan—or the plan of God—for this situation. To interpret any card appearing in this position correctly, it cannot be viewed from a petty or personal point of view. It must be dealt with impersonally, with a sense of the big picture.

5. The fifth card, located to the left of the first card, is **the endowment.** This card indicates what strengths or skills you bring with you that can be used in managing this situation. In some cases, it may indicate issues brought forward from a prior life; in other cases, it may just show earlier forces and actions that have led to the present consequences.

6. The sixth card, positioned to the right of the first card, is **the destiny.** It tends to indicate where the forces governing the situation are heading at the present time. It is important to understand that this may or may not be the same as the final outcome; it is more an indication of what will happen if absolutely nothing is done to act upon the forces already set in motion.

These first six cards form what I call the "cross of definition." They reveal the situation as it is, but do not necessarily demonstrate what can be done to control or redirect it. This part of the message is left to the final four cards, which form the "pillar of revelation" and are laid out in a vertical column to the right of the sixth card.

7. The seventh card—placed at the bottom of the pillar of revelation—is **the real question.** This card recognizes that the questions we ask are often fragmentary and incomplete, because we do not yet understand the broadest perspective of the situation at hand. The Tarot generally knows far better than we do what question we should be asking, and this card in the pillar of revelation gives it a chance to show us the fuller picture and implications. If you ask the question—"Why don't I have more friends?"—and the seventh card comes up as Temperance from the major arcana, the Tarot is probably telling you that the real question ought to be: "In what ways do I drive off friends by making demands of them that go beyond friendship?"

8. The eighth card—the second from the bottom in the pillar of revelation—is **the unseen forces.** This card indicates to you what subtle or hidden forces are at work in the situation that have not yet been taken into account. It may suggest, for example, that a friend you have been counting on is not trustworthy. Or it may indicate that your feeling of hopelessness is totally unwarranted, because there is great help and support being given you from the inner levels of life.

9. The ninth card—the second from the top of the pillar of revelation—is **the spiritual ideal.** It represents the ideal quality or force that you should be working with in order to obtain your goal. It is important to define this quality clearly and fully, so that you understand it as a spiritual force, and not just in personal terms. The 4 of Pentacles in this position would tend to suggest the need

44

for spiritual initiative, especially in service. But that does not mean that we should just go out and throw ourselves into the work of a conspicuous charity. The 4 of Pentacles clearly indicates that the service and work we do must be linked with our own goodwill and the plan and intent of God. So we must act, but it must be wisely and lovingly.

10. The tenth card—at the crown of the pillar of revelation—is **the fulfillment.** It represents the full achievement of the plan for this situation. This full achievement may be very much different from our goal, however; it represents the fulfillment of the divine plan or the plan of our higher self. This is therefore not a card representing our personal emotional fulfillment, but rather spiritual fulfillment.

As you come to the card occupying each position on this map, it is important to interpret it in the context of the position, as described here. Obviously, if the same card appears in two different positions in two different consultations, the interpretation of that card will probably be very much different in each case. The Knight of Rods appearing as the starting point in one reading might well indicate that we are dealing with a problem of our values and priorities toward service or work; found in the position of unseen forces in another reading, it may indicate that we have a chip on our shoulder which is straining an important relationship.

The point to keep in mind in working with the ten-card layout is to treat it as a map to understanding. Each position on the map gives you a clue or a hint to the answer you are seeking; if you follow the map as laid out, it will lead you to your destination.

As you develop proficiency in working with the Tarot, you will gradually come to appreciate the inner dynamics of this map. Relationships among the various positions on the map will quickly be established in your own mind. You will see, for example, that the cards in the positions of purpose and the real question often parallel each other, as do the cards in the positions of challenge and fulfillment. The endowment card almost always leads naturally to the destiny card, giving a major clue concerning the basic direction in which events are heading, while the unseen forces and spiritual ideal cards often form a similar pair, revealing the resistance you are facing and the energy you must harness to tame it. Indeed, the four cards in the pillar of revelation will often have a common theme running throughout all of them. Finally, in many cases, the fulfillment card will just be a restatement of the starting point, yet with something vital and new added to it.

As you become alert to these relationships, you will also begin to grasp that these are not static images on cards. They are living, dynamic forces which impel you from the starting point to fulfillment. Each step along the way is important and must be understood, but it is the overall force and flow of the entire map that is the key.

We do not live in a one-dimensional world. We inhabit a multidimensional sphere, and the problems and events we encounter are multidimensional as well. Only simpletons can be satisfied with simplistic answers. For the rest of us, we need a means to probe the multidimensional nature of our questions and challenges.

The Tarot lets us map these many dimensions of our thinking and acting, and harness the forces that govern our lives.

LINES OF MOVEMENT IN THE TAROT

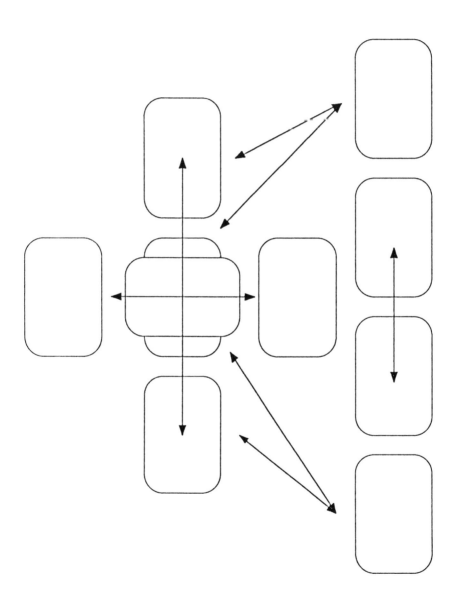

47

CHAPTER FIVE

Formulating Questions

The Tarot cannot function without a question. This may be a startling declaration to many people; in the fortune telling applications of the Tarot, after all, it is common to do "readings" without a question at all. The reader picks a card called the significator which represents the client, places it on the table, and then proceeds to lay out the cards by placing the first one on top of the significator and the other cards around it, as dictated by the spread being used. The resulting "reading" is supposed to tell the client what he or she needs to know.

Unfortunately, life is not designed to operate in this simplistic way. The basic esoteric principle at work in the use of any tool of divination is the science of invocation. At the risk of oversimplification, it can be stated that nothing can be drawn forth from the inner dimensions of life without the formulation of a proper invocation. The invocation is, in part, a recognition that the inner reality exists; even more importantly, it is a confession that we need it in our physical life.

In a Tarot reading, the act of invocation is performed by formulating an intelligent question. Without a question, no invocation will occur; nothing will be brought from the archetypal dimensions of life into our personal awareness. The process of formulating a proper question is therefore of great significance to the outcome of our use of the Tarot.

If this is true, then how do the fortune telling uses of the Tarot produce results? The answer to this question is simple. They do not produce the kind of results being described here. At worst, the fortune telling use of the Tarot is an outright fraud, a tool used to intimidate and manipulate superstitious clients, not enlighten them. At best, this use of the Tarot is limited to answers and insights from what is known esoterically as the astral plane—the level of our emotions. Since these "readers," even at their best, are only picking up the feelings and attitudes of their clients, no question is actually needed. Nothing substantive is being invoked—or revealed. The "readings" never rise above the most specious level of superficial living.

This limitation does not apply, however, if we sincerely want to work with the archetypal forces of the Real Tarot. When this is our goal, we must learn to work with the principle of invocation and take the process of formulating questions seriously. Actually, this is the most critical stage of using the Tarot. If you formulate your question correctly, the answer will flow smoothly. You will be able to interpret it with hardly any strain at all. If you fashion your question sloppily, the Tarot becomes congested. You will have to fight and struggle for every insight you gain, and then you will still not be sure if you have interpreted the answer correctly.

What are the ingredients of a good question? There are several. The key points to consider are these:

1. It cannot be a yes or no question. We are not expecting the Tarot to do our thinking for us or make decisions on our behalf. We are looking for insight. Questions that are designed to be answered with a yes or a no tend to cut off the thinking process, not stimulate it; they remove us from the decision making process. They induce fatalism. So it is unfair to both the Tarot and our own selfhood to look for this type of answer. The Tarot is a tool designed for use in exploring life and examining its meaning. We should limit ourselves to questions that harness this great potential.

2. We should only ask questions that have answers. This may seem a flippant condition at first, but there is a great deal of truth in it. The Real Tarot is a system of archetypal forces; our personal use of the Tarot is meant to teach us to interact with this abstract system. We can therefore make the fastest progress by asking the kind of questions that our own higher intelligence wants to answer. In this way, we establish a meaningful dialogue between the personality and the higher self.

It would be silly to ask a question such as—"Why don't cows have six legs?"—of the Tarot; because there are no cows with six legs, the question really has no answer. Few of us would ask such a dumb question, of course. But some of us might be tempted to ask questions such as:

"What is the purpose of my grief?"

"Why doesn't my higher self support my efforts to grow more?"

"Why have I not experienced happiness in my life?"

On the surface, these seem like reasonable questions. Yet the Tarot would find it almost impossible to answer them, for the following reasons:

There is no purpose to grieving. Grief is neither a spiritual quality nor an archetypal force. It is a natural reaction of the emotions to loss, but this loss is meant to be controlled by our awareness of and thankfulness for all the blessings of our life. Dwelling on losses estranges us from the rich abundance and joy of living.

The higher self *does* support us and encourage us to grow. At times, however, we fail to register this support and may even feel abused or neglected. This is an illusion, not based on reality.

Happiness is not something we experience; it is an emotional state that we generate in reaction to certain stimuli. What these stimuli are will vary from person to person. It is true that the average person believes it is his or her right to be happy, but in fact, we will be only as happy as we allow ourselves to be. Expecting life

51

to provide us with happiness is an illusion that is impossible to fulfill.

The Tarot would find it difficult to answer these questions because they are based on illusions or mistaken assumptions. It would try, of course, but the way the questions are structured, the only answer the Tarot could truthfully provide is one that would indicate that we are deceiving ourself and falling victim to illusions. Since most people do not like to hear such a message, it is unlikely that we would interpret the answer correctly. In any event, we would find such a layout to be a great test of our capacity to understand the Tarot!

It is for this reason that we should only ask questions we can reasonably expect to be answered. This rule teaches us to think the question through before we ask it, and state it in such a way that an answer can easily be provided. One of the best ways to meet this requirement is to get in the habit of asking for the ideal solution to our particular problem:

"What is the ideal way I should treat my spouse?"

"What are the most important themes to stress in raising my child?"

"What should be our keynote for success as a company next year?"

"What is the best way to defend the lawsuit that has been filed against us?"

"What is the ideal attitude for me to take in tomorrow's job interview?"

3. We should ask because we have a genuine need to know. Whenever we ask the Tarot a legitimate question, we can be sure of receiving the answer we need. But with the answer comes more than insight—it is accompanied by a responsibility to act and the power to do so. We will be expected to use the new wisdom and power we have tapped. If we are unwilling to do so, it would be better not to ask in the first place.

The Tarot can be used for less noble purposes, of course. But if our motivation in using it is to snoop on others, to satisfy our idle curiosity, or just to find shortcuts to life's problems, we can expect the Tarot to increase the difficulty of our life, not lessen it. Like any tool, the Tarot has power. If we abuse it, we will probably dislike the consequences.

4. Our questions should identify our real needs. Instead of asking: "How can I get a promotion at work?"—it would be far better to ask: "How can I improve my skills and broaden my responsibilities so that I will be able to make a greater contribution to my work?" We are bound to learn far more from the second kind of question than the first. In addition, we are creating a framework or mental structure that will assist us in interpreting the cards that comprise our answer.

5. Our questions should open doors, not impose limits. If you ask a question such as—"Why is Johnny such a poor student at school?"— you are making assumptions about Johnny that may be highly misleading. He may not be a poor student at all; he may have a condition such as dyslexia or poor eyesight that is keeping him from expressing his ability. It is therefore far better to phrase the question in a different way: "How can we help Johnny realize his full potential as a student?" The answer to this question will probably be profoundly different than the answer to the first one.

6. To the best of our ability, we should let higher intelligence dictate the question. You may be used to thinking in terms of using intuition to interpret the answers to your questions, but it is equally important to use the intuition in phrasing the question. After all, the higher self—or the mind of God, as the case may be—knows far better than we do what we ought to be asking. For one thing, it knows the answer! Therefore, it likewise knows what question will best elicit the answer we need—and best assist us in the intuitive process of interpreting it.

For this reason, it is important to take your time in formulating the question. It is silly just to jot down the first thing that enters your mind. Shape it and reshape it until it feels right intuitively. Ask the higher self, or friends you may have on the inner side of life, to help you with the wording. And always remember, once you start laying out the cards, your question is frozen in time. It cannot be changed. So make sure it reflects your true need to know.

These few rules illustrate the importance of phrasing questions carefully and intelligently. But one more point needs to be added. Be sure to write down the final wording of the question, so that you have a record of it. While shuffling the cards, focus your whole awareness on the question and your need to know the answer. This act of focusing will help create a suitable invocatory vortex which will draw to you the insights you need. Maintain this level of focus while laying out the cards. It should be as if you are praying to your higher self for the guidance you need. Indeed, it is a good idea to ask specifically that the answer come from your higher self—not from your wish life, your fantasies, your subconscious, someone else, or mass consciousness. This will help focus your attention on the Real Tarot, not the lower levels of the fortune telling or academic Tarots.

Once you begin the process of interpreting the cards, keep referring back to the question as you wrote it. One of the biggest problems people have in working with the Tarot (or any tool of divination) is that they tend to "forget" the question they have asked and invent a new one to fit the answer as they choose to interpret it. As an example, we might ask the Tarot: "How can I improve my relationship with my spouse?" The resulting spread may indicate the need to redefine our expectations of marriage, learn to be more caring, and eliminate certain patterns of selfishness. But we may have a strong resistance toward hearing such advice. In our mind, we may be convinced that the problems of our relationship all stem from our mate's inability to respect our needs and give us the independence we crave. So, without even realizing what we are doing, we begin to interpret the cards in terms of what our mate needs to do, not what we need to do. As a result, the question we end up answering is—"How can I continue to perpetuate my blind spots about my marriage, and blame my spouse for the problems I have created?"—rather than—"How can I improve my relationship with my spouse?"

The tendency to reinvent the question is a strong one. The only cure for it is self-discipline and a well-cultivated habit of constantly referring back to the original question, as written down, making sure that we are indeed answering the question we asked.

As an extension of this principle, it may be useful to keep track of the questions you have asked and the answers you have received, at least in the beginning stages of learning to use the Tarot. By keeping a journal of your Tarot inquiries, you can track your growth over a period of time. You can see not only how your interpretations of the cards grow and mature, but also how your ability to ask and answer intelligent questions improves. A journal of this nature can also provide an effective safeguard against self-deception. It is often difficult to spot self-deception in a single question and its answer. But when similar patterns appear over and over again in a collection of consultations, they become easier to detect.

CHAPTER SIX

Decoding the Answer

Once the question has been formulated and the ten chosen cards laid out, all that remains is to interpret the answer. The Tarot has spoken to us; its message is spelled out right before our eyes. We simply have to decode it.

To do this, we must understand a little bit about symbols. Symbols are a kind of language that allows us to communicate with superliteral ideas, forces, and patterns. We speak and write English. We may know a foreign language or two besides. But the mind of God—and our higher intelligence—does not use English or any other language of modern humanity to think and communicate. When the mind of God thinks, It thinks abstractly—without employing words, images, or any of the concrete forms we traditionally associate with the awareness process. At the personality level, our awareness is defined by *what* we are aware *of.* At the abstract, spiritual level, awareness requires no object. It just is.

This presents a problem in becoming aware of the inner dimensions of life. How do we bridge the gap between concrete and abstract? This is why tools such as the Tarot have been devised. Through the intelligent use of symbolism, our minds are gradually trained to become less and less dependent upon concrete forms and more and more attuned to abstract forces and movement.

It is important to understand that symbols are not abstract nor archetypal. They are images, and as images, they are as concrete as words and memories. Should we forget this basic truth, we might run the risk of becoming drunk on symbols and visualizations, which is not desirable. What we need to understand, instead, is that symbols are a special kind of image or pattern. Although concrete, they stand for inner or abstract realities. As we work with symbols, therefore, we can gradually move from an intensely concrete focus, where we find it impossible to envision any inner reality, to an abstract focus, where we begin to suspect that it is indeed possible to think without words, pictures, associations, or even memories.

The key is understanding that symbols are *multidimensional.* They can have many different levels of meaning simultaneously. A flower is a good example. At its literal level, a flower is a physical plant that grows in our garden. At a social level, it is a symbol of caring—we give flowers at weddings, on Mother's Day, on birthdays and anniversaries, and on many other occasions, as a token of our affection. The flowers are not our affection, but they represent it. They demonstrate it. They are a symbol.

A flower can also have personal meanings. Perhaps when we were young we were deeply impressed by an Easter service in church. From that moment forth, lilies might have a special meaning of devotion to us. Whenever we think of lilies, it would trigger an emotional release of devotion. How can a symbol have that kind of power? Again, the answer is a simple one. Symbols are the language of the subconscious. As we grow up, we construct a basic structure of symbols in our subconscious. Our feelings, attitudes, memories, and habits are all tied to these symbols. As we encounter outer manifestations of these symbols in daily life, they induce a corresponding release of memory and response subconsciously.

In much the same way, a symbol such as a flower can have many cultural meanings. Perhaps you come from a state in which the state flower is a rose. In that state, the rose is a symbol of citizenship and pride. More generally, the rose is a symbol of natural beauty. It is the emblem of Venus, as well as the primary flower in the garden of Eros. As we delve into these levels of symbolic meaning, we attune ourselves to the thoughts and associations the whole of humanity has had with the rose. We leave the personal behind, and begin dealing with the universal. We are no longer dealing with a single flower that lasts a few days and then wilts; we are tapping a level of meaning that has endured for centuries and embraces the whole of humanity.

But even this is not the ultimate symbolic level. For a rose also serves as a symbol for the archetypal realities of perfection, completion and divine beauty. When we tune into the image of the rose at this level, we can actually touch the full power of these forces as they flow through the mind of God. We have left the form level far behind; we are now dealing directly with the formless essence of all true Ideas. It is as though we are dealing with the essence of the perfume of the beauty of the rose.

The key point to understand about symbols is that they can be plugged into at so many different levels—literally, socially, personally, culturally, esoterically, and archetypically. Every true symbol will function at all of these levels—but just because we work with a symbol, there is no guarantee that we will indeed plug into each level. If we work with it intelligently, the symbol can help us do just this, but the level of our success depends entirely upon our individual effort. If we are a dense materialist, believing only in the physical plane, we will find it a struggle to understand personal and cultural meanings of a symbol—and absolutely impossible to comprehend the esoteric and archetypal meanings.

The Tarot is a complex collection of symbols. Each card portrays a primary symbol and a variety of minor symbols. Every card in the Tarot deck can lead us to an archetypal reality—if we are willing to follow. But it is also quite easy to get bogged down in much lower levels of interpretation, if we are not discerning.

As an example, one of the dominant themes in the illustrations of most standard Tarot decks is the medieval setting. There are, after all, pages, knights, queens, and kings. They ride horses, drive carts, live in castles, and dress like they came straight out of the Middle Ages, which they did. If you interpret this recurring imagery in terms of duty, honor, service and the other noble ideas of the Middle Ages, these images will serve their symbolic purpose of linking you with archetypal realities. But if you get bogged down instead in interpreting these images in terms of class struggles, militant crusades, and the quixotic idealism that leads to jousting with windmills, you will have taken a nose dive into the murk of mass consciousness and pseudo-sociological sophistry.

The multiple level of symbolism in the Tarot is what gives it its richness. A single card appearing in ten different readings can have ten levels of meaning. Take the 6 of Cups, for instance. In the Aquarian deck, a man and a woman are sniffing and admiring six pots of flowers. These flowers are arranged in three tiers, with three pots on the bottom tier, two on the middle, and one at the apex. Together, they form an equilateral triangle of beauty. But yet another distinction needs to be made. All the flowers are beautiful, but the flowers on the second tier are more refined and delicate than those on the first tier, and the flowers in the pot on the top level are the most elegant and radiant of all. If this card appears in a consultation on business matters, it may suggest the need for hierarchical thinking and an intelligent ordering of priorities. In a consultation on personal growth, it may emphasize the need for developing intuitive senses that can grasp the subtle and sublime essences of life. In answer to a question about healing a chronic illness, it may indicate the need for homeopathic remedies. In answer to a query about a relationship, it may well tell us to look for common activities we can share, as a way of strengthening the bond. If we are searching for

insight into ways we can improve our meditative skills, it may be suggesting that we should work with seed thoughts. If we are trying to discern what archetypal qualities we need to work with to improve our creative efforts, this card's message is probably encouraging us to fill our life with beauty. In answer to a question about how to deal with excessive energy, it probably is advising that we learn to sublimate it. If our inquiry deals with motivating a group of people, this card may well be encouraging us to build up their enthusiasm. Should the inquiry involve a habit we need to change, the 6 of Cups may be telling us that the habit in question is not the real source of difficulty; it is merely a symbol for an inner problem that must be rooted out and confronted. If we are trying to define a goal, the card is probably telling us to base it on our highest and noblest ideals.

The card is the same in each of these ten situations. So is the archetypal force; being a part of the reality of God's mind, it does not change from question to question. What then, is the cause of these ten different interpretations—and, presumably, the potential for many more? Quite simply, it is the multidimensional nature of the Tarot. Out of a single divine Idea, thousands, if not millions, of applications can arise. When we use the Tarot skillfully, we are able not only to tap into the divine force which can resolve the problem at hand, but also into the understanding of the ideal way to apply it, given the circumstances as they exist—even though tomorrow, when we need to work with the same archetypal force again, the application will differ from the one we needed to use today. When used correctly, the Tarot has the power and the flexibility to reveal to us all these minor variations on the major themes of our life.

You do not have to memorize any of these meanings and variations in order to be able to interpret the 6 of Cups—or any other card in the Tarot deck. In fact, only three of the ten interpretations listed in the paragraph above are ones that I drew from my memory storehouse of interpretations, and only one of them is what I would label a "stock" or "generic" interpretation. All the rest came to me spontaneously as I wrote the paragraph; as I thought of each question, the symbolic association arose in my imagination.

The key to interpreting the Tarot, in other words, does not lie in an enormous capacity to memorize traditional meanings. It involves training and nurturing a healthy, active *associative mechanism* in your imagination. What is an associative mechanism? It is almost exactly what it sounds like—a capacity to use the imagination to associate freely with any image, word, or idea. The writer who is able to think rapidly of a wide number of synonyms for a word he has overused is employing his associative mechanism. He does not necessarily have a better memory than other writers—just a better imagination. An artist who is able to see the moon, a wheel, the end of the barrel of a gun, and King Arthur's knights all sitting at the round table in a simple circle is likewise employing his associative mechanism.

The associative mechanism is developed by exercising it. In working with the Tarot, for example, you can exercise your associative mechanism by picking up any card at random and letting your imagination see how many different associations you can make with it. Do not try to actually answer a question in this exercise—just see how many rich associations you can uncover as you reflect

62

on the images on the card. Start with a card that is already filled with rich imagery, such as the High Priestess or the Wheel of Fortune. It may even be helpful to write down your associations, and see how many you can tabulate. There are no right or wrong answers to this exercise. To some degree, you will discover something about the content and organization of your own subconscious, as well as the meaning of these cards, through this exercise. Once you have developed some ability to associate easily with the cards that are rich in imagery, then go on and work with some of the more abstract ones in the deck, such as the 3 of Swords or the Ace of Pentacles. In this phase of the exercise, you will be forced to stimulate your associative mechanism more abstractly.

Activating the associative mechanism in this way will also help you understand why I prefer the Aquarian Tarot. In studying a card such as the Ace of Cups, for example, your attention will first be drawn to its obvious features—the cup, floating as it were on the surface of a pond, the lotus flowers around its base, and the rising (or setting) sun peeping out of the top of the cup, radiating yellow light in an upward direction. But as your reflection deepens, you will notice details that are not present in other Tarot decks. Look at the pattern on the cup itself—what does it mean? Does this pattern appear in other cards in the Aquarian Tarot? What does it mean there? Why is the surface of the pond a clean white? What associations do you make with that? What is under the surface of the water? Why are two lotus blossoms yellow and one tan or pink? Why is the background white?

Again, we are not looking for right or wrong answers; this is not a quiz. We are simply looking for the associations you would make with these details. You may be surprised what you come up with!

Once the associative mechanism is activated, the next step is nurturing it. We need to feed our imagination the kind of associations that will help us interpret the symbolism of the Real

Tarot accurately. It is for this reason that we should shy away from books that are steeped in the traditional fortune telling interpretations of the Tarot. These interpretations would only pollute our associative mechanism and trap us in the astral dimensions of this device.

Nurturing our associative mechanism is not something that can be done in forty-eight hours, or even a few months. It is a life-long adventure that involves feeding the mind with a wide range of cultural, psychological, and esoteric structures that will enrich and expand the structure we are building with the Tarot. It is not possible to list all the possible sources for nurturing the associative mechanism in this way. Some of the best places to start, however, would include:

• Reading the Bible, especially the New Testament. You will be surprised how easy it is to see parallels between Biblical stories and principles and the various cards of the Tarot. The 2 of Pentacles, for instance, contains echoes of the woman at the well. In certain contexts, drawing a parallel between the story of the Good Samaritan and the 10 of Swords might be helpful in interpreting this card. Temperance, from the major arcana, certainly is suggestive of many of the references to angels in the Bible, and their role in bridging the gap between God and man. Just so, the World, the Wheel of Fortune, and the Chariot all have obvious roots in the visions of Ezekiel. As such, one potential meaning these cards might have when they appear in the spread is the admonition that the higher self is speaking to you through this message; do not ignore its true significance.

• A study of world mythology, especially Greek and Roman, Egyptian, Norse, and the Arthurian legend. These stories all deal with archetypal forces presented symbolically. Even where there is no direct reference, therefore, a basic understanding of any codification of archetypal patterns will be helpful in working with the Tarot.

It will be even more beneficial when the imagery of the Tarot evokes a specific myth. A knowledge of the story of the Phoenix, for instance, is helpful to understanding the full significance of the Star. There are many parallels between the Empress and the Egyptian goddess Isis. An awareness that wings denote the ability to use the intuition in certain mythologies may help you interpret cards like the Wheel of Fortune, the Knight of Cups, and the Six of Swords. A knowledge of creation stories from different cultures will also enrich your use of the Tarot.

In this light, special mention should be made of the movie *Excalibur*, which is a dramatization of the King Arthur story and easily available on videocassette. In many ways, this wonderful movie is a three-dimensional study in the Tarot. Scene after scene brings specific cards to life, almost as if they were deliberately patterned after the Tarot. When Lancelot is leading Guinevere to her wedding, for instance, her maids in waiting ride on a cart rigged up very much like the scene in the 4 of Rods. When Arthur drives the sword between the sleeping bodies of Lancelot and Guinevere, it brings the symbolism of the Ace of Swords dramatically to life. The misty scene of the funeral boat carrying the body of Arthur out to sea, in the final moments of the film, is highly reminiscent of the 4 of Swords. Part of the remarkable parallelism between this film and the Tarot is due to the obvious fact that the movie is set in the Middle Ages, and the Tarot is likewise medieval in flavor. But the symbolic parallels are not just superficial; the words Arthur utters as he plunges the sword into the earth, shattering the spine of the dragon, are profound: "A king without a sword; a land without a king." These words touch on an important facet of the meaning of the Ace of Swords.

• *The Greater Trumps*, by Charles Williams. This is the one book in print dealing with the Tarot that is recommended. While it pays homage to the role of the gypsies in preserving the Tarot, it does not in any way fall prey to gypsy fortune telling influences. Written as a novel, *The Greater Trumps* deals with the Tarot not as a deck of cards but as a set of primordial, archetypal forces that can actually be invoked and harnessed for specific uses. In the context of the novel, this use happens to be murder, but it is also a superior knowledge of the Real Tarot which blocks the murder and reveals God's redeeming love. More can be learned about the archetypal realities behind the Tarot by reading this book than in any other way.

A less successful, and not recommended, novelization of the Tarot is *The Tarot Trilogy* by Piers Anthony. Although many other novels by this author, especially *The Magic of Xanth* series, are excellent, he did not succeed in avoiding the influences of the fortune telling Tarot in this set.

• A study in alchemy. Being a product of the Middle Ages, the Tarot is heavily steeped in the esoteric traditions of that time. Alchemy is one of them, and many of the symbols in the Tarot have alchemical correspondences. The four suits, for example, correspond to the four alchemical elements of life: the Pentacles represent earth, the Cups represent water, the Rods represent fire, and the Swords represent air. In addition, many of the images on some of the cards, such as the Moon, are so steeped in alchemical allusions that it would be difficult to penetrate to their archetypal significance without some knowledge of these sources. Alchemically, the Moon represents volatility and mutability—the feminine principle. When the Moon appears in a spread, therefore, it almost always carries with it a sense of transitory appearance and susceptibility to the illusions and superstitions of humanity. It also suggests vulnerability to mass consciousness and global "waves" and "tides" of influence.

• A knowledge of the Kabalah. The Kabalah is the esoteric tradition of Jewish mysticism. It forms the foundation of the

66

Western esoteric tradition. Its influence upon the Tarot can be felt at every turn. The twenty-two cards in the major arcana, for instance, correspond to the twenty-two letters in the Jewish alphabet, each of which represents one of the paths in the Kabalistic Tree of Life. The ten numbered cards in each suit can be compared to the ten sephira of the Tree of Life. The three pillars in the 3 of Pentacles correspond to the three pillars of mercy, mildness, and severity in the Kabalah. The same pattern is repeated in the High Priestess, with its depiction of its twin pillars, Jachin and Boaz, from the Temple of Solomon. The apparently missing pillar, in the middle, is known as the Invisible Pillar. It supports the Holy of Holies.

One must explore the Kabalah with restraint, however. It is easy to get too caught up in what amounts to relatively unimportant parallels and correspondences and forget that the purpose of the Tarot—and the Kabalah, too—is to help us discover and examine the archetypal realities of life. Filling our heads with too much esoteric trivia is a good way to trap ourselves in the intellectual Tarot—and many a student who has delved too deeply into the Kabalah has done just that. The Kabalah and the Tarot both are systems that must be used intuitively; we must learn to identify with the moving forces these symbols represent, and learn to work with them at their own levels. We can memorize all the words, letters, and signs, but if we cannot use them archetypically, we have learned nothing at all.

For this reason, the only books on the Kabalah that I recommend are *The Mystical Qabalah* by Dion Fortune and *The Bible and the Tarot* by Corinne Heline.

• Numerology. Numerological symbolism is one of the basic structures of the Tarot. At least a working knowledge of numerology can be helpful in making sense of recurring patterns. Nonetheless, most of the numerological correspondences that anyone needs to know in order to operate the Tarot are given in my upcoming chapter on the ten spiritual lessons.

- Astrology. The usual approach to natal astrology can add some interesting tidbits of esoteric trivia, but not much useful information. Nonetheless, an approach to astrology such as Dr. Robert Leichtman and I take in *Forces of the Zodiac* will enrich the associative mechanism tremendously and prepare you to work more skillfully with the Tarot.

- Other Tarot decks. It is interesting to compare other valid Tarot decks with the one you are using, not so much to see how they are similar but rather to see how they differ. In the Aquarian Tarot, for example, the woman in The World is fully clothed, whereas she is nude in most other decks. This may seem like a trivial difference, except that in esoteric symbolism an unclothed woman represents the archetypal force of Truth. The decision to portray the woman as fully clothed in the Aquarian Tarot therefore suggests that the views of the world—"worldly wisdom," as we call it—hide the truth rather than reveal it. We hide our eyes from esoteric realities and become like an ostrich, burying our heads in the sand of materialism, so that we will not have to confront what we know to be true. Much the reverse is the case with the High Priestess. In most Tarot decks, she sits in front of a veil that hides us from inner secrets. In the Aquarian deck, the veil has been pulled back to reveal a vision of what we are to obtain. These are significant variations, and as such, they reveal a great deal about the meaning of these cards.

- Other tools of divination. The use of the I Ching, the Runes, and similar tools of divination can greatly enhance the use of the Tarot. Each of these is a symbolic system representing archetypal forces; as we learn to work them, they shed light on our understanding of the archetypal forces we encounter with the Tarot.

- Knowledge of the steps involved in personal growth. The

Tarot is a tool for examining our inner selves and exploring the inner dimensions of life. Being archetypal in design, the use of the Tarot will reveal to us a steady progression of lessons, first in personal growth and later in spiritual growth. Having been developed originally by initiates for use in their training programs, the Tarot is designed expressly to encourage this kind of growth. To whatever degree we can learn about the basic steps and lessons of esoteric growth, therefore, we will better understand the symbolism and dynamics of the Tarot. Studying the twelve labors of Hercules, especially as interpreted by a writer such as Alice Bailey, is an excellent way to accomplish this. Working with the Muses and the Graces, as described in essays in volumes IV and V of *The Art of Living* series by Dr. Leichtman and myself is also recommended. Another good source of insight into the lessons of growth would be my book, *The Light Within Us*.

• Other sources describing archetypal realities. In interpreting the Tarot, it is important to give our associative mechanism free reign, to associate with whatever images or patterns strike us as relevant. But even though we must be open to virtually any kind of association that would be relevant, we cannot afford to let this process become disorderly or chaotic. We must work always with a sense of purpose—to discern the archetypal realities these symbols represent. So we must nourish our associative mechanism with as much information about these divine forces as possible. This requires a certain amount of digging on our part, because there is no readily available anthology of archetypes we can consult. We must search for our clues in good poetry, great artwork, and inspired music, as well as in sources already mentioned—the Bible, the scriptures and myths of other cultures, and the inspired writings of enlightened people. The more we can mold our thinking and values in harmony with archetypal forces, the more profound our ability to use the Tarot will become.

Once the associative mechanism has been activated and nourished, all that remains is to begin creating a structure of associations based on the Tarot itself. In other words, we start interpreting the cards as they appear in answer to actual questions. Each question we work with in this way will give us new insights into the meaning of the cards. As we file these insights away in our associative mechanism, consultation after consultation, we begin to build an elaborate structure of meaning and insight in our own subconscious. It is almost as if we are building a replica of the Real Tarot within our own awareness!

There are a number of tricks we can use to help us in decoding the message of each individual card as it arises in response to our questions. One of the best is to establish a dialog with the card itself, just as I did with the Page of Rods a few chapters ago. Personify the primary symbol on the card as a human being you can talk with and then, in your mind's eye, engage in conversation. Ask him or her to explain the card's meaning to you, its origin, its archetypal nature, and how it applies to your question. Let the personification ask questions of you and challenge you to view your situation from different perspectives.

A second method that can be used is identification. Instead of chatting with The Magician, for instance, it can be even more powerful and informative to become The Magician in your imagination for a short while. What forces are at your disposal? What do you plan to do with the symbols of the elements on the table? Where are you heading? How does all this affect the question at hand?

A third suggestion is to speculate on the archetypal force this card represents, and then look at the situation at hand from its perspective. This approach takes you one step closer to the archetypal meaning and power of the Real Tarot than chatting or identifying with the image. Perhaps the card you are decoding is the

Queen of Pentacles. In studying her face and robe, you are struck by the sublime elegance of this woman. You also note the wing on her helmet, which indicates strong intuitive abilities. From this basis, you try to speculate on the archetypal force the Queen represents. The idea of the divine grace that understands our weaknesses and flaws and helps us overcome them begins to take shape in your thinking. You can then take this idea and look at your question and see how the Queen of Pentacles, embodying this divine principle, would solve your problem.

Beware of superficial, easy answers, however. The object of using the Tarot is not to see how quickly you can zip through all ten positions and come up with a plausible answer. Our goal is to produce a thorough understanding of the forces and hidden factors influencing this situation, and how to work with them. So gear your efforts accordingly. I often spend as much as 90 minutes on a single Tarot layout. This averages out to about nine minutes a card.

Above all, learn to rely on your intuition. Do not use formulas—think! In the traditional use of the Tarot, if a card appears upside down in a layout, it is interpreted differently than if it appears upright. In most cases, the meaning is reversed; for example, if the Ace of Cups is said to represent wealth in the upright position, it supposedly represents bankruptcy if it appears upside down. This is an example of the kind of formulistic thinking that weakens the effectiveness of the Tarot. There *can* be significance in whether a card is upright or reversed, but it is nothing that can or should be reduced to a formula. In point of fact, far less harm (indeed, none at all) would be done by ignoring the difference between upright and reversed than by ascribing the silly meanings cited in the usual fortune telling Tarot text. If you want to include these factors in your interpretations, do it intuitively. Once the cards are laid out, but before you begin to interpret them, try to discern what upright and reversed cards imply for this particular question. In many cases, this will give you a vital clue toward interpreting the cards.

In some instances, the upright cards will indicate the situation as viewed by the personality, while the reversed cards will reveal the perspective of the higher self. In other cases, the upright cards may indicate things you are doing correctly, while the reversed cards point to false assumptions or self-deceptions. In two-part questions, such as—"What are the origins of my health problem and what can I do to cure it?"—the upright cards will often pertain to one half of the question, and the reversed cards will deal with the other half.

Also keep in mind that while all of the archetypal forces in the Real Tarot are constructive, divine energies, the messages you receive from any given card will not always be positive. Indeed, the Tarot may often seem to scold you or issue you frank warnings. The Sun is a very pleasant card to look at, for example, but if it appears in a reading concerning your relationship with your children, it may be a warning that you are misusing your authority. You are demanding their respect without necessarily treating them in ways that command respect. In much the same way, an unpleasant card such as Death may bring you a very positive, uplifting message—for instance, that a cycle of worries and stresses is about to come to an end, leading to a time of rebirth and renewal.

Generally speaking, it is best to start the work of decoding these messages by interpreting the first card in the map and working in sequential order through the rest of the layout, culminating with the tenth card. But feel free to deviate from this order whenever appropriate. If the first card is one of the cards from the suit of Cups, and there are three other cards from that suit in the layout, you may want to examine all four of these cards at the same time, to see how they relate to each other—and the answer.

As you proceed, do not worry if you are proceeding correctly or not. Trust in your intuition to guide you. Once you have formulated a question and laid out ten cards, only one thought should guide you: discerning the answer. Do not fall into the trap of thinking that you must interpret every detail on every card. The cards themselves have no meaning, except to the degree that they reveal to you an intelligent answer to your question. So look for the common meanings and associations among these cards. Look for patterns and repeated images which unite them. Keep on looking at the cards, both one by one and as a group, until you have distilled their innermost essences, and your answer is revealed.

Another Visit with the Tarot

The doorbell rang. I went to answer it. There was the artisan from the 3 of Pentacles, standing on my front stoop.

"I thought I gave you fair coverage back in Chapter Four," I said.

"Is that any way to welcome an old friend? Show a little hospitality."

"Excuse me," I replied. "I'm a bit worn out from writing all day, and you were the last person—uh, force, or whatever you are—that I expected to see."

"That's why I was sent. Frankly, we images are worried that the process of learning the Tarot may be sounding overwhelming to some of your readers."

"Overwhelming?"

"Exactly. I know you don't intend to give that impression, but you have to understand that one of the charms of the usual way of interpreting the Tarot is that it is so easy. People can lay out a spread, look up the meaning in their guide book, and crank out an interpretation."

"A very superficial interpretation!" I cried.

"I know that and you know that. But you also know that many people would rather have a superficial interpretation, or even a wrong one, than none at all. There are all kinds of people in the world, and some of them are not looking for the best way, just the easiest way. That's why fortune telling is so appealing."

"Well, there is no easy way to develop real competence in using the Tarot. But if they follow my suggestions and practice enough, they will find that it is not really hard to use the Tarot, even if it is not easy."

"Is that a Zen koan?" the artisan asked. "It ain't hard but it ain't easy?"

"Something like that. How would you get the message across?"

"I would ask them to keep the 3 of Pentacles in mind. It's the image of a lovely cathedral or temple, almost completed. It is filled with arches and naves and must have required outstanding genius to design and enormous organizational skill to build. The prospect of building a cathedral like this would be overwhelming to almost anyone. But you know, it was actually built by ordinary people, very much like the readers of your book. We built the temple brick by brick, stone by stone. We were guided by blueprints, but anyone who ever had a set of blocks as a child would have been capable of doing the actual work. When you look at it on that scale, the project is still mammoth, but not overwhelming.

"The same is true about learning to use the Tarot. Your readers do not need perfect knowledge of these cards before they begin. They can build their understanding of the Tarot brick by brick, stone by stone. And that is the way they ought to do it. If they try to use someone else's interpretations—even yours—they'll never discover the power of the Tarot. But if they use their own associations, and build them as they get to know each card, they will soon comprehend the mystery of the Tarot. They need to realize, of course, that the Tarot is guided by an inner design, just as the building of a cathedral is. But the work of building it in their own awareness is something they must do for themselves."

"Very nicely put," I said.

"There's one more thing," added the artisan. "They should have fun doing it. Let me tell you a story. It's an old story—you may have heard it before—but it is still a good one. There was a construction crew working on a new building. A fellow walked by and began to watch them work. Finally, he went up to one worker and asked, 'What are you doing?' 'I'm a mason,' he said. 'I'm laying the stone for this wall.' The fellow walked over to another man and asked, 'What are you doing?' 'I'm a carpenter; I'm building this form where they will pour concrete.' He went to a third man, who didn't seem to be doing anything, and asked the same question. 'I'm a foreman; I'm supervising a part of the crew.' Finally, he went up to a young fellow who seemed to be nothing more than a gopher for the more skilled workers. 'Can you tell me what you are doing?' the fellow asked. 'Me?' the gopher asked. 'Why, I'm building a cathedral!'

"Just remember," said the 3 of Pentacles, who was now starting to fade from view. At least, I could see the sky and the clouds right through him, just as you can see through the cathedral of the 3 of Pentacles. "We are building a cathedral, somewhere, somehow, in our lives. And we should behave as such. We should have fun! What good can ever come of any structure, inner or outer, unless it radiates the joy and inspiration with which it was built?"

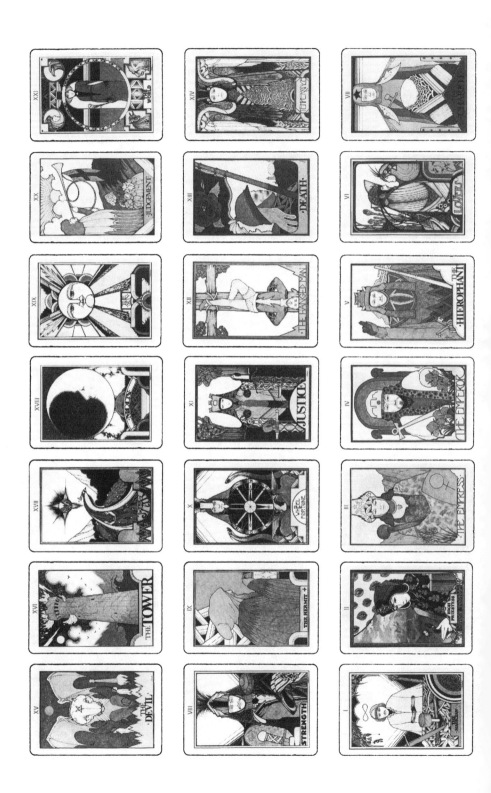

CHAPTER SEVEN

The Major Arcana

Of the seventy-eight cards in the Tarot deck, twenty-two form what is known as the major arcana, or the greater trumps. Each of these cards has a descriptive label—such as The Tower or Justice—and symbolically portrays an archetypal force. There are many ways these cards can be interpreted. I regard the major arcana as the primary expressions or emanations of divine life—the basic creative forces of life, in a sense. By comparison, the cards of the minor arcana represent the steps we human beings must take in learning to use these forces—the steps on the spiritual path as we move from novice to initiate.

In trying to understand the major arcana and how the cards that form it are to be interpreted, it is helpful to divide them into three groups of seven cards. The cards numbered 1 through 7 form the first group, those numbered 8 through 14 form the second group, and those numbered 15 through 21 form the third group. The Fool, which is numbered "0," stands by itself as the card of synthesis—the card that unifies the rest of the major arcana.

I call the first group of seven cards the Divine Personas, as each one represents a personification of some aspect of divine life. As such, they evoke comparisons to the muses and graces of Greek literature; they embody a divine principle. The seven Divine Personas are:

1. The Magician.
2. The High Priestess.

3. The Empress.

4. The Emperor.

5. The Hierophant.

6. The Lovers.

7. The Chariot.

In my terminology, the second group of seven are the Divine Attributes, as each one represents a quality or force of divine expression. They embody the forces that influence our lives and that we need to learn to work with, as we strive to grow spiritually. In one sense, they represent the tools that God—or an advanced Initiate—works with in pursuing His creative goals. The seven Divine Attributes are:

8. Strength.

9. The Hermit.

10. The Wheel of Fortune.

11. Justice.

12. The Hanged Man.

13. Death.

14. Temperance.

I refer to the third set of seven in the major arcana as the Divine Spheres, as each of these cards represents a sphere of divine influence, a dominion. It is almost as if these are the divine kingdoms or principalities in which each of the seven Personas rules. The seven Divine Spheres are:

15. The Devil.

16. The Tower.

17. The Star.

18. The Moon.

19. The Sun.

20. Judgment.

21. The World.

It can be most interesting to lay the cards out in three rows of seven, as described here, and study the parallels from one row to the next. The High Priestess, the Hermit, and the Tower, for example, all fall in the second position in each of the three rows. In the High Priestess card, the inner vision is being unveiled; in the Hermit, the vision or truth is hidden at dimensions he has not yet penetrated. The Tower card implies that the process of discovering the inner vision and applying it to our life often involves crisis; the curtain is rent by a direct strike of lightning, as it were. We must know who we are and what we stand for before we start exploring the true nature of the plans of the higher self.

In reading the Tower card as it comes up in a spread, therefore, it may often be helpful to remember its relationship with the High Priestess and the Hermit. These other cards may not appear in your map, but their presence should be felt intuitively, through the appearance of the Tower.

Similar patterns can be seen among the Magician, Strength, and the Devil, all of which appear in the first position of each row. Note in particular the V-shaped lines which appear in the background of the Magician and Strength, and which are formed by implication by the wing pattern of the beast representing the Devil. The Magician and Strength are the only two cards in the whole deck in which this pattern can be found so distinctly, although it does appear in a subdued fashion in the background of Temperance and by allusion in others. It also appears inverted in The Fool and The Wheel of Fortune, and as static, horizontal pattern in The Chariot and The World. To me, these lines represent divine force. In the V-shape, they represent God Immanent, or the expression of divine force through our creative talents. When inverted, they represent God Transcendent, or the expression of divine force through the whole of life. When horizontal, they suggest the interface between heaven and earth. This could imply a stagnant condition, or it could imply that factors are ripe for a major breakthrough into a new arena or sphere of life.

Because of the repeated pattern of God Immanent in the Magician and Strength, it would be silly to believe that the Devil was a negative, sinister card. As has been stated, all of the cards in the Tarot represent archetypal realities; as such, they are neither inherently positive nor inherently negative. They are forces we are meant to learn to use. The force symbolically portrayed as the Devil must therefore be construed as a part of the immanent nature of divine life. It is not necessarily a sign of sin or temptation, although this certainly can be a valid interpretation in certain consultations. As the Magician learns to work creatively with the force of divine Strength, he must pass through stages of imperfection before he achieves perfection. He may suffer loss, criticism, opposition, humiliation, and even a sense of separation from the higher self. These are the byproducts of humanity's efforts to grow. If we leave them behind us, they do not hinder us. But if we allow them to traumatize us, they can trap us in the "sphere" symbolically known as The Devil. This is the human capacity to create illusion and glamour and believe it to be real. It is the source of cruelty, bigotry, anger, and malice, but also the source of our wish life, escapist fantasies, and self-deceptions, individually and collectively.

The cards in the major arcana are not just random symbols. They are designed to relate to one another, and often the clues of relationship and association are the smallest, seemingly most insignificant details in a card. The intricate designs at the top of The Magician suggest an awareness of archetypal patterns and designs; this symbolism is repeated in a cruder way in the headdress of the dog in Strength, and is completely absent in The Devil. Part of the drama of the Devil, therefore, seems to involve such complete absorption in form that divine origins are forgotten. Whether this is a blessing or a curse will involve other factors, and quite probably our own orientation.

Parallel patterns can also be spotted in the three cards in the fourth position of each row. In this case, the primary theme is balance or equilibrium. Few cards of the major arcana are more symmetrical than these three. Each of the cards is framed by twin pillars. In justice, the pillars are sheaves of rods on either side of the goddess. In the Emperor, they are the ram's head rods which grace either side of his throne. In the Moon, they are more abstract, being part of the art deco ornamentation at the bottom of the card, which represents the monolithic, unredeemed force of materialism. A strong sense of mercy and grace is conveyed by these three cards. In the Moon, we are at the mercy of environmental forces and raw materialism— meaning, in effect, that there is no mercy. In Justice, we come under the laws of life, and begin to understand how hardship and suffering can help us grow. We learn, and taste mercy for the first time. In the Emperor, the potential for mercy and grace reaches its fullest expression, as we harness the impulse to grow in its fullest scope.

For readers with a background in esoteric studies, many other associations will suggest themselves. There is an obvious correlation, for example, with the seven positions in the major arcana and the seven days of creation, as well as with many other septenates. In pursuing some of these correspondences, however, it is important not to overdo them, nor force meanings on the cards that do not naturally emerge out of them. It is all too easy to slip into the trap of esoteric trivia, where you become so absorbed in finding parallels and correspondences that you forget the active purpose behind your studies. Our goal here is only to enrich our associations with each card—not to become so bogged down in trivia that we paralyze our capacity to think! We want to challenge and stimulate our thinking—not fill our minds with formulistic thinking that might clog our associative mechanism.

Keeping this in mind, we shall explore the inner meanings of each card in the major arcana in more detail, starting with the seven cards known as the Divine Personas:

The Magician

The "bookends" of the major arcana are The Magician and The Fool. The Magician is numbered one; The Fool is numbered zero and is placed at the end of the arcana, in the twenty-second position. The Magician is a symbol of God Immanent; The Fool is a sign of God Transcendent. The Magician possesses all of the tools of the Tarot—the Pentacle, the Cup, the Rod, and the Sword; The Fool possesses only the Rod and a pure white rose.

The Magician is the epitome of creative skill in bringing heaven to earth. He is capable of both abstract and analytical thought; he acts under the sign of infinity, which hovers over his head like a halo, but is girded at the waist by the serpent, the sign of wisdom in action. He knows how to harness and control the natural forces of life, both within his own system and within his environment. He is likewise able to penetrate and work with archetypal forces, represented by the ornate decorations at the top of the card and translate these forces into inspired plans and projects, represented by the pattern of the table-top, which is reproduced in The Hermit. The circular pattern in the lower right-hand corner, with the bubbly design of red and black, indicates that he is able to act as an agent of God in unlocking the secrets of nature and finding new uses for the resources of planet Earth. The rod in the background suggests that the magic he performs is all done "behind the scenes," at the level of the mind.

86

This is the card of genius and mastery of esoteric forces.

When the Magician appears in a spread, it tends to indicate competence and skill in the endeavor under exploration. There is also a strong suggestion that the higher self is in control, directing and guiding events from an unseen level. Depending upon the question asked and the position the card occupies in the map, The Magician could mean:

• You need to acquire greater competence or skill.
• You need to utilize the skills you have to a greater degree.
• This issue demands competence and skill, not just hope and faith.
• There is a need for greater professionalism.
• You are over-estimating your competence and skill.
• You need to express the wisdom and guidance of the higher self.
• You need to evaluate the larger picture, not get bogged down in details.
• You need to stop expecting a miracle to rescue you, and tackle your problem with old-fashioned hard work.
• Work with a greater awareness of archetypal patterns.
• You are accountable for the quality of work being performed.

The High Priestess

The High Priestess is the feminine counterpart of The Magician. Whereas The Magician veils his true identity as a priest, the High Priestess does not. In this way, the esoteric and the exoteric are joined. The High Priestess sits on an altar chair in front of a curtain decorated with symbols of fertility. The curtain is drawn, revealing a vision of a castle in faraway mountains, with a river running from it through the valley toward The High Priestess in the foreground. Her face and left hand are perfectly white, suggesting a transition from the physical plane to the inner, invisible dimensions of life. In her hand, she holds beautiful flowers; a butterfly is resting on one. Her headdress is adorned by a pattern similar to the table-top pattern of The Magician; her cloak is covered with images of leaves. Her headdress has a beaded string descending from it and draped over her shoulder. In the right foreground are two canisters which represent the twin pillars of discipleship, Boaz and Joachin. In the Rider deck, she wears a cross as a necklace, holds a scroll labeled *Tora*, and sits with a crescent at her feet. In that illustration, also, the curtain is closed, not open.

The High Priestess represents the intuitive side of our nature. When we are working correctly with this force, it will be as though we are able to draw aside the curtain of any issue or question and see the reality behind it. To develop our intuition to this point, however, we must undergo much instruction and many tests. We must enter the temple of Solomon (the wisdom of our own higher self) and stand before the twin pillars. From that point on, we must rely on our intuition to guide us, as we make our way toward true intuition and the capacity to use it in exploring the inner dimensions of life. We must learn to discover and balance the masculine and feminine principles within us; we must learn to discern the presence of God within every living thing; we must learn to identify so fully with the archetypal forces and patterns of life that we begin to embody their beauty, joy, and grace. In this regard, note the decorative design at the bottom of the card, below the actual illustration. It is almost as though the knowledge of the archetypes has become so ingrained in consciousness that it has "dropped below the threshold." The High Priestess, in other words, would not use the Tarot; she *is* the Tarot.

When The High Priestess appears, it tends to indicate the need to be inspired and guided by an inner plan or vision. There is a strong suggestion that new growth will be required to understand and implement this plan. In specific situations, The High Priestess may imply:

- You have cut yourself off from your true sources. Re-establish contact.
- This situation is a test of your discernment and capacity to respond to inner guidance. Act wisely.
- You need to achieve better balance in expressing both the masculine and feminine sides of your nature.
- You are behaving somewhat like a "wicked witch." Soften your behavior and learn to act with more grace and goodwill.
- The answers you seek lie within yourself. Seek within.
- You need to learn basic lessons in spiritual growth and develop a stronger sense of awe for the mysteries of life.
- You have inner connections you are unaware of. Rely on them.

The Empress

The Empress and the Emperor combined represent the authority of mankind on earth, just as The Magician and The High Priestess represent our spiritual nature and responsibility. What is the authority of mankind on earth? Primarily, to serve as the paraclete or link between heaven and earth, the channel by which divine inspiration can flow into the lower planes. The exercise of this authority requires us first of all to establish dominion over ourselves, confirming the authority of the higher self over the personality, and second of all to extend this dominion to the work we do.

The Empress derives her authority from the archetypal force of goodwill; she is meant to express her dominion over the earth by nurturing growth wherever it is needed. This may be the growth of new humanity in her womb; it could be the growth of wheat in the fields, as represented by the sheaf in the lower left hand corner. It may be the growth of order and intelligence throughout life as well, for The Empress embodies many of the facets of the Mother aspect of God. The signs of her authority are the staff (a stylized rod) and her shield, by which she protects that which she nurtures, but the essence of her authority is the headdress of starry fire, which emphasizes that she is the agent of divine intelligence on earth. It is important to note that the image of The Empress in the Aquarian Tarot stands in the midst of a barren canyon, with only a waterfall in the background breaking the monolithic rock. This is in stark contrast to other decks, in which The Empress is seated on a throne and surrounded by symbols of luxury. It suggests that the work of the Empress—and the nurturing love and intelligence of all of humanity—is to transform that which is barren into a garden of Eden, not just inherit the garden and preserve it. True creativity and love exerts its dominion by making the desert flourish.

When The Empress appears in answer to a question, it probably indicates a need to nurture and protect the work at hand. This is the card of the enlightened parent, not in the sense of the "earth mother" but in the sense of the divinely inspired guardian of our creative work. In the Golden Dawn deck, a dove of the Holy Spirit hovers over The Empress's left shoulder. This is a significant enrichment of the symbolism of the card. In specific cases, the presence of The Empress may indicate:

• A need to exercise authority and dominion over our subconscious.

• The need for more self-discipline in learning to use the mind.

• The need to express more care and nurturing love in the situation.

• The need to protect that which is cherished or sacred.

• You are behaving like a spoiled child; heed the higher self.

• The work at hand requires feminine input.

• The issue at hand is barren; unless you can find a way to touch its inner life with nurturing love, nothing will come from it.

It should be added that The Empress neatly states that love is not something expressed only through the heart. It is expressed by the fiery mind as well, the fully developed intelligence that guides and leads expertly while nourishing our growth potential.

The Emperor

The second half of the story of mankind's authority on earth is portrayed in the symbolism of The Emperor, the fourth card in the major arcana. Whereas The Empress derives her authority from the nurturing power of love, The Emperor derives it from the building, creative power of the will. He penetrates to the heart of purpose in any issue, and from this identification with purpose derives the power he needs to act in harmony with divine intent. "Thy will be done" is the mantra of The Emperor as well as the Christ.

The Emperor sits on a throne flanked by ram's heads. Only the upper portion of the throne can be seen in the Aquarian Tarot, whereas in other decks the throne itself is as important as The Emperor, sometimes more so. The throne is often described as a cubic stone and laden with extensive esoteric and masonic symbolism. The Aquarian interpretation helps us remember that we are dealing with the force of authority, not the tangible representations of it. The Emperor holds a scepter in his right hand and a fiery globe, almost a miniature sun, in his left hand. The scepter represents human acceptance of his authority, whereas the fiery ball represents divine right. The headdress is one of the most unusual aspects of this card. The orange cap includes an outline that is undoubtedly meant to represent a crown but reminds me of the skyline of a modern city. From this descends a brown vestment decorated with brown and black dots. There is a sense of identification with the community spirit and public weal of those he leads—not just his own ego. The Emperor represents enlightened leadership at its highest level, as testified to by the flowers in the foreground, which bask in the glory of his power and presence. The

card is saturated with a profound awareness of the responsibility of leadership and authority.

The ram, by the way, is of more than passing interest. In the Golden Dawn deck, the Emperor's feet rest on a living ram. In other decks, the ram is part of the throne. As such, it indicates that The Emperor is working with the same creative forces that set new cycles in motion during the sign of Aries—but only achieves full control of these energies when he learns to set aside personal needs and considerations and sacrifice them for the good of humanity as a whole. The ram embodies both impulse and humility.

When this card appears as part of a layout, it tends to represent the need for enlightened leadership, a benevolent exercise of authority, and a deeper sense of responsibility. It may also indicate a need for forgiveness and mercy. In specific situations, it may imply:

• You can achieve your goal only by making an intelligent sacrifice.

• You need to expand the scope of your responsibility.

• There are people who depend upon the wisdom of your actions.

• You need to base the decisions you must make on an understanding of purpose.

• You must respond to demands with the fullest measure of integrity, mercy, and the capacity to forgive that you can muster.

• You are failing to fulfill the responsibilities given you.

- You are mistaking authority for aggressiveness and domination of others. There is a need to learn inspired humility.
- There is a need for greater respect for true authority.
- There is a rare opportunity to initiate new cycles of creative action.

The Hierophant

A hierophant is not actually an ancestor of the elephant; he is an Initiate of advanced degree who is designated as the keeper of the mysteries. In ancient Greece, the hierophant was the individual who had the official responsibility of interpreting the rites and sacrificial rituals of the mystery schools. In more modern days, the hierophant would be the individual who preserves the accuracy and integrity of the rituals of a lodge. He would not be the one responsible for leading magical ceremonies, but for preserving the traditions of the lodge intact.

The Hierophant is dressed in a blue-gray cloak of oriental character, suggesting that the inner mysteries transcend cultures, religions, and rituals. He wears a crown or helmet with three tiers and carries a triple cross. The crown indicates conscious awareness of spirit, soul, and personality; the cross indicates a capacity to work with the three fires of divine life: cosmic fire, solar fire, and fire by friction. Esoterically, it is the work of the Hierophant to "step down" or translate the energies used in any true ritual so that they can be safely used by the participants in the rite. If this stepping down of energies is performed correctly, without distortion or coloration of the archetypal force, then it can be said that the mysteries have been preserved. The right hand of the Hierophant is raised in blessing, with two fingers extended and two fingers closed, indicating that he knows what to give forth and what to hold back. The base of his cloak is marked by sharp angular designs, indicating that he is well aware of the opposition of the world to the knowledge he guards. He will not "cast his pearls before swine." There are two keys in the immediate foreground, forming a cross. This is a symbol that wisdom must be combined with love—ability must be combined with responsibility—before the secrets of life can be unlocked. The secrets of the Hierophant cannot be acquired forcibly.

When The Hierophant appears in a layout, it is usually an indication that there is much to be learned about the true workings of the situation at hand. There are inner dimensions and forces at work that have been overlooked or ignored. We must gain some knowledge of these elements before we can master the situation—and we must rely on the higher self to guide us correctly. In specific situations, the Hierophant may indicate:

• You are being blinded by prejudices, narrow thinking, or self-deception. Open your eyes to the reality before you.

• You should seek guidance from someone who knows more than you.

• You are facing obstacles greater than yourself. Cultivate the inner resources that will enable you to handle them effectively.

• Increase your trust in the higher self.

• You are learning valuable lessons about the inner workings of life through this situation.

• Learn to tap the rich power in the traditions you have been taught.

• There is a tendency to condemn, criticize, or reject that which you do not understand. You need to become more tolerant.

The Lovers

The sixth card of the major arcana, The Lovers, has nothing to do with human romance. Nor does it have a direct reference to divine love, for that matter. It deals instead with the male and female dualism of all divine energies. In a very real sense, creation is made possible by the interplay of opposites. This dualism has

94

already been referred to in the major arcana by the pillars of Joachin and Boaz in The High Priestess and the crossed keys of The Hierophant. The challenge of the spiritual aspirant is to find "the Noble Middle Way" which reconciles the opposites, and thereby completes creation. This Noble Middle Way is not just the midpoint between the two poles; it is more the apex of an equilateral triangle from which both extremes—and every point on the baseline in between—can be harnessed and directed. It is therefore *the union* of The Lovers which is most significant, not the maleness or femaleness of either one.

The symbolism of The Lovers is especially rich in the Aquarian Tarot. It portrays the two people almost as though they were from the bird kingdom, the male bedecked in peacock-like finery, the female beautiful and yet subdued in color by comparison. There is a sheaf of growing rods in the left background, indicating that the union of the opposites is something that can occur only as the mental principle grows and matures. The ornamentation in the lower right corner emphasizes that we are exploring archetypal principles in this card, not issues of sex and romance. The swirling pattern of the woman's hair, coupled with the long strands descending from the man's hand, suggest ties of relationship. The decorations on the woman's headband imply that she possesses both intuition and a knowledge of archetypal life; the imagery in the solar plexus region of the male anticipates similar patterns in The Chariot and Temperance, and suggests a tremendous inner power to act, fueled by ancient fires.

The portrayal of The Lovers in the Aquarian Tarot differs significantly from other decks. In the Rider deck, the lovers are presented in the form of Adam and Eve before the fall, overshadowed by an angel of God. In the Golden Dawn deck, the woman, naked, is chained to a stone in the sea, threatened by a sea monster. The male, sword in hand, reaches down from the heavens to defend her against the threat. This emphasizes the inner meaning of sex—the polarity between the personality (compliant) and the higher self (dominant)—but this meaning is likewise included in the Aquarian portrayal, plus much more.

When The Lovers appears in a spread, it should not be interpreted in terms of human romance or sex. It should indicate, instead, that the question involves a duality or set of opposites which must be united. This duality must be defined, reconciled, and then harnessed, so the two can act as one. At the very least, we should view the two halves as a single, united whole in our thinking. In specific situations, this can mean:

• You are not acting in harmony with the higher self. You must learn to look at this issue as the higher self does, and then act on it.

• There are inconsistencies in your values, principles, or habits which are tearing you apart. You need to eliminate these inconsistencies.

• You need to define the divine ideals that should be guiding you and learn to cherish and serve them unreservedly.

• Something vital is missing from the situation and must be supplied.

• Look for people with ideals similar to your own, and incorporate them into your plans.

• Take care not to get caught in an extreme. Seek the higher perspective which harnesses both extremes.

The Chariot

The last of the seven Divine Personas is The Chariot, which perhaps ought to be known as The Charioteer. Especially in the Aquarian Tarot, the driver becomes as important as the vehicle. Of course, the driver represents the higher self, with its plans and goals, and the vehicle represents the personality, with its skills and aptitudes.

The Charioteer is a massive figure—his cloak extends off both sides of the card, seemingly embracing the whole of life. In fact, subtle lines following each shoulder suggest a tremendous capacity to radiate love, wisdom, and joy. There is a black star in the center of his forehead, and horizontal lines of the divine emanation extending from both sides of the upper head. Two half moons, one smiling and one frowning, appear in lieu of breastplate; they seem to have replaced the traditional sphinxes (or horses) as the motivating power for the chariot. The charioteer wears a sword on his right side. The chariot itself is a strange vehicle. Red and gray stripes form a V which introduces a thematic reference to conflict; just above it is a black and white bubbly design which introduces a thematic reference to ancient weaknesses and unredeemed evil. The top of the chariot is pure white. It is almost as though this is a portrayal of a furnace in which the dross of our past is ignited and burns white hot, providing the thrust for the chariot.

When The Chariot appears in a Tarot spread, it tends to indicate that we need greater detachment. We have been caught up in the endless "rat races" of humanity and are just going in circles, without accomplishing anything. We need to see the distinction between the driver and the vehicle, and realize that the driver—the higher self—is able to remain changeless even as the chariot speeds toward its destiny and undergoes both change and transformation. In specific instances, The Chariot can mean:

• There are hidden, possibly repressed issues to be dealt with. These need to be discovered, confronted, and redeemed.

• You are being driven by circumstances. You need to take control and become the driver.

• You are dangerously close to conditions of psychological "burn out."

• The situation is not the mystery you are trying to make it. You are a victim only of your own self-deception.

• The patterns of conflict found in present conditions can be traced to far earlier events. The antecedents must be resolved before the present can improve.

The Chariot completes the story of the Divine Personas. But the tale of the Tarot continues with the seven cards of the Divine Attributes. Keep in mind that these are abstract archetypal forces. They are used by God continuously in the work of divine creation, and they are meant to be used by us as well, as we gain skill in working intuitively and creatively. The seven Divine Attributes are:

Strength

There is a human tendency to think of divine strength in terms of the wrath of God—something to fear. This is unfortunate, because it alienates us from the divine strength we can find within ourselves—the inner strength of courage, steadfastness, determination, and a value-based character. This is the strength to express our talents and abilities, not hide them shyly lest others criticize us. It is the strength to affirm the presence of God within us through everything we do.

The Aquarian portrayal of Strength captures its essence extremely well. It depicts a soldier in sleek armor with a sword in his right hand. In the right foreground is a highly-trained dog with a headdress with triangular decorations. The dog is joined to his master by a leash. There is a metallic epaulet on the soldier's shoulder, and feathers extending from the top of his helmet. In the background are the V-shaped lines of divine immanence which appear also in The Magician. This portrayal is a radical departure from the standard Tarot representation of Strength, which is a woman with a lion. But symbolically, the difference is less radical. Both the soldier and the woman represent the higher self; the soldier of the Aquarian Tarot simply reminds us more forcefully of the enormous strength to be drawn from these inner dimensions. Both the carefully manicured dog and the lion represent the personality, under full control of its master but able to translate its strength into the physical plane. This is not a card of authority (which is sometimes confused with strength), but more a card of integrity and the power to act in accord with directions.

When this card appears in response to a question, it probably indicates that we need to draw on the strength of the higher self and learn to act with greater courage, strength of character, or determination. It does *not* mean that we should become more aggressive, pushy, or selfish. In specific situations, it can mean:

• You need to become more consistent in your efforts to act. You have good ideas, but too often fail to act on them.

• You need to defend your creative ideas and projects from sabotage.

• There is a need for greater discipline; you are squandering your energy and opportunities.

• There is a danger of betrayal; hold fast to your ideals.

• You lust too much for power and strength. This is self-destructive.

• You need to deal firmly with others, holding to your values; nevertheless, you must treat them benevolently and kindly.

• Your course is a proper one: overcoming the obstacles before you will strengthen your position.

The Hermit

The Hermit is one of the most misunderstood cards of the entire Tarot. It is often interpreted in terms of the seeker of Truth or the lonely isolation of the spiritual aspirant. In fact, The Hermit is something of a code name for humanity as a whole. It is the spiritual destiny of humanity to develop its true individuality while simultaneously learning to identify with the spiritual essence of all of life. It is for this reason that we endure the seeming conflict between ego and altruism. Ultimately, we resolve this conflict and achieve a state of consciousness Alice Bailey labels "isolated unity." It is this state of consciousness, and its corresponding capacity for action, that The Hermit embodies.

The Hermit is an old man dressed in a mauve stocking cap and a flowing purple robe. He has a long white beard but we can see little of his face, for he is turned inward. He holds in his right hand a lantern lit by a star. In the right background is a tan void; in the left background is a black and white structure which resembles the table-top of The Magician. It is clear from this portrayal that The Hermit is not seeking truth—he has found it. The black-and-white lattice work represents the abstract archetypal patterns of the divine mind. The star in the lantern indicates that not only can The Hermit explore divine archetypes, he is able to translate them into specific work and activities. He is able to light the world through his actions. He has withdrawn from the world only to the degree that he bases his thought and understanding on the divine plan; otherwise, he is active, involved, and productive. He is the role model for humanity.

When The Hermit appears in a Tarot spread, it tends to suggest that there is a need for greater understanding of the underlying issues involved. Current actions may be based on false assumptions or wrong information. There is a need to appeal to the higher self for new insight and direction. In specific instances, it can also indicate:

100

- You are too cynical or nihilistic. You have spent more time looking into the void than exploring the realities of life. This has unbalanced you.
- You pay too much attention to "the wisdom of the world."
- You are distracted by trivial issues. Focus on substance.
- The mind is an important resource. Develop and train it.
- You have many talents and abilities you are not expressing. Let your light shine into the world!
- There is a tendency toward misanthropy. This is unhealthy. Open up new contacts by which you can share your humanity.
- You are too dogmatic and strident. Adopt gentler methods.
- You have a good mind, but do not always use it to its fullest. Learn to penetrate to the core of ideas.

The Wheel of Fortune

Divine intelligence and order pervades all of manifest life. It governs the growth of trees, the flight of birds, the emergence and extinction of species, and the rise and fall of nations. Life does not unfold at random; it is the embodiment of a divine plan. As humans, we have the free will to choose our own direction and course, but even these choices are made within a context of divine intelligence and the cycles of divine activity. If we act wisely, we will draw to us a harvest of future opportunities; if we act foolishly, we will draw to us a crop of future problems and hardships. It is not necessary to believe in this; because all of life is permeated with divine intelligence, it happens automatically. The ancients believed in Fate, and felt that it governed our lives; the spiritual aspirant knows that the wheel of fortune is nothing other than divine intelligence, operating in accord with the divine plan.

The Wheel of Fortune in the Aquarian Tarot is embodied in the chest of a man, whose headdress of fire and will radiates upward off the top of the card. The inverted V-design of lines appears from

above the card, indicating that we are dealing here with an aspect of God Transcendent, the universal divine force which governs the whole universe. Two serpents flank the wheel; they might be opposing forces that set the wheel in motion, but in reality they are complementary forces. They embody the principle that for every action, there is an equal and opposite reaction. At the base of the wheel a winged bull and a winged lion stare at one another. These represent Taurus and Leo on the Fixed Cross of the zodiac; the same portrayal is repeated in The World, where symbols for Aquarius and Scorpio, the other points on the Fixed Cross, appear at the top. (In other decks, these two signs appear on The Wheel of Fortune as well.) Alchemically, Taurus, being an earth sign, represents the fixation that permits spirit to manifest in form. Leo, being a fire sign, represents divine activity and rhythm. The combination of rhythm and resistance makes the wheel go around. The Wheel itself has eight spokes, forming two crosses. At the end of each spoke is a letter. The Hebrew letters spell *Jehovah*; the English letters spell *rota* (wheel) or *taro* (Tarot), depending upon how you unscramble them.

The primary meaning of this card is that the individual events of life, which occur on the outer rim as the wheel turns, cannot be interpreted by themselves. We must penetrate beyond the superficial implications of events and pierce to the core of life's pattern;

102

only there can we see the *words* that the individual letters form. To understand the principles of cause and effect and the creative workings of duality in our life, we must always keep in mind that the wheel is whole, and its rotation emanates from the central hub. Just so, the events of our life only have meaning when viewed from the perspective of the higher self and its plan for our lifetime. Even this plan, in fact, must likewise be viewed in the larger context of the divine plan, which the zodiac reveals.

We must realize, however, that the wheel is not static. It is constantly in motion, spun by divine intent. "Experience" is the intangible residue of what we have learned from the events that have come our way. We need to realize that there are very definite consequences to the actions we take—in a real sense, it is we who choose where the wheel will "stop," taking shape as a specific event. What we experience may at times seem unfair, but it is just an outgrowth of earlier actions and omissions. Experience, in other words, is the building block of our character and talent, and ought to be viewed in this way.

When The Wheel of Fortune appears as an answer to a question, it most likely suggests that there is a guiding, benevolent plan behind the problem, issue, or situation we are involved in. We need to look for this plan, try to understand the lessons we are learning, and then address these real issues. *It is not a sign that we are going to experience good or bad luck!* In specific instances, it can mean:

• Events are unfolding with precise timing. Invoke the guidance of the higher self, so you can be in the right place at the right time.

• The answers you seek lie buried in experiences from earlier in this life.

• Little happens by chance. You have earned what you are experiencing.

• You are not acting in harmony with the cycles of this time.

• The mistakes you have appeared to make are actually steps leading toward an ultimate achievement. Learn the lessons of your life!

• Learn to harness conflicting forces and put them to work toward common ends.

Justice

We usually think of justice in terms of right or wrong; justice is either served or betrayed, depending upon whether wrongs are ferreted out and punished, and rights are rewarded. But this is a limited, superficial understanding of justice. It allows us to misconstrue the whole idea of justice and confuse it with "fairness"—which is often something we evaluate with our emotions. Juries, for example, often pass judgment on their sense of fairness, not justice. Our common notion of justice also orients us more toward wrongs and punishment than it does toward rights and rewards. "Justness" might be a better word for the real spirit of justice—the mental capacity to perceive the correct and proper way to express any divine force and to conform to its divine plan. It judges not on the rightness or wrongness of an act, but on whether or not this act fulfills or betrays inner purpose.

Justice is a woman, symbolizing our need for intuitive perception, who holds the sword of truth in her right hand and the scales of justice in her left. She is not blind. Sheaves of rods serve as pillars on either side of her, reminding us of the great importance of mental discernment and objectivity in issues of justice. The cloth draping from her helmet contains the symbols of archetypal awareness found in The Hermit; her breastplate opens in the center to reveal signs of conflict (the black, bubbly pattern). But her sleeves indicate that these issues can be transformed into correct patterns through the application of justice. In addition, the V-shaped parallel lines at the base of her breastplate subtly suggest that Justice is a living expression of God Immanent. In other words, we are meant to be agents of justice or justness in the way we conduct our lives.

When Justice appears in a Tarot spread, it probably indicates that there are patterns of misconduct or lapses of integrity in the present situation. They will have to be corrected or adjusted. If these are honestly faced and resolved, it will be possible to discover the force of mercy. In specific instances, Justice may indicate:

• You are deceiving yourself. Stop making excuses and rationalizations.

• Your actions are not consistent with your values. Restore balance.

• You are judging others—and yourself—on the basis of prejudices and biases. As a result, you are making a fool of yourself.

• You are holding on to some evil from the past. Learn to forgive.

• Your actions are just and proper. Do not be upset by opposition.

• You must act with the utmost integrity.

• Learn to make the examined life the central pillar of your growth.

The Hanged Man

The duality of life eventually becomes defined as two poles or points of view: the perspective of the personality, grounded in the material world, and the perspective of the higher self, dwelling in spirit. The personality tends to think of itself as a child of the world, its true home and roots being the family and race from which it sprang. The higher self, by contrast, knows it is a child of God whose true home and roots are spirit, the family of man. As the spiritual aspirant struggles to understand this duality, there comes a time when he or she must reverse polarity and begin looking at life from the perspective of the higher self. Once this has happened, the aspirant becomes The Hanged Man.

In the Aquarian deck, The Hanged Man is suspended from a wooden cross that is nonetheless still a living tree. He is tied by his left foot with a rope that ascends straight up the vertical post. His arms are tied behind his back; his right leg is bent underneath the left calf, thereby forming an inverted triangle. This, too, gives us a powerful hint into managing duality. He wears orange hose, red shorts, and a blue-gray jersey with symbols of conflict on the arms and shoulders. A red bolt of lightning fire races along the front of his chest, along the route of the spine. It should be understood that the rope is not a restriction in this card; on the contrary, it symbolizes our true connection to spirit. When we have made this connection and reversed the polarity of our perspective, we can take any risk or make any sacrifice spirit demands of us, because we know we can rely on its support. We do not challenge it to prove this support (as Jesus was asked to do in His three temptations); we simply know from past experience it will be there. The symbolism of the reversal of polarity is also subtly underscored by the bolt of fire on the chest, which indicates that the lower energies of the personality have been lifted up, redeemed, and focused in higher, more creative arenas. The lines at the very bottom of the card suggest a connection to the cards of God Immanent as well.

When The Hanged Man appears in a Tarot layout, it most likely implies that we need to make a major shift in our attitudes, convictions, or polarity in order to act wisely and properly in the situation at hand. In particular, we need to start looking at this situation through the eyes of whatever spiritual force is indicated in the ninth position of the map. But this will not necessarily be an overt shift, say in lifestyle or career; it will more likely be an inner, subtle shift, as we move away from the Shallow Life and begin identifying more and more with our spiritual nature. In specific situations, The Hanged Man can mean:

- Your hands are tied in this situation. You do not control it.
- You need to act as though you were guided by the very best and noblest qualities and skills within you.
- Remember your true tools and sources of power; do not betray them.
- Your grief or suffering is not meant to imprison you; it is meant to inspire you to open a door to a new understanding of life.
- Do not look for the outer elements of life to give meaning to your life. Look within.
- You are being too weak and permissive. Stand upright; voice your convictions.
- You need to identify more with your inner values and principles.

In a very profound way, The Hanged Man as a whole represents the spiritual path each of us must find and follow. Much insight can be gained by reflecting on this card with this idea in mind.

Death

Death is one of the great creative principles of life. It refers not to the end of our physical life, when we transfer our awareness from a physical form to the inner dimensions of life, but rather to the capacity to bring one cycle to an end and prepare the way for a new one. The capacity to summarize the gains of a cycle and fuse or synthesize them into new seeds for the next round of achievement is the work of death. As such, the card Death foreshadows many of the key elements of The Fool.

In the Tarot, Death is portrayed as a soldier riding an unseen horse. The dawn is breaking on the far horizon, with an orange sun rising between twin towers. Death carries a flag emblazoned with a symbol of fertility and new life; he wears a brown hat with red plumes. His face is just a skull; his coat is covered with the pattern of archetypal life seen in The Hermit and The Magician. The ground is brown; the sky is white. Death leads inevitably to rebirth and a new cycle of opportunity. This card is saturated with the joy of achievement.

When this card appears in a Tarot spread, it is not to be construed as a sign of death or misfortune. It probably suggests the need to reform habits, attitudes, methodologies, or approaches. Some area of life has outlived its usefulness, and now it is time to put it to death, before gangrene sets in. In specific situations, it can imply:

• An opportunity you thought to be very much alive is actually dead.

• You have an opportunity to plant seeds from earlier successes.

• Do not bemoan losses in the physical plane.

• Certain ideas are being entertained that ought to be eliminated.

• Elements of fear are crippling your efforts to succeed.

• There is an unparalleled opportunity for growth in the present situation.

• Do not reawaken elements or issues that have already died.

For more insight into death as a creative principle of life, read "The Role Death Plays in Life" from *The Life of Spirit: Volume II*, by Robert R. Leichtman, M.D. and myself.

Temperance

Members of the angel kingdom act by absorbing the divine energies coming to them and then focusing these radiations directly into the lower forms under their supervision. In this way, there is a constant bathing of all life forms with divine life. The human kingdom works in a very much different way, trying to create new physical forms which approximate, ever more closely, the divine pattern that originally inspired them. Eventually, we learn to tap the real power at the heart of the pattern—the archetypal Idea—and we begin working as the angels do, with the added ability to shape forms. Until then, however, we can nevertheless learn an important lesson from the

way the angels work. This lesson is temperance.

We normally think of temperance in terms of abstinence and restraint from any temptation which might cause us to lose our self-control—for example, indulgence in alcohol. This is a distraction from the real meaning of temperance. In its fullest sense, temperance is the ability to hone and sharpen the raw forces of our skills and talents so that they are able to perform at full effectiveness—just as we would temper the blade of a sword. We therefore temper our character in the forge of human experience, we temper our love in the trials of personal relationships, and we temper our joy and steadfastness through the hardships of life. We learn to control reactiveness not through restraint but through a highly refined sense of what is right. We become motivated by nobility and elegance and choose to honor these elements of life, instead of dishonoring them. Temperance does not diminish our humanity in any way; it refines it, purifies it, and polishes it. The key idea to remember is that a "temper" is any mental state; temperance, therefore, is the ability to regulate or modulate our mental state in such a way that it can express divine force at its highest possible level.

As portrayed in the Tarot, Temperance is an angel through which the full force of God Immanent flows. This angel has lovingly and carefully drawn into herself the unredeemed residue of human misdeeds, human negativity, and human pessimism and has transformed them into a honeycomb of enlightened structure. She has filled the dark corners of human character and awareness with light, so that not only can the light of the soul shine through the personality and its work, but even the light of the monad or spirit can be glimpsed. There is a constant, uninterrupted flow of spiritual energy into the outer form.

When Temperance appears in response to a question, it implies that new methods and breakthroughs will be required. You cannot just rely on what has worked in the past; you must break through to new understandings, new measures of love, and new expressions of talent. You must grow. In specific situations, Temperance might mean:

• The situation is marred by impurities and selfish motives. These must be removed before true progress can occur.

• You have contaminated your thinking and feeling with poisonous attitudes. These are the roots of your difficulties.

• Act as though you were expressing the best and noblest within you.

• You have harmed yourself with excessive guilt and self-condemnation.

• Resentments are eating away at your character.

• You need to make a daily habit of filling your awareness with the highest kinds of stimuli—uplifting music, spiritual reading, and so on.

• Center yourself in the highest perception of spirit you are capable of.

• You need to observe rules of etiquette or protocol more carefully.

Temperance is the final card in the series of cards known as the Divine Attributes. The stage is now set for considering the third series of cards in the major arcana, the Divine Spheres. Each of these cards represents an arena or dominion in which the Divine Personas act. The seven Divine Spheres are:

The Devil

The great sin of humanity is separativeness—the belief that we are estranged or alienated from God's love and wisdom. We forget that we "live and move and have our being" in divine light, and fill ourselves with all kinds of weird substitutes for His presence. We entertain self-doubt. We question the benevolence of life. We criticize. We cling to materialistic signs of security. We lust for what we do not have. We become neurotic and paranoid. And in this troubled brew of self-absorption, we create what might be called "the devil's playground." Having reached a state where we are certain God must reject us, we open ourselves to whatever we believe is the alternative. In reality, there is no alternative, but we do not know this yet, so in our imagination, we invent one. But the devil can reign only where we willingly engage in separativeness. Once we reunite with the God within us—which has never abandoned us nor left—the problem of separativeness (and the devil) evaporates.

In the Tarot, The Devil is a fantastic figure, part bat, part animal. He has an inverted star on his forehead. His staff of power is an inverted, flaming phallus. Before him, an unclothed man and woman stand, back to back, separated. They each have tails, indicating a reversion to animal instincts. The bottom of the card is filled with the red flames of hellfire. A wan moon is directly overhead; the background is a cloudy gray. The figure of the devil is intentionally unreal; no such figure exists, nor does it represent any archetypal force. The images of the devil and the flames of hellfire are just projections of our own uneasy beliefs and fears. The archetypal reality of this card is the duality which seems to produce a schism between the man and the woman—and, by extension, between the personality and the soul. As such, it is a study in contrasts with The Lovers. The archetypal quality implied by this card, although obviously not stated, is therefore the redemptive and healing power of divine love—the love that will bridge the gap of our separation and draw us back to the Godhead.

When The Devil appears in a Tarot spread, we should immediately examine the situation at hand to determine where schisms and separations have occurred, and if they are in harmony with the intent of the higher self. Where they are not, we must then invoke the divine redemptive love which will heal the schism, and try to understand how we must learn to express it. We should also consider the possibility that we are misinterpreting life's messages to us. Sometimes the immense force of divine will appears to be destructive, especially when it cleans away the old debris of our life so we can get on with new lessons. It is easy at these times to label these events as "evil," but they are not. They are a further manifestation of God's benevolence. In specific cases, The Devil can mean:

• You have become trapped in the forces of materialism.

• You have allowed anger to dominate your emotions.

• Your actions are leading to a schism you ought to avoid.

• You have succumbed to "the line of least resistance." But you can reverse this backsliding by acting again with nobility and integrity.

• Beware the temptation to lower your standards.

• You are polluting your understanding of life with unreal fantasies and dreams. Fill your imagination with more wholesome thoughts.

• There is strong opposition to your work. Do not take this lightly.

• You need to replace self-centered love with altruistic benevolence.

- The conflict you are enduring is the result of your own adversarial stances.
- Not everything that seems mean or nasty to you is necessarily evil.

The Tower

One of the great times of opportunity, both microcosmically and macrocosmically, is what is known as a point of tension—a time when several lines of force intersect and open the door for new progress. Human beings usually label these points of tension as "crises" and develop a strong emotional antipathy toward them. Nonetheless, the crises of our lives are usually the moments of greatest growth and achievement. They force us to take stands, initiate projects, and learn lessons we otherwise would ignore. We should therefore come to appreciate the crises of our life—and be grateful for them, even if we cannot quite welcome them. We should see them as a moment of divine opportunity. In a very real sense, indeed, the point of tension is a Divine Sphere of action.

In the major arcana, The Tower embodies this drama of crisis. It is a tall pillar, very much like a rook in a chess set, dominating the middle of the card. A storm is beseiging it; waves are lapping all around it at its base, while lightning strikes it at its top, as though Zeus had hurled a thunderbolt and shattered the tower. Fire has broken out and is ravaging the top. Birds fly in the background, silhouetted against the clouds. At first glance, this seems to be a card of obvious disaster, but first glances can be erroneous in working with the Tarot. The fire, after all, is burning at the top of the tower. If the tower is thought to be the human fortress (our character), then it is only the mind that has been ignited by the fire, and since fire is an element of the mind, this is actually a wonderful sign. Indeed, the birds flying in the background tend to confirm this idea, representing qualities of the spiritual self. If the tower itself is also seen

as a symbol for the spine, or the integrity of the human system, it is not too hard to see that this crisis is actually an intentional stimulation of the whole character. On an esoteric level, this card has profound implications for the process of energy distribution throughout the form and the inner meanings of initiation.

When it appears in a layout, The Tower generally indicates that the situation at hand provides us with an esoteric point of tension. We should therefore prepare for a new stimulation and expansion of consciousness. This may come in the form of meeting a crisis—but as we look for its true meaning, the danger of crisis will fade and be replaced by its opportunity. In specific cases, The Tower may indicate:

• Forces are underway that will bring an abrupt change in your attitudes, convictions, or lifestyle.

• It is time to initiate projects that have been on the shelf for a while.

• The emotions are unusually roiled; be conservative in your actions.

• The structure of your business is in disarray; it needs to be reshaped.

• A weakness in character will make you highly vulnerable.

• Do not be overwhelmed by the sequence of events; take a step at a time.

- Your values are coming under fire; be sure they are firmly established.
- The disillusionment you are undergoing is a step in the right direction; open your eyes to reality!

The Star

Jesus said, "There are many mansions in my Father's house." A similar statement could be made about human consciousness. We tend to think of the thoughts, feelings, and sensations of our waking hours as the sum of our awareness. But we exist at psychic and spiritual levels as well as the physical, and there are dimensions of our humanity that are active and productive even though we are not aware of them. These dimensions of our being operate in what might be called the sphere of intuition—one of the seven Divine Spheres of activity. The sphere of intuition is symbolically portrayed in the Tarot as The Star.

In the Tarot card The Star, the star is portrayed as a brilliant heavenly body of red, orange, brown, and black, dominating the sky. On earth, the usual image of a nude woman has been replaced by a peacock—or perhaps a Phoenix—which glows with the same colors as the Star, plus an extra touch of blue. The horizon is reminiscent of that in The Empress (which likewise occupies the third position in its septenate), but is distinctly more V-shaped, bringing in once again the idea of God Immanent. On either side of the bird are two blue-gray decorations which are probably abstract representations of the jugs usually found in this card. At the bottom of the card are sharp, jagged red and black designs, suggesting acute conflict in the physical life. This same pattern, however, is also found in a more subdued form in the heart of the star itself, suggesting that in this case the conflict is part of the archetypal pattern. Darkness covers most of the land, suggesting nighttime. In more traditional presentations of this card, water from the

115

wellsprings of life is being poured into the sea and onto the land. The same idea is more abstractly presented in the Aquarian symbolism of the life essence of the star being embodied in the peacock. Through the peacock (representing humanity, as we saw in The Lovers), the light of the star shines forth and illuminates the shadows of earth.

When The Star arises in a consultation, it probably suggests a need to become aware of the inner dimensions of the situation, through the use of your intuition. You have not yet discerned the true implications of the condition at hand. In specific instances, it can mean:

• You need to express the nurturing love of the higher self.

• The part you play in a larger group is a vital one. Define your responsibilities and execute them.

• The problems at hand can be traced to improper energy distribution. Examine your wish life, desires, and urges to see where you are focusing too much attention.

• Do not seek vengeance for injuries done to you. Leave that to heaven.

• Do not be impressed by superficial displays of wisdom or insight.

• Sharpen your intuition so it becomes a more useful, reliable tool.

• Pay heed to your dreams; they are guiding you.

The Moon

One of the great mysteries of life, that science has not yet plumbed, is that of instinct in animals, the subconscious in humans, and the innate life of matter. These mysterious currents govern the world of form, yet can be controlled and directed by focused thought. Humans, for instance, are still conditioned by ancient racial memories—yet are able to use their emerging intellects to transform and enlighten these patterns. Nonetheless, when we fail to do so, we can quickly fall prey to the superstitions, fears, and fads of mass consciousness. The Moon, owing to its role in affecting the ebb and flow of tides as well as the emotional stability of humans, symbolizes the Divine Sphere of Instinct—the innate life of the body, the emotions, and thought-forms. It is the materialistic counterpart to the sphere of Intuition.

In the Aquarian deck, The Moon is a quarter moon, with the illuminated portion colored white and the dark portion blue. The Moon has a human face and is situated in a stormy sky. It almost seems to sit on a globe-like pedestal rising out of the sea, which is rough and choppy, indicating stress and turmoil. There are decorations suggesting twin pillars on either side of the card at the base, plus other designs suggesting rocks or boulders. In the middle of the card at its base, there are faint horizontal lines, somewhat reminiscent of the lines at the top of The Chariot. All in all, The Moon portrays the forces of unredeemed humanity that influence unenlightened people through mass consciousness—superstition, fear, and anxiety. There is an underlying current of hysteria that can be whipped up in an instant, if circumstances lend themselves. We need this bond of instinct in order to preserve the race and the memory of what we have accomplished, but there is no real divine presence here. Pessimism reigns, instead of joy; sorrow reigns, instead of triumph; envy rules, instead of compassion.

When The Moon appears in response to a question, it most likely implies that we are being heavily influenced by mass consciousness or are relying on the innate desires and fears of our emotions, rather than inspiration. We need to see how easily our own thinking can be influenced in these ways, and work to regain control of it. In specific situations, The Moon can mean:

• Your current behavior is being influenced by subconscious patterns from long ago.

- You are sailing directly into the headwind of popular opinion. Unless you are careful, it will blow you off course—or sink you.
- You are going through the paces like an automaton, but you have not actually committed yourself to this challenge.
- Your thinking is being adversely affected by psychic interference.
- The impressions you are receiving are not from the higher self; they are just from your wish life or from undisciplined psychic sources.
- The nightmares you are having are rooted in mass consciousness.

The Sun

If you arrange the three septenates with the first seven cards on the bottom, the next seven above them, and the third seven at the top, an interesting pattern emerges in the fifth position. The up-raised arm of The Hierophant points to The Hanged Man, who hangs upside down, but is supported by the rope that leads to its true source—The Sun. The Sun therefore can be thought of as the Divine Sphere of support—the dominion or kingdom that supplies all that we need to sustain life and pursue our creative and spiritual goals.

The Sun is a card filled with yellows, reds, and white, as befits its subject. The sun itself is a white globe of fire with a yellow ball for a chin, rosy cheeks, and smiling eyes and mouth. White fire radiates outward horizontally; orange fire radiates upward; and yellow fire pours down to the earth. The middle column of descending energy is also white. These distinctions not only symbolize the different kinds of fire which nourish our lives, but also thematically unite God Immanent with God Transcendent. At the bottom of the card, there is an open book facing the sun, supported on some kind of pedestal. This reminds us that the Light of the World is not the physical sun, but rather the spiritual sun that we contact through what Patanjali called "spiritual reading." The proper use of the Tarot is one example of spiritual reading.

When The Sun appears in a Tarot layout, it tends to imply that we must harness the true source of the energies which have led to this situation. Our problems in life are not usually caused by the presence of an obstacle, but more commonly by the absence of some spiritual quality. A poor relationship, for instance, is not caused by our bitchiness but rather by our lack of caring, nurturing love. If we went to the source and acquired this ability to truly care, our bitchiness would vanish and the relationship would improve. In answer to specific questions, The Sun can also mean:

• You are confusing issues. Clarify your thinking.
• There is a tremendous opportunity at hand for growth. Seize it.
• You are putting too much pressure on others. Correct this.
• Your self-confidence is blinding you to real problems that need solving.
• Conditions are favorable for achieving greater unity of effort. Define common purpose.
• You can be a healing force in this situation.
• The abundance of divine life is shining on your efforts.

Judgment

Religion portrays Judgment as something that is experienced after death, as we review the sins and achievements of our physical life. Esoterically, however, judgment is an experience which occurs every day of our life, as part of the work of redemption. If we have an opportunity to help another person, and ignore it, we judge ourselves. If we have an opportunity to grow, and seize it, we judge ourselves. Even while watching television or engaging in athletics, we constantly judge ourselves, by how we choose to respond to ideas, problems, and opportunities. This judgment either closes

119

down or opens up new doors for growth, service, and creativity. If we understood this phenomenon in the fullest, we would recognize that these "tests" by which we judge ourselves are actually a summons from the higher self—a call to us to respond with the best and the noblest within ourself. And when we do respond in this way, we in turn are summoning the divine qualities of spirit. In this way, we enter into the Divine Sphere of Redemption.

The card of Judgment again illustrates dramatically why I prefer the Aquarian Tarot. In other decks, this is a morbid scene of physical humans rising out of caskets on a mythical Judgment Day. The angel Gabriel is blowing His trumpet from the heavens, summoning the worthy, all of whom have ended up in a sea (the astral plane). In the Aquarian version, by contrast, Gabriel is standing on the earth blowing His trumpet—or perhaps it is not even Gabriel. Perhaps it is us; having sensed the opportunity for judgment, we have replied to the higher self by summoning its help. We have blown the trumpet, and the clouds have parted, so that the sun may shine on our life again. The darkness that has covered the land is now receding, and flowers are beginning to bloom again. We are ready to redeem the darkness within ourselves with the light and power of spirit. The decoration at the bottom of the card once again brings in the theme of God Immanent.

When Judgment appears in response to a question, it suggests

120

that we are being tested in this situaton by the higher self. We therefore need to respond by summoning the highest and noblest qualities within ourself, and expressing them to the best of our ability. In addition, we need to examine what old habits, tendencies, and beliefs need to be redeemed, so that we can grow. In specific cases, Judgment can also mean:

• You cannot stand all by yourself in this situation. You need to call on the help of the higher self.

• Your judgments are faulty in this situation. You need to look at the facts from a higher, less biased point of view.

• You are accidentally calling back to life issues that are better off dead.

• Your ambition is driving you in directions you are not meant to travel. You are in danger of overloading your abilities.

• The mind needs to be trained to make accurate, objective judgments.

• Do not dwell on failures. They are the building steps of success.

• Be careful what you ask for, lest you get it.

Esoterically, Judgment also suggests a great deal about the science of sound.

The World

As has been described, each of the cards in The Tarot represents an archetypal force which is in turn a key part of the plan of God for creation. And yet, if any one card in the deck embodies the plan as a whole, it would be The World, the final card of the third septenate, or Divine Spheres. It is in specific the plan for human development, enlightenment, and service, and as such, is an integral part of the full plan of God for this cycle. It can therefore be studied by the individual who is interested in discerning the plan of his or her higher self for this lifetime, by a group to determine its plan for

121

manifestation, or by a nation. And as you study it, you enter into the divine dominion of God's Plan.

The World is one of the most elaborate cards in the major arcana. There is a braided circle which represents the world or the "ring-pass-not" of God's plan for the world; in its center is a clothed woman (in the Rider Deck, she is nude, symbolizing truth) holding a rod. There is a tiny orange sphere on her forehead and an orange triangle at her throat, indicating an ability to be aware of the plan creatively and spiritually. In the four corners of the card, there are the bull, lion, eagle, and woman that were referred to in The Wheel of Fortune. There are designs which seem to indicate a magnetic attraction between the bull and lion and between the woman and the eagle. These four beings, coupled with the circle, which could be a wheel as easily as a world, suggest obvious references to the vision of Ezekiel, but also to the fixed cross of the zodiac (the eagle is an alternate symbol for the scorpion). These allusions enhance the imagery of The World, but the meaning of this card does not depend on them. The allusions merely suggest that any prophet such as Ezekiel, or any system such as astrology, that is capable of tuning into the divine plan will naturally tune into some aspect or facet of The World. To them, the woman or goddess of Truth would be naked; but to the rest of the world, she is veiled. Just so, it may seem to many people that divine creation is static, unchanging; but to the eyes that can see, the wheels of the world are in rapid motion, and evolution is moving forward apace.

Looking at the final cards of each septenate from last to first, the plan of The World is translated through the angelic-like consciousness of the chosen agents of God and becomes manifest through the skillful actions of The Chariot.

When The World appears in a Tarot spread, it probably indicates that we need to consider the inner plan for the situation at hand and try to understand the forces we are meant to work with.

122

We must place intelligence above hope, comprehension above enthusiasm. In specific situations, The World can mean:

- You are paying too much attention to "worldly wisdom" and are not heeding the subtle voice of your higher intelligence.
- There are natural limits to your activities that you need to respect.
- You are not fulfilling your responsibilities.
- You have become trapped in your own private world. You need to find constructive ways to serve humanity and the larger plan.
- You are excessively sensitive to the problems of humanity. Do not take all of these woes on your own back.
- Your efforts are not actually helping the plan of God unfold. Reform!

The World completes the third septenate of Divine Spheres. With the three aspects of divine force fully explored, there is just one final card of the major arcana to consider. Its unique position in the major arcana is underscored by its number, which is the null cipher, Zero.

The Fool

The final card in the major arcana is The Fool. This card cannot be understood except in the context of the other twenty-one cards, for there is a part of every card in The Fool and, in a most sublime way, The Fool synthesizes all of the forces represented in the major arcana. He unifies the Tarot. As such, he represents the spiritual aspirant who must learn to work with the forces of the Divine Personas, with the tools and methodologies of the Divine Attributes, and upon the stage or platform of the Divine Spheres. We cannot become The Magician, for that is a divine force, but we can become his agent on earth, The Fool. It might even be said that the Fool has been made in the image of The Magician (and all of the Divine Personas), but until we can see this truth, we erroneously mistake him for a simpleton.

The Fool is a card of God the Transcendent, as we can see from the inverted V design at the top of the card. The fool himself carries a rod over his shoulder, indicating that the principle of mind is active in him and his primary characteristic. His face is white, his hand is pure white, and he carries a pure white rose. The background is white. This suggests that the true essence of this level of attainment is found entirely at the inner levels of consciousness. He wears an orange toque with a yellow plume, tied under his chin with a gray veil. A medal hangs from the cap with designs that suggest archetypal awareness. His cloak is of a very rich design, in contrast to the motley found in most interpretations of The Fool, and its subtle patterns suggest that he has completely conquered the forces of materialism. There are two strands flowing from the toque, evidently linking him to his higher self. The decorations around the lettering of The Fool suggest that while The Fool is a sign of God Transcendent, he likewise reveals God Immanent, and thereby fuses the two, but in an individual, human way, not in a cosmic way as was the case in The Sun.

The Fool is one of the most powerful cards in the Tarot, and when it appears in a layout it should not be dismissed flippantly. It implies that there is an unusual intersection of forces at work, not producing a crisis, as in The Tower, but rather producing a rare opportunity for synthesis. It will require all of our skill, understanding, and inner insight to pull these forces together and get them to work harmoniously, but if we do, the accomplishment will be enormous. Other meanings, as they apply to specific situations, might include:

• You do not know your own values and beliefs. Examine them first before trying to understand your difficulties and obstacles.

• You need to learn to take sensible risks.

- Listen to the guidance of your inner self.
- Look for the presence of God within those you deal with, and treat them accordingly.
- Hold to the highest, purest motives in what you are undertaking.
- You are richly blessed. Invest what you have in serving God.

The Fool completes our exploration of the major arcana. The brief descriptions and suggested interpretations are meant only to serve as clues and introductions to each card. Keep in mind that the card is just the outer appearance of a living, powerful divine force. It is one thing to read the cards, and quite another to "read" the archetypal realities they symbolize. It is the latter ability which signifies a true working knowledge of the Tarot.

CHAPTER EIGHT

The Four Suits

Not only does The Fool summarize and synthesize the major arcana, he provides a bridge to the minor arcana as well. If the major arcana describes the divine forces The Fool must learn to work with, the minor arcana describes the spiritual lessons he must undergo and the stages of growth he must master in learning to harness these energies. Since The Fool represents the prototypical spiritual aspirant, it can be said, only slightly with tongue in cheek, that the four suits of the minor arcana represent the four sets of "clothing" he must wear as he "goes about his Father's business." These four sets of clothing are, of course, the physical body, the emotions, the mind, and our spiritual nature. In a more cosmic, impersonal sense, they could also be listed as the four elements: earth, water, fire, and air.

The four suits of the minor arcana are:

Pentacles—corresponding to everything physical. Its element is earth.

Cups—corresponding to everything emotional. Its element is water.

Rods—corresponding to everything mental. Its element is fire.

Swords—corresponding to everything spiritual. Its element is air.

These suits should be seen as representing the raw materials from which the spiritual aspirant—The Fool—learns to weave the perfect vestments of the mature spiritual person. Nothing in the life of spirit comes ready-to-wear; we have to spin the threads and weave the garments ourselves. We achieve mastery when we are able to weave beautiful cloaks without any seams—radiant minds, flawless emotions, and healthy, productive physical bodies, all serving a spiritual nature that dedicates every fiber of its being to service as an agent of God.

Learning to use the Tarot is much the same. The cards come ready-made, but not our capacity to interpret them. We must discover the Real Tarot on our own, weaving a tapestry of associations that will lead us to inner wisdom. It is therefore important to acquire a sound understanding of the symbolism of the four suits.

We can examine them one by one.

Pentacles

This suit is sometimes called "coins"; the term "pentacles" derives from alchemy and magic, where a pentacle is a five-pointed star enclosed in a circle. In either case, the Pentacle is symbolic of the material world and the things of physical life. This includes money and possessions on the one hand, but also our work, physical health, and home on the other. Memory and instinct are aspects of life touched by the Pentacles, as are the structure of organizations, the development of the brain and nervous system, and the inner potential of all of earth's resources.

All of the cards in the Pentacles are drawn with a light blue sky and fluffy white clouds. In many instances, the sky pattern either overlays the physical image (as in the 3 of Pentacles) or the physical form is suspended without support in the sky (as in the 5 of Pentacles), thereby reminding us that the physical level of life is the least tangible, the least solid, and the least durable. It only appears to us as solid and durable because our perceptions are limited; from a spiritual perspective—and certainly from the perspective of the Real Tarot—it is possible to see clear through physical forms and substance. As a suit, the Pentacles are meant to be interpreted in this spirit.

Esoterically, the purpose of the Pentacles is to serve as a "ground" for spiritual energies. Nothing of the physical plane has much significance in and of itself; its significance can be found primarily in the inner, spiritual purposes associated with it. When we allow ourselves to get caught up in some facet of the physical plane—i.e., worrying about finances—we are forgetting the invisible nature of physical substance. We are forgetting to look at the inner patterns which would allay our worries and fears. In interpreting the Pentacles, we must constantly look for these inner patterns that enrich the meaning of the outwardly obvious.

Cups

In many presentations, the cups portrayed in this suit become something of a Holy Grail. This appeals to the wish life of many people, who like to think that fulfillment of the emotions is the ulti-mate spiritual fulfillment. Unfortunately, this is just a glamour or self-deception. The cup symbolizes the vessel of our emotions—what is known esoterically as "the astral body." It can be filled, empty, or partially full, but that is generally not the secret to inter-preting these cards. The key to the cups is what we do with the liquid the cup holds. It may be water—or fine wine; the issue is the same in both cases. What do we do with it? Do we share it with others? Or are we just trying to fill our own cups? Do we rejoice in the joys and triumphs of others—or do we fill our cup with jealousy and envy? Do we pour our love and enthusiasm into the work we do—or do we expect our job to please us?

All of the cards in the suit of cups are drawn with a plain white background, with the exception of the 5 of Cups, which is more a pale overcast background. This artistic device focuses our attention on the cups themselves. They are orange except in two cases: the 2

129

of Cups (yellow) and the 7 of Cups (red). In the 2 of Cups, there is the added emphasis of a yellow border around the background, indicating that the atmosphere itself is filled with the quality that is contained in the two cups. The different shade of color in the 7 of Cups underscores the bizarre arrangement of the cups. The decoration and positioning of the cups will be of great importance as we interpret the cards in this suit, one by one.

Esoterically, the purpose of the cups is to provide us with a vessel by which we can help others. The dominant keynotes of our emotions should therefore be goodwill and helpfulness. To the degree that the cups in these cards are filled with these qualities, and used to slake the thirst of others, we will be able to taste spiritual fulfillment. But to the degree that we use the cups of our emotions to "grab for all the gusto we can," we will find that the higher self, along with Saki, has turned down the empty cup.

Rods

In some decks, this suit is known as "wands," the reference being to the wand of the magician. The word "rod" embraces that meaning, in that the rod of power is a standard symbol of authority, enlightenment, and initiation, but also includes many other ideas. The rods of the Tarot are actually growing trees, not sticks, with a very healthy flower at the end of each one, and in many cases, buds about to open along the trunk. The flower is actually a living symbol of the fire of the mind as it flows through the nervous system (esoterically, the etheric body). The rods can also be collected together, as in the 10 of Rods, and used to build structures. In all these ways, the rods make an ideal symbol for the enlightened human mind. They have stability, as do our values and convictions. They have strength, as does the logical, orderly mind. They grow, as should a healthy mind and the ideas it contains. They can provide structures for creative work and service, as does the mind that is capable of working with archetypal patterns.

Like the cups, the background of all the rods is plain white, but unlike the cups, the background on all the rods is also outlined by a single thin line. This is an important thematic variation, because the human mind is the only part of our system that can operate both in the world of form and the world of abstract forces simultaneously. The mind bridges form and spirit. But unless infused with spirit, represented by the swords, the mind will be focused concretely, in form. The subtle outlining of the upper portion of the card reminds us that the mind will act concretely, unless inspired and directed by spirit.

Another thematic note that can be observed in the rods is a tendency for many of the people in these cards to become somewhat like the object they carry. This is most obvious in the 7 of Rods, where the man seems to be carved out of a tree trunk. But it is visible to a lesser degree in the 3 of Rods, the 10 of Rods, and others. This feature reminds us of the degree to which our thoughts influence us and shape our lives.

Esoterically, the purpose of the rods is to enable us to build a sound structure of thought upon which we can establish our values, our character, and our identity. If the structure is loose and chaotic, our lives will be filled with confusion. We will tend to trip over the rods, not be guided by them. Ideally, however, the rods will be well defined and filled with the fiery light of inspiration, so that our mind can truly serve as a light on top of the hill.

Swords

It may seem odd to some that the sword, a weapon of warfare, should be used to symbolize our spiritual nature. Yet if we accept the medieval nature of the Tarot, it is not odd at all. It was the nobility of that time, not the peasants, who fought the battles of war, and no knight or king would ride into battle without his sword.

In this context, nobility is a symbol of our higher nature. The sword, therefore, is a symbol of spirit. In the Middle Ages, in fact, the sword was held to represent the word of God. The sages of that time saw the cross embodied within the design of the sword.

It is not just the image of the cross that lies hidden within the sword, however. The two-edged sword of the crusader can be thought of as three vertical pillars—the two edges plus the blade in between. As such, there is a strong parallel to the three columns of the Kabalah, mercy and severity flanking mildness. In the case of the sword of spirit, it can cut with both mercy and severity, as the need demands. In this sense, a parallel can also be drawn to the Pharaohs of ancient Egypt, who ruled with a crook and flail, the crook serving to help their people, the flail serving to punish. This pattern is repeated in medieval mythology, where an upright sword symbolizes destruction but a sword planted in the ground symbolizes protection.

I view the sword in a more abstract sense as a living flow of energy sent from heaven to earth. The spiritual aspirant—The Fool—must learn to wield these bolts of energy with as much skill and dexterity as a swordsman handling his weapon. The obviously symbolic uses of swords in the cards of this suit tend to reaffirm this view. One would hardly plant six swords in the bottom of a boat, for example, as in the case of the 6 of Swords, unless those swords were actually sources of spiritual energy which had been harnessed to impel the boat across the waters.

Spirit is not a static quantity like a loaf of bread. It is living, moving force. As such, we can harness it only by identifying with it, absorbing it into our awareness, and then translating it into dramatic action of our own. This idea is portrayed time after time in the suit of swords in the Aquarian Tarot.

Two artistic themes characterize the swords in the Aquarian Tarot. The first is the background of each card, which is a purplish cloud pattern. This reminds us that the element of swords is air, and that the real substance of our life is to be found in the heavens, not on earth. Therefore, the sky of the swords has more substance than in any of the other suits. In addition, there is no hint of the transparency of form which we found in the pentacles. It is form that is transparent, not spirit. The swords, therefore, are depicted with clarity.

Second, the swords are virtually the only cards in the minor arcana that embody the monolithic patterns of ancient mischief that appear in several of the cards in the major arcana (the King of Pentacles, the Ace of Rods, and the Knight of Rods being the only exceptions.) This is the black and blue or black and white pattern that dominates the 2 of Swords and the 9 of Swords and resembles mountains of remorse, fear, or pessimism. It is present in every card in the suit of swords except the 4 of Swords, the 7 of Swords, and the Page, Knight, and King of Swords—and all but two of these have the emblem of conflict in its place. Indeed, in many of the cards this pattern is an ingrained part of the cloak or body, as in the 8 of Swords. This reminds us that spirit has a definite purpose in manifesting on earth—to redeem materialism and free us (and the rest of creation as well) from its limitations. The sword is the weapon spirit uses to confront the sometimes overwhelming denseness of materialism.

One other thematic pattern deserves mention as well—except in the case of the royal family, all of the people in the suit of swords are either blindfolded, looking away from us, or have their eyes closed. This is a symbolic clue that spirit cannot be found in the physical plane or the worlds of form; it can only be found by developing our inner vision and exploring the actual dimensions of spirit.

Esoterically, the purpose of the swords is to show us reality. We can pretend that negative emotions are all right; we can believe that false ideas harm no one. But we cannot pretend that reality is not reality, when it cuts through our illusions and pretensions like a two-edged sword. The sword is not meant to intimidate us—it merely gives us a tool or weapon by which we can discern reality.

PAGE of PENTACLES

KNIGHT of PENTACLES

QUEEN of PENTACLES

KING of PENTACLES

PAGE of CUPS

KNIGHT of CUPS

QUEEN of CUPS

KING of CUPS

PAGE of RODS

KNIGHT of RODS

QUEEN of RODS

KING of RODS

PAGE of SWORDS

KNIGHT of SWORDS

QUEEN of SWORDS

KING of SWORDS

CHAPTER NINE

The Four Faces

Within each suit, there are ten cards, numbered ace through ten, which represent the ten spiritual lessons the aspirant must learn in working with each type of energy, and four face cards—the page, knight, queen, and king. These are the four faces of the minor arcana, and they represent the different stages of maturity the aspirant or The Fool attains as he learns the lessons of the path. The symbolic meanings of these face cards can be stated as follows:

The Page represents the novice in working with the energy of his suit. He is the student, the learner, and cannot yet be trusted with any responsibility. Whenever the Page appears in a layout, it is an indication of immaturity and the need to grow in understanding and expertise.

The Knight has learned the basic lessons of working with the energy of his suit, and has achieved a journeyman status. He is competent and skilled and can be trusted. In addition, there is a strong sense of dedication and commitment to service. Whenever the Knight appears in response to a question, it strongly suggests that altruism and service to an ideal should play a key role in the answer.

The Queen is an actual embodiment of the force or energy of her suit—she has learned to individualize it in its highest degree. She does not just serve the ideal; she lives it. She demonstrates the fullest meaning of responsiveness, which includes using the energy of a divine ideal to nurture and enrich life. Whenever the Queen

135

appears in a spread, it indicates that we must embody the force of the ideal in our own character—and actions. She represents the feminine aspects of God.

The King is one who has achieved full mastery of the energy of his suit. He is able to take full responsibility for and initiate creative work and service. He is a source of inspiration, guidance, and authority. Whenever the King appears in a spread, it suggests that nothing less than total mastery will suffice. He represents the masculine aspects of God.

These general guidelines can be applied to each of the four suits. While each suit does suggest a different focus, nevertheless the basic message of each face card remains remarkably consistent from suit to suit.

The Four Pages

One of the striking artistic themes in each of the four pages is the scarf that swirls down from the hat or the neck to the bottom of the card. This suggests an inability to control and discipline the downward-flowing energies of spirit seeking manifestation. In the Page of Pentacles, this is a downward swirl of gray, representing a difficulty in handling duties at work, money, sexual energies, and the like. He can easily be caught in downward spirals, where one problem leads quickly to another, and then another, and so on. The Pentacle is only half visible on the card, indicating that he is very limited in his perceptions. When this card appears in response to questions, it will tend to suggest inconsistencies in work habits, a lack of diligence, crudeness, and a high degree of sensuality. It can also mean:

• The person in question is not reliable.

• Your understanding of the problem is heavily influenced by materialistic concerns.

• You are still just a novice in your field of inquiry. Work hard and you can improve your skills.

In the Page of Cups, the scarf is like a flow of blood or passion which is so intense it has scrambled and confused his thinking, symbolized by the dirty brown hat and its chaotic brown plumage. A fish, a sign of deception and illusion, is emerging out of the cup, catching his entire attention. He ignores the two flowers in the background, which stand for reality, in favor of his fantasies and wish life. When this card appears in connection with spiritual issues, it strongly suggests that we are mistaking emotional fulfillment and psychic glimpses for profound spiritual experiences. In other situations, it indicates an intensity of passion and pursuit of the wish life. There is a strong measure of superficiality and lack of emotional control. The card can also suggest:

• You can easily be swept away emotionally.
• You are deeply immersed in "The Shallow Life."
• You have a tremendous capacity for devotion and adoration. Use it wisely.

In both the Page of Rods and the Page of Swords, the scarf has become cream colored, indicating that the individual is less controlled by desire and more by values and ideas. The Page of Rods has emerged from the swamp of mass consciousness and popular beliefs, where he mistook the reeds of opinion for rods of understanding, but is now determined to walk the razor's edge. His eyes are covered by the brim of his hat, suggesting that he is still largely blind to reality but trying to turn his vision inward. The strings on the front of his garment imply that he is the cause of most conflict in his life, but gradually he is learning to see the consequences of his acts. He has reached the point where he does learn from his mistakes—but continues to make plenty of them. When the Page of Rods appears in a layout, it suggests that we are learning our lessons the hard way, through the school of hard knocks, but we are learning. We need to train the mind to think more clearly and logically. We dare not assume that we know enough to make our way in the world. It may also imply:

• You have caught a fragment of the truth but may be over-emphasizing it. Look for the larger context in which it makes sense.

• There is a danger of becoming intoxicated by ideas. Practice common sense.

• You are on the right track—don't give up.

The Page of Swords has taken the first step onto the spiritual path, but he is still a novice and likely to do more harm than good. He wears conflict as though it were a badge on his sleeve and is anything but subtle in his righteousness and strong beliefs. He has very little understanding of human nature and overestimates the level of his achievement.   He is almost one-dimensional in his pursuit of spirit.   When this card appears in a spread, it probably suggests that we need to review our spiritual beliefs and principles and refine them, so that they lead us to the reality of the life of spirit, not mislead us into distortions of it. We have much to learn when it comes to spirit. The Page of Swords can also mean:

• Do not presume too much. Practice inspired humility.

• You need to learn to judge people by the presence of spirit within them, not by their beliefs or even their actions.

• You need to learn to redeem the child within you, not indulge it.

The Four Knights

Two key themes distinguish the knights from the pages. The downward flowing scarf, draped over the shoulder, has been replaced by the emblem of the suit, resting on the shoulder or emblazoned on it. The one exception to this is the Knight of Cups, where a tiny patch of gray fear or superstition still keeps him from using the cup as fully as it was designed to be. This implies that even the person who would use the cups (the emotions) to serve cannot do so fully, because society's understanding of the emotions is so distorted that it makes true service at this level all but impossible. The other three knights, however, are ready and willing to serve to the best of their ability.

The other important distinction is that the cap of the page has been replaced by the helmet of the knight. These fellows take their work seriously, and guard against avoidable danger. Moreover, all of the helmets are plumed, indicating the need to rely on intuition for guidance and direction. The plume of the Knight of Swords almost resembles a periscope into the inner dimensions of spirit.

The Knight of Pentacles is riding a horse, but only the smallest tuft of hair is visible. By implication, we can assume that all four knights are mounted, but the horse is no longer important. The focus is on the service the rider can perform. For the Knight of Pentacles, this service would involve the responsibilities and duties of his work, his home, his church, and his community. When this card arises in a consultation, it most likely implies that we should be asking ourself: what physical contribution can I make to the proper unfoldment of this issue? How can I apply my talents, skills, and labors to resolving this situation? The Knight of Pentacles can also mean:

• You are not matching your spiritual aspirations with effective work in the earth plane. Become a true agent of God!

• The creative work you are engaged in is well-supported from within. Rely on this support.

• You are not alone in your work or trials. You are part of a much larger group.

In the Knight of Cups, the two flowers that were being ignored by the page appear once again, but now they are correctly positioned so that they become the source of motivation for the knight. He is driven by the ideals of beauty and growth to make his contribution, but as mentioned above, does not have a real grasp on the nature of the emotions—the cup is floating in mid-air. His efforts to help are therefore highly colored by the expectations of society. When this card appears in a spread, it suggests that there is an eagerness and willingness to help others, but not necessarily a clear idea of the best way to proceed. There is also a strong acceptance of belief, opinion, and consensus. It may likewise imply:

• There is an excellent opportunity to enrich the quality of life in this situation.

• You are being influenced by people or ideas contrary to your interests.

• You must be a pillar of calm strength in the midst of chaos and panic.

The Knight of Rods has discovered that expanded awareness not only makes him more aware of the great ideas that have inspired men and women for eons and eons, but also of the ancient residue of mischief, hostility, and conflict that has poisoned our relationships with one another. He carries the rod in service, but finds himself intimately involved in the struggle of casting out darkness wherever it exists. Indeed, the pattern of ancient residue that appears so prominently in the lower right hand of the card is reflected in a subdued way in his vest. When this card appears in a spread, it implies that we have a good mind and are able to think clearly and lucidly on issues. But we must base our understanding on the benevolence and intelligence of life, not on our perceptions of cruelty, stagnation, and indifference in humanity. In addition, we must learn the vast difference between hating evil and honoring good. An obsession with hating and condemning evil actually aligns us with darkness; the only way to fight evil effectively is to become an agent of light. The Knight of Rods also suggests:

• Do not become too cocky. Always remember that your power derives from spirit, not your personal strengths.

• Practice gentleness. There is no reason to clobber people with your insights and creative ideas.

140

• Your understanding of the situation is accurate. Do not be undermined by the opinions of the lesser-informed.

This obsession with conflict and the ancient residue of evil has been corrected in the Knight of Swords, who represents the true knight of service. He knows of the problems of earth but keeps his focus fixed firmly on the qualities of spirit he serves, and therefore fills his life with beauty, joy, grace, goodwill, peace, and wisdom. He serves the plan by the way he lives his life, and touches the lives of others through the qualities he expresses day by day. He has found the presence of God, lives it, and expresses it. When this card appears in a layout, it implies that the situation can only be solved spiritually, and will require our full range of spiritual skills and talents. It can also indicate:

• Do not worry if others cannot comprehend your motives. Do not try to explain yourself—let your actions do that for you.

• The struggles you are experiencing may seem greater than you can handle. Invoke the inner life of spirit to help you meet them.

• Make sure that the methods you use match the ideals you serve.

The Four Queens

In the Queens, the skill of working with the energy of the suit reaches such a high level that the queen herself embodies the energy. She becomes almost angelic in her capacity to radiate this energy into her work and throughout her dominion. Thematically, it should be observed that each of the queens except the Queen of Pentacles has a flower, and it is not too much of a stretch of the imagination to construe the Pentacle she holds as a floral sub-stitute. The flower emphasizes the nurturing power of the Queen—the ability to infuse forms and structures with the divine force she represents. She can make life flourish.

141

The statement of the Queen of Pentacles is contained mostly in her robe, a flowing, seamless gown of great elegance. This is a woman of refinement, style, and beauty. As such, she embodies the glory of God which the enlightened physical plane is meant to reveal. When this card appears in a spread, it tends to suggest that we need to pay more attention to revealing the light within us through the quality of work we do, the graciousness with which we act, and the manner by which we meet life's hardships. The Queen of Pentacles is the personification of divine beauty and grace. She can also mean:

• You are too passive. Take more initiative and responsibility.

• You may be overemphasizing superficial appearances.

• Do not be afraid to express the beauty and charm within you.

The major clue to the message of the Queen of Cups is to be found in the warm glow around her heart. She converts the electric fire flowing down from behind her head into the benevolent, caring warmth that flows through her heart. In this way, she nurtures all of life around her, and it is able to reveal the love of its inner design just as a flower in bloom reveals the love of its higher nature. In this card, we are able to grasp more fully the real purpose of the emotions, which is to help us enrich life. When this card appears in response to a question, it is an indication that we need to learn to express the true essence of affection, goodwill, and benevolence. If we harbor resentments, we need to learn to forgive. If we tend to be angry, we need to learn compassion. The Queen of Cups presents the gift of love. She can also signify:

• You are too dependent on others. Become more emotionally self-sufficient.

• Do not fall into the trap of self-pity.

• This is an opportunity to express the full depth of your caring love.

The image of the Queen of Rods inspires respect for maturity and wisdom. She does not live in the abstract; the ancient patterns of residue hidden in the shadows to her left and right at the base of the card testify to that. Yet in spite of the trials and tribulations of the world, she stands serene and upright, the personification of true nobility. The enormous flower, which almost seems like the world itself, represents the full maturity of her insight, her support, and her work. When this card appears, it suggests that we need to work with the greatest measure of maturity and dedication to truth that we can muster. This is no time for inexperience. The Queen of Rods expresses the essence of dignity. This card can also mean:

- The truth of this situation is obvious. Face it and accept it.
- You are blinded by an inconsistency in your values. Rectify this.
- Do not jump to conclusions. Work patiently until you can understand the full picture.

The most striking feature of the Queen of Swords is her long hair, which streams downward from her head to the bottom of the picture. There it embraces the symbolic images of evil and negativity, so that they can be transformed and illuminated. She carries the presence of God with her everywhere, and so she is never without it. She is never empty; she is always complete. She is never alone; she is always in harmony with God. When this card appears in a spread, it suggests that we should make the plans and projects of spirit our highest priority, and align other projects or needs to this central one accordingly. The Queen of Swords is the embodiment of harmony. This card can also suggest:

- The work we are involved in is not quite the spiritual service we believe it to be. We need to review our assumptions.
- This activity can be an avenue for serving God, if we approach it with an awareness of its underlying purpose.
- Be not afraid; there is an inner force of spiritual protection embracing this venture.

The Four Kings

The story of the kings is one of mastery—the ability to harness the force or energy of the suit and use it creatively. This is not something that is accomplished by brute force. It is the result of long practice in harnessing the many forces and energies within. This theme is portrayed in the images of the four kings by the peculiar button-like ornamentations on their caps, which suggest that the spiritual centers of the head are fully awake and organized; each king is therefore in control of the energies of his own system.

In the King of Pentacles, this mastery includes control of environmental forces as well as personal urges, as represented by the bull. Instead of fearing the bull, the king has harnessed him, and draws upon his strength for proper motivation. The circle of the yoke on the bull is repeated in the clear circle on his chest. The power of the pentacle flows through his heart. As a consequence, he gains complete dominion over the ancient residue of evil at the bottom of the card. He has transformed aggressiveness into creative action, selfishness into authority. When this card appears in a spread, it is a call for self-control and mastery in our use of physical energies. We must harness our resources wisely and use them productively. The keynote is self-dominion. The King of Pentacles can also mean:

• Having unleashed your ambition, you are now its slave.

• You have taken on more responsibility than you can handle. Cut back.

• You have a talent to help others learn self-control.

The King of Cups reflects the peculiar problem of gaining mastery of the emotions. It is always tempting to believe that the master of the emotions is the one who can indulge in all manner of selfish excess without apparent effect—the "grab all the gusto you can" syndrome. In one sense, the King of Cups does appear to be grabbing the cup tightly, seizing control by usurping pleasure that does not belong to him. This can, therefore, be the card of the master hedonist. But true mastery of the emotions is actually much different—it is the ability to control and direct the emotions from the higher level of spirit, and use them to enrich our work, the lives of others, and our efforts to serve. This is symbolized by the presence of the staff on the right side of the card, which replicates the design found on the cup. This truly is a ruler of the emotions—a fact that is confirmed by the symbolism for God Immanent in the background, behind the king's throne. When this card appears in response to a question, it most likely indicates a need to direct our emotions constructively—to offer affection, kindness, forgiveness, or support unilaterally. The keynote is helpfulness. The King of Cups can also imply:

• Your rationalizations for self-indulgence are fooling no one, not even yourself. Clean up your act!

• It is up to you to offer the help you can give. Do not wait to be asked.

• As you give of your abundance, you also receive of God's abundance.

In the King of Rods, there is a subtle allusion to the science of heraldry, which still plays an important role in diplomatic relations. The symbolic value of this reference lies in the fact that heraldry is a way of communicating priority, structure, and degrees of privilege. As such, it underscores the importance of a mind that is able to think hierarchically and is based on a strong foundation of noble values and principles. It also suggests that the king is able to act multidimensionally; he is able to think on several levels of subtlety at the same time. When this card arises in a layout, it suggests that we must understand the many levels of meaning in this situation before deciding on a plan of action. We must approach our problem with as much wisdom and comprehension as we can muster. The keynote is brilliance. The King of Rods can also indicate:

• Use whatever intuition you have to decide on a course of action. Intellectual reflection is not enough to reveal the right decision.

• Do not hesitate to begin your creative work on only a fragment of guidance. The rest of your inspiration will develop as you proceed.

• Your thinking is erratic. Some mental skills are well developed; others are deficient. Train your mind to work more consistently.

The connections of the King of Swords are unimpeachable, as both the plume of his crown and the tip of his sword reach up into the highest spiritual realms. What is more remarkable is that his shield is emblazoned with the sign of conflict—but the imprint of his crown over the conflict signals triumph. The King of Swords is continually engaged in the struggle between good and evil, but the good within him always triumphs. When this card appears in a spread, it reminds us that joy *is* stronger than depression, peace *is* stronger than hate. There is also the suggestion that we are not acting on our own in this situation, but on behalf of inner spiritual connections. We should therefore embody the impersonal life. The keynote is salvation. The King of Swords can also signify:

• The loneliness you experience is not a badge to wear on your sleeve. It is the result of your self-imposed isolation.

• It is not enough just to love God. We must express God in all we do.

• It is not necessary to defend your personal honor when everything you do is solely to honor God.

A Trip with the Tarot

I thought I would take a day off—go visit the art museum or something. I was beginning to have visions of Pentacles dance in my head. I needed a break.

So my wife and I got in the car and headed into town. We didn't make it very far, however. There was some kind of obstruction in the traffic. We figured it might have been an accident, and slowed down. But it wasn't an accident at all. It was the image of The Hierophant, acting as a traffic cop. Once he saw me, he let all the other cars proceed.

"It's you we want," he barked, leaning into the open car window.

"Why me?" I asked, trying to sound as plaintive as possible.

"Something to show you," he replied. "Mind if I get in?"

I apparently had no choice, since he was already in. "Kidnapped by the Tarot," I thought to myself glumly.

"I heard that," The Hierophant said, disapprovingly.

"How could you hear it?" I asked. "I thought it to myself."

The Hierophant said nothing—at least out loud. But a voice in my head said, loud and clear, "The poor lad probably thinks he thought up the whole book by himself, too." I let the issue drop.

The Hierophant had me drive to a nearby park. It was nearly deserted, which was not too unusual for a weekday. "I would take you to Tibet, but it would take too long, cost too much, and it's a little dangerous right now. This will do just as well, though. Almost any quiet place away from the city is a good place to contact divine forces. We don't much care for cities, you know?"

"They're a nice place to visit, but I wouldn't want to live there," I quipped.

"Ah, that's right," said The Hierophant. "You were driving into the city for a day's leisure. Sorry for the inconvenience. But you may find this more refreshing."

"Did you want to show me something?"

"Exactly. We've been watching what you've been writing with some interest; we've got a stake in all this, you know. We all got together last night and took a vote. I was appointed to come here and show you."

"Show me what?"

"The meaning of my two keys," The Hierophant replied, as though the answer should have been obvious.

"Ahh—now that would be interesting," I admitted.

"There are two keys to just about everything," The Hierophant continued. "One human and one divine. The divine key is the only one that will open the genuine doors of understanding, of course. But mankind is always looking for shortcuts. You always try to find a way to get what you want without putting forth any effort. So you invented the second key. It's a fake, of course—it only works on the astral plane, but that's good enough for most people, I guess."

"How can you tell which key is divine and which is human?" my wife Rose asked.

"That, my dear, is the test of discernment," The Hierophant answered. "Here, see for yourself."

He handed my wife the two keys that had been dangling from his waist. She picked them up, holding one in each hand.

"This key is solid," she said, referring to the one in her left hand. "It feels real. The other one—I don't understand this, but I can't feel it at all. It's almost as though it doesn't exist, but at the same time, I know that it does. I can't feel it, but I can understand it." She paused. "It seems to be telling me that it is the one and only key."

"Excellent," said The Hierophant.

"But the other one seems so much more real," said my wife.

"It's all done with mirrors," The Hierophant chuckled. It must have been a private joke, because we didn't get it.

"What does the key open?" I inquired.

"The Real Tarot, of course," The Hierophant replied.

He took the key and held it upright in his hand. I felt a rush of power surge through my mind; I was filled with a sense of self-control. Instantly, the key turned into the image of the Six of Rods; before our eyes had a chance to adjust, it had turned into a burning column of fire. Then, almost as quickly, it was the key again, but as I stared at it, I was flooded with a deep sense of triumph and responsiveness to the inner plan. I had touched the essence of the Six of Rods—and I knew it.

I was at a loss for words.

"Fine time for that," The Hierophant grumbled.

He held the key upright again; I gulped involuntarily, as a chill raced up my spine. The key became the Ace of Swords, turned into a shimmer of electric blue, and then became itself again. Yet as I looked at it, I seemed to see the whole of heaven. I understood a fragment of what has been, what is, and what is to come.

"This is how we did it for the Old Testament prophets, you know," The Hierophant joked. It was nice to see someone who so obviously enjoyed his work. "Would you like to see a burning bush or two?"

He continued his demonstration, turning the key into pentacles and cups, as well as swords and rods. From time to time, images from the major arcana appeared as well. Our favorite was the 6 of Pentacles—we still have the gold coin the chap gave us before he dissolved into the ether again.

Then, suddenly, almost abruptly, The Hierophant announced, "That's enough. You've been shown the key. It's up to you to show it to your readers. Inspire them to look only for the real key, not the fake one. Admonish them to cherish the doorways it will open for them."

"How do I do that?" I asked.

"I think you just have," The Hierophant chuckled, and he disappeared from sight, leaving my wife and me standing in the midst of a deserted park, by ourselves.

I looked down on the ground. Stooping, I picked up a key that wasn't there. And then we left.

CHAPTER TEN

The Ten Spiritual Lessons

In many Tarot decks, the pip cards of the four suits of the minor arcana—those numbered ace through ten—are treated almost like a poor relation. Instead of having a rich, symbolic illustration, as the cards of the major arcana do, they are often just five swords or eight cups arranged in a geometric pattern. A fortune telling meaning has been attached to them, but they are in no way invitations to deeper exploration. Even as good a deck as The Golden Dawn Tarot is guilty of trivializing the minor arcana in this way, although its cards do at least hint at energy distribution and spiritual connections. Still, its treatment of the minor arcana is a major reason why I do not recommend it as a practical Tarot deck. It has value for purposes of study, but lacks the flexibility of other decks in use.

The symbolism of the minor arcana is one of the great strengths of the Rider and the Aquarian decks. Especially in the Aquarian deck, there is such a continuity of artistic themes in each suit that it becomes obvious, after working with the cards for a while, that the minor arcana tells a definite story. This is the story of spiritual growth and development, and it is told in ten chapters, beginning with the Ace and ending with the Ten. In addition, it is a story the Tarot tells four times over, because it is told for each one of the four suits.

The ten chapters are the ten lessons the spiritual aspirant—The Fool—must learn as he makes his way from novice to initiate. This is a path he must follow in learning to use each of the four key energies of human mastery—our physical energies and resources, our emotions, our mental energies, and our spiritual energies. These lessons are not necessarily learned sequentially; nor does any one aspirant learn all of the physical lessons first, then all of the emotional lessons, and so on. The typical aspirant may be working on the sixth or seventh lesson of the Pentacles, the fifth lesson of the Cups, the third lesson of the Rods, and the fourth lesson of the Swords. Each one of us is working somewhere on this spectrum, from Ace to Ten, in each of the four suits.

The problems and challenges that come to us in life give us practical experience in mastering these lessons. They are not the lessons themselves, but are more like tests which show us how well we are learning our lessons. The true lesson in each case involves learning to express more of some divine ideal or spiritual principle in our daily living. If a card indicates that we have been behaving irresponsibly, for instance, the true lesson to be learned is how to act more responsibly—how to respond to the guidance and wisdom of the higher self.

The ten lessons of the spiritual path can be summarized as follows:

Ace—Grasping the Ideal.
Two—Harnessing duality.
Three—Discerning duty.
Four—Grounding spiritual force.
Five—Creativity.
Six—The right use of energy.
Seven—Achievement.
Eight—Sacrifice.
Nine—Inclusiveness.
Ten—Service.

The potential meanings of each card in the minor arcana are

much more extensive and profound than these brief descriptions, of course. But by working from this structure of spiritual lessons, to be cycled through in each suit, we can quickly build a set of associations for each card that will lead us to the Real Tarot. And we insure that our use of the Tarot for asking questions and receiving answers will be a constructive one that accelerates our growth. We know that it will, because we are building a structure of associations based on the principles of growth.

The story of the ten lessons of spiritual growth, as is true with all stories, begins at the beginning.

The Four Aces

Each of the four aces represents the primary spiritual ideal to be contacted and harnessed as we learn to work wisely with the energies of its suit. By nature, these are very abstract cards. They are much like the first few bars of music in a concerto or symphony; they introduce the basic themes that the piece of music will explore and develop. The aces introduce the basic themes of living that the divine plan expects us to explore and develop in the symphonies we call our lives.

In the Ace of Pentacles, the divine ideal is glory. Through the skills and talents we develop, we are meant to contribute to the richness of human civilization. This may be a minor contribution, through the faithful execution of our duties at work, or it may be a major contribution, through creative expertise. The scope of the contribution does not matter, so long as we see it as a revelation of God's glory here on earth. God has given us plenty of demonstrations of His glory and beauty through nature. It is our role, as humans, to demonstrate that we are responsive to this glory and able to contribute to it through the work we do—not for our personal glory and fame, but because our awareness of God's glory is so strong in our heart and mind that we are impelled to share it

with everyone we can. When the Ace of Pentacles appears, it is probably an indication that we need to evaluate the contribution we are making to the work at hand, and make sure it fulfills the ideal. It can also mean:

• You are being led too much by your own desire for glory. You need to curb this vanity and ambition before it destroys you.

• You are claiming a level of authority you do not possess. Practice humility.

• The work you do is being supported by sources on the inner planes.

With the Ace of Cups, the ideal is goodwill. The astral plane, or plane of the emotions, is very much like a pond. The water may be clear and calm at the surface, but as you descend, it can become murky and dark. Water lilies or lotuses can grow on the surface, but their roots extend to the mud at the bottom of the pond. All too often, our emotions are like that, rooted in the darkest muck of our reactiveness. Ideally, they should be like the cup, standing on the surface of the water, radiating the light of spirit, not the darkness of our anger, grief, or selfishness. The light in this case is goodwill, the ideal of the emotions, which is meant to be expressed through kindness, helpfulness, benevolence, tolerance, and compassion. When the Ace of Cups appears, it suggests the need for exercising greater control of our emotions, enriching them with goodwill and caring. We need to improve the quality of our emotional expression to the point where the presence of God can be seen through them. This card can also mean:

• You are being excessively confident. Be sure confidence and enthusiasm are matched by reliable skill and opportunity.

• The glowing prospects that have been laid before you are not matched at inner levels by substance, quality, or support.

• Others depend on you to act as a pillar of strength.

With the Ace of Rods, the divine ideal is wisdom. We have been given a mind with which to comprehend life. For long eons, the mind is capable only of observing life in its most superficial levels. But as our training of the mind begins, we learn to use the mind to penetrate to the heart and essence of ideas, not just take them on face value. We develop the capacity to look at a barren piece of ground, filled only with boulders and scrub grass, and see what it could become if we cleared it, irrigated it, planted it, and cultivated it. This is how we are meant to use the mind to discover the Garden of Eden within every idea. When the Ace of Rods appears, it suggests that we need to re-evaluate certain key assumptions and beliefs that we have made, and try to make better use of the wisdom we have. It can also indicate:

• You will have to stand by yourself in defending or promoting this idea.

• Do not overdose on a single Big Idea, no matter how significant it is.

• Your patterns of thinking are heavily influenced by cultural patterns. You do not think for yourself as much as you believe.

In the Ace of Swords, the divine ideal is individuality. The Ace stands alone, in the midst of massive patterns of the residue of ancient mischief, with a white rose on either side. And yet it is not alone—three strands flow from the tip of the sword's handle, two to the left and one to the right. These strands can be interpreted in

157

two ways—as the higher self's connection with the mind, emotions, and body of the personality, on the one hand, and as connections with the rest of humanity, on the other. In other words, although we are designed to develop the capacity to stand alone as an individual, the true attainment of individuality makes us aware of our spiritual communion with the rest of humanity. We do not take on the work of redeeming the material side of life alone—it is a joint effort involving the whole of humanity. When the Ace of Swords arises in the Tarot, it tends to indicate that we need to take a stand which clearly expresses our dedication and commitment to spirit. This is not a time for vacillation or shyness—it is a time to stand up and respond to the summons of the higher self. It can also mean:

• Although you have lofty spiritual ideals, you seldom exercise them.

• You have become too rigid spiritually—too dogmatic. Be more flexible.

• Rely on the strength of the higher self for the courage and steadfastness you need.

As we work with the four aces, we will eventually come to realize that these divine ideals that they each represent are actually the initiating impulses of divine life that motivate us to learn the lessons of the spiritual path. We can therefore draw great strength and support from them, as we become familiar with them. In a very real sense, they are our true spiritual home, from whence we came and to which we shall return.

The Four Twos

The second card in each suit portrays the drama of duality. As mentioned in the chapter on the major arcana, duality is one of the most fundamental principles of all life. Every facet of human life and divine creativity is characterized by duality. This should not be hard to understand—after all, the only way it is possible to define

good is in terms of evil, and vice versa. The only way to define maleness is in terms of femaleness. But the purpose of duality is not to split everything into its component halves. It is to show us the interaction which can occur between two polar opposites, thereby uniting them. And so, the lesson to be learned, always, in working with duality is to find a way to unify the two extremes, whether they are complementary or conflicting.

The theme of unity is certainly very much in evidence in the 2 of Pentacles. A woman contemplates the two pentacles, which together form the sign of infinity. The ocean is in the background, reminding us that one of the primary dualities of life is between the life of form and the life of abstract force. Her large pink hat suggests that she has great expectations, while the lacing of her tunic implies that she is embroiled in entanglements and conflict. She must try to understand the circumstances of daily life as one pole of a duality; the other pole is the spiritual purpose which shapes these experiences. To grasp both poles, she must train her thinking to perceive the unity they both share—the lessons she is learning. But this perception may well be obscured by her expectations, conflicts, and past experiences. When the 2 of Pentacles appears in a layout, it probably indicates that we are in danger of misinterpreting the meaning of events connected with the issue at hand. We are too close to our problem; we need to back off and distance ourself, or

159

we are likely to take harmful actions. It can also mean:

- You are being paralyzed by indecisiveness. Take a stand!

- Do not get caught up in the details of the situation, lest you never understand it. Look at the big picture.

- You have generated the conflict you are encountering. It can be resolved by making unilateral changes in your conduct.

In the 2 of Cups, more action is implied. There is a recognition that the dualities of life must be bridged, but there is still an incomplete understanding of how. It is not yet recognized that common purpose and synchronized actions will indeed achieve unity. Intellectually, the possibility of separation or schism is still very much a real factor. To the human in this condition, making a pledge or troth of unity is therefore the logical step to take. This is what the image of the 2 of Cups portrays—a man and a woman confirming their commitment or dedication. This could be a marriage troth, or just an agreement to work together toward a common goal. But it indicates a very human attempt to achieve unity, even though it also sows the seeds for betrayal. It is still true, unfortunately, that the majority of people do not take their commitments and pledges very seriously. They view them as something to break at their convenience. As a result, the unity that is achieved, so long as the bond is primarily emotional, is more an illusion than a reality. It has the appearance of unity, but lacks the reality of it. When the 2 of Cups appears, it suggests that any commitment, pledge, or contract should be entered into only with extreme caution. Is this a sign of true unity and shared purpose, or something that will be discarded without thought for the other party? The subtle yellow outline on the inside of the upper border of the card reminds us that commitments and pledges can only be made to our higher self, not to others. If we break a pledge to another, we break it with our own soul. The 2 of Cups can also mean:

- Rebuild this relationship on a foundation of your common

values, not mutual attraction. The potential for a healthy bond still exists.

• The responsibility for the problem at hand is shared; there-fore, the solution must be as well.

• You are projecting your own inadequacies onto others, blaming them for problems you have caused.

In the 2 of Rods, the theme of unity becomes more pronounced, being represented by the sphere or globe. There are two rods, each representing a different point of view on the subject at hand (a different extreme of the duality). When most people think about an issue, they simply take sides and choose between one or the other. They then label the side they have chosen as "right" and the other side as "wrong." This is how arguments arise. The person who has learned to think with his mind instead of his feelings, however, recognizes that there are always more than two sides to any issue. Indeed, the only way to understand an issue is to embrace its wholeness and then determine what kind of practical action can express this wholeness. He puts his emphasis on growth and pro-gress, therefore, as symbolized by the emblem on his sleeve, rather than rightness or wrongness. When the 2 of Rods appears, it suggests that we need to broaden our thinking to include possibili-ties we have previously excluded. We have probably been too narrow and dogmatic—if not bigoted—in our approach to this issue. We need to learn to look at life through the eyes of others. It can also indicate:

• If you gave as much time to being thankful for the blessings of your life as you do to grumbling about problems, you could restore balance to your attitudes and feelings.

• You need to learn to direct the emotions and the physical body from the level of the mind and higher self.

• You are wasting time on idle speculation.

The 2 of Swords completes this lesson of duality by emphasizing the need for spiritual discrimination. A nude woman stands with two swords pointed upright, one over each shoulder, behind large boulders of ancient evil. She is blindfolded; her hair flows down to embrace the boulders. The fact that she is nude indicates that she stands for spiritual Truth; the fact that she is blindfolded suggests that she perceives it intuitively. She is surrounded by the falseness of ancient cultural patterns and assumptions, and yet she is non-receptive to them, because she is able to discriminate between falsehood and reality, between the wheat of spirit and the chaff of form. When confronted by the duality of life, she explores each pole, to see how it leads back to spiritual purpose, and then harnesses the reality behind it. She is immune to the false lures of materialism. When the 2 of Swords appears in a reading, it tends to indicate that there is a danger of succumbing to the temptations of worldly thinking. We must carefully review our spiritual values and principles and reorganize our thinking so that we know what is real and substantial and what is not. The 2 of Swords can also mean:

• You have repressed many feelings and memories, and have therefore lost control of them.

• You have indulged in falsehoods so often you have blinded yourself to the truth.

• Your attitudes are acting like a lightning rod for conflict.

The Four Threes

The third card in each suit of the minor arcana portrays the spiritual lesson of duty. This in not the duty imposed by an employer on an employee, or by society on its citizens (although it is expected that the spiritual aspirant would perform such duties automatically). Rather, it is the measure of obligation or responsibility that we feel in any situation. There are therefore three aspects to this lesson of duty. The first is the measure of how much duty we are able to sense, and how this corresponds to the definition of duty

162

by our higher self. Many people feel no obligation or duty other than what is imposed on them—but ought to. The second is the measure of how faithfully or fully we respond to this sensed duty. The third is the measure of the quality of our attitudes, behavior, and work as we perform these duties. In many cases, it would actually be better to leave a duty unfulfilled than to perform it with bitterness, unhappiness, or regret. From a spiritual perspective, the failure to perform a duty, even if it is not recognized as such, is a sin of omission which can be just as serious as an overtly harmful act.

The 3 of Pentacles clearly underscores our duty to build—our duty to make a constructive contribution to humanity in whatever ways we can. Our primary duty in this regard lies in the way in which we perform the work by which we support ourselves. Our first duty as humans is to be self-sufficient and not a drain on society. Our second duty is to be sure that we make a real contribution to the quality of human life through the work we do. Our third duty is to put as much of our humanity into the work we do as possible. In a day and age when it is popular to strike at a moment's notice, file lawsuits against one's employers, and grumble and complain freely, these ideas of duty may seem antiquated. But they are the key to a spiritual understanding of duty. Of course, they are not limited to the workplace, either. They also apply to our duties as parents, as spouses, and as citizens. As the 3 of Pentacles suggests, human life is like a massive cathedral or temple, and we are all engaged in the building of it. But it is not just any building; the physical work or activity is actually transparent. What actually matters is the way in which the life of spirit is being served by it. When the 3 of Pentacles appears, it indicates that we need to carefully define our duty and role in the issue at hand. What does the higher self expect us to do? Are we doing it? How can we expand our role? It can also suggest:

• You need to fill yourself with a greater respect for others and the genuine achievements of civilization.

• You are overdosing on fears and worries about the future of mankind. There is an intelligent plan for humanity's future; try to discern it.

• Don't try to redeem others, when there is so much transformation that you need to do within yourself.

The 3 of Cups reminds us of our duty to honor the presence of God wherever we find it and to learn to use it to heal, both ourselves and others. Three women raise their cups in a mutual toast, with a giant yellow flower in the background. One of the cups is decorated with the symbol of conflict; the other two are plain. In the foreground is a hint of the design for the ancient residue of evil. The flower is a symbol of growth, but more than growth; its tremendous burst of vitality suggests an immense potential for healing and helpfulness. It is therefore our duty to learn to use the emotions constructively, to worship, adore, and pay homage to God's life in whatever shape or form it appears, and to help others in any way that is practical. Whenever the 3 of Cups appears, it suggests that we need to examine, objectively, whether we are a constructive or a destructive presence in the issue at hand. It can also mean:

• You are not treating friends and colleagues as equals.

• You are too caught up in hedonism and "looking out for number one."

- You need to develop a more mature capacity for sharing.
- Jealousy or envy is threatening to divide something of great value.

The message of the 3 of Rods is a bit more subtle. A man stands in the center of a triangle formed by the three rods, gazing out at the horizon—but the horizon is completely undefined. It is just white sky. This suggests that he is gazing into the inner dimensions of life, trying to discern the subtle patterns that guide and influence him. This interpretation is reinforced by the bubbly designs on his hat, which are similar to those of the kings and suggest that the centers of consciousness in his head are open and active. He is intuitive enough to be centered more in the inner life than the physical plane. He is therefore exercising his duty to be discerning—to make sure that his activities and plans are in harmony with the plan of the higher self, and that his methodologies will be effective. When the 3 of Rods appears in a Tarot layout, it suggests that we need to speculate on the unknown variables of the issue at hand, and try to discern what they are. It can also mean:

- You have made a number of false assumptions that are misleading you.
- The methods that have worked for you in the past are no longer sufficient. You need to develop new approaches to the problem at hand.
- You have been trapped in your own inconsistencies (or lies).

The 3 of Swords is one of the most dramatic cards in the minor arcana. It is the image of a pink heart pierced through by three swords, all pointing downwards. There are fluffy clouds in the upper portion of the card and the usual image of the ancient residue of unredeemed evil in the lower half. The immediate reaction of most people is to interpret this as a sign of something heartbreaking. But further reflection reveals a deeper meaning. The heart stands for "the heart of the issue," while the three swords indicate our ability to penetrate to the core. So this is actually a card of penetrating to the heart of the matter, or dealing with the innermost essence of an idea, feeling, concept, or event. In terms of spiritual duty, it suggests that one of our primary duties as a human being is to be involved in life and participate actively in the struggles of humanity to improve itself. We are a child of God and need to "be about our Father's business." When the 3 of Swords appears, it reminds us of the need to act as an agent of divine life in our own life. We are the only way in which the light of heaven can enter into our own personal sphere. As appropriate, therefore, we must be willing to take correct action. It can also mean:

• New spiritual energies are being poured into this situation. Unless correctly handled, they may cause a sense of overloading.

• Do not be fooled by superficial appearances. Examine the innermost level of motives for a true understanding.

• The present time is a "window of opportunity" for cleaning up ancient patterns of conflict, jealousy, and resentment.

The Four Fours

The fourth card in each suit embodies the lesson of grounding spiritual forces. By nature, divine forces are abstract. They cannot be applied to the problems of physical, emotional, and mental life in the same way that icing is spread on a chocolate cake. They must be absorbed by the spiritual person, integrated into his or her values, principles, and goals, and then expressed through creative or healing activities. Only once the spiritual force has been harnessed in this way and transformed into productive work, helpfulness, or common sense does the abstract and divine become alive and active in the worlds of form. This process is called "grounding spiritual forces." It is the process of making the intangible tangible, the idealistic practical.

This lesson is nicely portrayed in the 4 of Pentacles, where an

166

  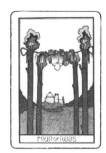 

individual—it could be either male or female—stands upright. A huge pentacle hovers over his head like a crown. A second immense pentacle emblazons his heart. The other two, of similar size, cover his hands like gloves. In the background is a vague horizon suggesting trees. This image clearly suggests that the individual is connecting with spiritual inspiration and force at the head, is able to integrate it into his values and talents at the heart, and is capable of expressing it through his hands, which symbolize his skills and hard work. When this card appears, it suggests that we need to follow through on the ideas and inspirations we have already received, and put them to work in constructive ways. It can also mean:

• You have let spiritual forces constipate at inner levels without expressing them. The congestion you suffer is the direct result of this.

• The opportunities for creative breakthroughs are excellent.

• An honest effort to do your work with skill and competence will be rewarded.

• You are a pawn being manipulated by others, either overtly or psychically.

The message of the need for grounding inner forces becomes even clearer in the 4 of Cups. In this image, the individual seems to have rebelled against the work to be done—or at least seems indifferent to the role of higher purpose. He or she has developed an

167

attitude of cynicism or nihilism, perhaps infected by the ancient residue in the lower right hand corner. As a result, the person is unable to see that opportunity is being withdrawn. Unless there is a change in attitude, more and more of the opportunities of life will be lost, and the growth symbolized by the tree will be stunted. When this card appears, it suggests that some form of blindness at the level of the personality, usually in the form of skepticism or nihilism, prevents the individual from seeing his or her work in terms of spiritual grounding. As a result, he gets stuck in the mud of his own indifference. The 4 of Cups can also imply:

• There is a danger of burn-out. Enthusiasm and dedication need to be rekindled.

• A long cycle of inactivity is about to end. New vitality is being poured into the personality by the higher self, to reawaken it.

• Do not ignore the guidance that can come from higher sources.

The 4 of Rods illustrates the role of the mind in the grounding process. It is the mind that perceives the abstract vision of the higher self, as portrayed by the castle across the river (the gap in our consciousness leading to the unconscious realms of life). It is likewise the mind that must then translate this vision into values and principles by which we can lead our life and then integrate the new values into the structure of our subconscious thinking. It must eliminate the residue of old patterns, reconcile inconsistencies, and update earlier patterns of thinking, feeling, and behaving. The resulting structure gives us a foundation on which we can act securely. When the 4 of Rods appears, it suggests that we need to review our values, beliefs, and principles and update them to meet the needs of the current situation. It can also mean:

• There are weaknesses in the logic of your position. You need to find these and correct them before they are pointed out by others.

• Your longing for security and comfort is too rooted in the material life. Seek out first the treasures of heaven.

• Your goals are the product of personal ambition. This limits the possibilities of your achievement.

The 4 of Swords introduces the notion that we must ground spiritual forces in time as well as space. It is the image of a knight in a suit of armor, laid out on a funeral bier in a cathedral. Three giant swords descend from heaven to earth, from ceiling to floor, as though suspended over the body of the knight. A fourth sword, looking a bit less gleaming, lies underneath the knight, either emblazoned on the side of his casket or perhaps buried in the tomb beneath the shell of his armor. The sword of greatest interest is the one buried in the tomb, suggesting an ancient pattern or habit that is buried or repressed in the depths of the unconscious mind. Before the new spiritual forces symbolized by the three upright swords can be harnessed by the spiritual aspirant, he or she must journey into the unconscious to cleanse and purify the ancient pattern. We must integrate with the past and the future, in other words, as well as with the present. When this card appears in a layout, it suggests that we are being held back in our growth and creative endeavors by an unresolved issue from the past. It can also mean:

• You are being distracted from the true focus of your service.
• There is need for greater psychological integration.
• You have invested far too much psychological energy in masking some element of your past. It is time to make a clean confession of it and proceed with the challenges of living.

The Four Fives

In the Tarot, five is the number of the spiritual lesson of creativity. Having learned lesson number three, the importance of making a constructive contribution, and lesson number four, the art of grounding spiritual forces on earth, the aspirant—The Fool—is now ready to learn to create new expressions on earth through his work and activity. This is the first bold step he takes in learning to absorb

the imperfections of the earth into his own experience and living-ness, add the higher perspective of spirit, and then transform the material and the imperfect into something new, enlightened, and useful. By definition, the work of creativity exposes the aspirant not only to duality, conflict, and opposition, but also to the deadening impact of materialism itself. The early stages of this lesson, therefore, are often marked by intense struggle and a loss of control. But as the lesson is mastered, it transforms the aspirant into a genius.

• In the 5 of Pentacles, the struggle of creativity is emphasized. The aspirant must learn to harness the male (pragmatic) and female (intuitive) side of his nature so they work harmoniously together, and then send them off on a figurative pilgrimage. In this instance, the pilgrimage is a quest for creative inspiration. Typically, the aspirant looks for this inspiration in the events and experiences of daily life; for many years, perhaps lifetimes, he struggles along the path, searching, looking. What he fails to realize is that the inspiration he seeks is not in some holy place or Mecca; it is within himself. Wherever he is, at whatever stage of growth or need, all he has to do is turn inward, and he can discover the inspiration, guidance, and support he needs. The musical designs in the church window hovering over the heads of the two pilgrims suggest harmony; the snow white ledge at the base of the window suggests a gap in consciousness similar to the one observed in the 4 of Rods. When this card appears, it implies that we are excessively caught up in the struggle of our creative work. We need to pause, reflect on the purpose we are seeking to serve, and then renew our faith that the higher self is indeed helping us fulfill this purpose. It can also mean:

• You are too literal and one-dimensional in your approach to creative and spiritual work. Become more multidimensional.

• There is a need for greater harmony in your relationships.

• You are trudging blindly toward your goals without pausing to enjoy and delight in the joys and treasures of each step along the way. Do not let yourself become grim and excessively sober.

The 5 of Cups paints a picture of an individual, little more than a brown pillar, gazing at three cups lying on the ground, spilled. Reeds blow wildly in the background, and birds fly in the sky. Two cups remain upright in the right foreground; the lines on the person's cloak form the symbol for conflict. The usual presumption is that these cups have been spilled accidently, and the individual is mourning his or her loss. When viewed as a lesson in creativity, however, it is far more reasonable to interpret this card to mean that the cups have been spilled deliberately, to irrigate and fertilize the soil, so that the wildness of this barren ground can be cultivated and transformed into a Garden of Eden. In this scenario, the individual is looking forward to the harvest, when the toils of his labors will be rewarded. Nevertheless, there is still a warning in this card that the emotions must be especially prepared to handle the challenges of creativity, lest a constructive and purposeful act be misconstrued for a damaging or threatening act. They must be trained as well to dwell on the two upright cups, rather than the three that seem to have been emptied. When this card appears, it implies that the emotions are rebelling against our creative efforts, because they do not understand them. We therefore need to correct this situation before we allow them to seriously damage our self-image or the work at hand. The 5 of Cups can also mean:

• You need to learn to take sensible risks without enormous self-doubt.

• You dwell too much on the seeming errors and failures of the past. You need to learn that there are no real failures, just lessons that lead you eventually to success.

• Your creative imagination dwells too much on fears and worries; you are poisoning your awareness.

The 5 of Rods is another card that is easily misinterpreted. On the surface, it looks as if the fellow in the middle (probably us!) is about to be beaten to a pulp by the guys who have encircled him. But these are not physical sticks—they are the rods of ideas and understanding. The 5 of Rods, therefore, is a card that tells us that creative efforts usually involve some kind of group effort. The mental lesson of creativity, therefore, involves learning to organize an effective, stable group through which the creative goal can be achieved. At the very least, this will be a group of ideas that needs to be organized, directed, and energized. More likely, it will be a group of similar-minded people who need to be assembled, given duties, and funded, so that they can perform the work that will bring your creative idea into reality. The keynote of this lesson, therefore, is congruity. When this card appears, it suggests that a variety of creative forces must be assembled and given a common focus. It is a test of creative leadership. The 5 of Rods can also imply:

• Differing opinions may tear the creative unity of your group apart.

• There are too many "experts" involved, each with his or her own opinion. The result is mental chaos.

• Your individual efforts are supported by an unseen group.

• Your judgment is blurred by unseen psychic interference.

These themes are brought nicely together in the fourth of the fives, the 5 of Swords. In this card, a knight stands alone on a battlefield. He holds one sword perfectly erect, its tip implanted in the soil. Two other swords are carried over his left shoulder. The final two swords cross one another in the foreground. In the distant background, two people are walking away from the scene. The foreground is a light cream color; the background is a dark brown. The creative connection, in other words, is complete. Both inspiration and power can flow from heaven to earth through the two swords over the shoulder, energizing the sword that is upright in the ground, and galvanizing into action the skills, talents, and opportunities represented by the two crossed swords. In this way, the ultimate purpose of creativity—the redemption of matter—is served. When this card appears in a layout, it indicates that the issue at hand is part of a larger creative plan. We need to understand what the goal of this larger plan is and adjust our behavior so that we can act in harmony with this plan, not contrary to it. The 5 of Swords can also mean:

- A creative plan you are involved in needs your support. Do not fail.
- The opposition you have encountered is a reaction to your creative work, not to you personally.
- The conflict you are experiencing is worthwhile, for it will lead to a true creative breakthrough.
- You are succumbing to professional jealousy. This will eventually poison your attitudes and work.

The Four Sixes

Once a new form or use of form has been created, it must be sustained. The sixth lesson of spiritual aspiration, therefore, is the right use of energy—from the generation of energy to its proper distribution. The keynote of this lesson is self-discipline. The creative person, whether an artist, a business executive, a government leader, or a spiritual teacher, becomes the focal point for the creative

173

energies he or she employs. Since the essence of creative work is bringing new energies from heaven to earth, the amount of energy funneled through the individual's structure of consciousness may become quite great—especially in the case of a business executive, the president of a large country, or a spiritual leader. In addition, these people often must be able to face and dispel tremendous amounts of opposition, criticism, and sabotage. The unprepared person will probably crumble quickly under the intense pressure—perhaps even die. The prepared person, by contrast, will seem to thrive on fulfilling his or her destiny. Working with large measures of creative energy, therefore, requires a strong measure of self-discipline, the ability to distribute energy effectively throughout a group, thereby sharing the burden (by delegating responsibility), and the ability to sustain a united effort toward a common purpose or goal.

In the 6 of Pentacles, the focus of the right use of energy is on money. This could pertain to personal finances, the budget of a corporation, or money that one administers on behalf of others. Symbolically, the issue of money also stands for other forms of physical energy, such as sex. The underlying message of the image of the 6 of Pentacles is balance in both the acquisition and the expenditure of money. A guild member sits before a balance that is weighing out coins. The pattern on his sleeves indicates that he is involved in building the structures of society. A pillar arises directly behind him, with two pentacles to his left, two to his right, and two on the table before him. The interpretation of this card is greatly enriched by reference to the 6 of Pentacles in the Rider deck, where the merchant is handing out gifts of charity. The two cards combined emphasize the responsibility of earning money, conserving it, and then using it primarily for the public good, not our personal satisfaction. The emphasis is clearly on philanthropy and public works. When the 6 of Pentacles arises, it suggests the need to redefine the funding and support of the issue at hand. It can also mean:

174

• You are too selfish. You must learn the lessons of generosity.

• The financial foundation of this enterprise is weak. Strengthen it.

• The issue of money is undermining the quality of your life. Change your basic attitudes—and develop some stronger ethics as well.

• Invest your resources into worthwhile, productive activities.

The 6 of Cups conveys two distinct messages. First, it affirms that the best structure for the distribution of energy is always hierarchical—power flows from the top through intermediate levels to the bottom. Second, it opens our eyes to the way in which energy flows from spiritual levels into form—that is, from the most sublime levels of essence into the somewhat more tangible levels of the subtle, and from that finally into dense physical reality. This is symbolized in the 6 of Cups as three tiers of cups. The flowers in each level of cups are all beautiful, but with each higher level the beauty becomes more refined, delicate, and brilliant. At the most sublime level, the male and female sides of being are sniffing the essence of the perfume of the beauty of the flower. As this applies to emotional expression, we must realize that it is not enough just to restrain from negativity and harm; we must also learn to work with the essence of the perfume of the beauty of our positive emotions—the real substance of love, joy, peace, and harmony. When

175

the 6 of Cups appears in a Tarot spread, it suggests that we must look beyond superficial appearances and tap the true level of energy at work at inner dimensions. Otherwise, we will probably be overwhelmed by it. This card can also mean:

• The hierarchical structure of a group needs reorganizing.

• You need to enrich your life with a deeper appreciation of beauty.

• Learn to share the burdens of responsibility.

The 6 of Rods reveals the importance of the mind in the work of self-discipline. A woman rides a horse triumphantly; on one rod there is a laurel wreath, a symbol of achievement and honor. The cloak is the bright pink of devotion. The harness on the horse suggests that the rider has perfect control and mastery of this animal. The horse, of course, stands for the desires and urges of the physical body and the wish life of the emotions, which will lead us astray unless we exercise self-control. The laurel wreath of triumph indicates that the aspirant has gained perfect self-control, not by repression or restraint, but by perfect training of the lower personality to cooperate. The woman, plus the fact that the robe is pink, underscores the basic truth that the single most important ingredient in self-control is a deep and perfect love for yourself. People who lack self-control and discipline are generally people with a very low self-esteem. People who truly care for themselves will not let themselves become undisciplined; their love and respect for the higher self is too great. When this card appears in a Tarot layout, it tends to suggest the need for enlightened self-discipline. It can also mean:

• You have restrained yourself so ferociously you are afraid to act. Loosen up!

• You must give the mind permission to control and direct the emotions.

• With perseverance and patience, you will triumph.

• Your attitude of superiority and arrogance is leading to trouble.

The most dramatic of the four cards in this position is the 6 of Swords. This is the image of a magician or wise sage guiding a noble vessel across a large lake, heading toward mountains in the background. His staff is dipped into the water, but it is obvious that he is not using it to propel the boat. The boat is being propelled mysteriously by the energy of the six swords, which seem to be stuck in the bottom of the boat. Somehow, they form a dynamo which translates the abstract force of spirit into a power that can impel this boat. Moreover, the pattern of ancient residue on the magician's coat suggests that he is going to encounter rough water as he sails along, but in fact the boat is gliding smoothly. This card stands for sublime mastery of energy and its distribution—the ability to control not only the physical energy (propelling the boat) but also emotional energy (he has calmed the rough waters of the astral plane). It suggests a capacity to use the mind to shape and influence the course of life in powerful ways. When this card appears, it implies a strong presence of the higher self in guiding and directing events of the physical plane. The 6 of Swords can also mean:

• There is a need for greater faith and trust in the higher self.
• You need to become motivated by the ideals and values of the inner life.
• Make sure the direction you have set for this activity is a spiritual one, so that you will not end up just going around in circles.

The Four Sevens

The seventh lesson of spiritual development is achievement, not in the sense of personal success (although these cards may indeed indicate that at times) but in the sense of being able to take a creative or spiritual inspiration, translate it into a specific goal, organize the effort to achieve it, and then shepherd the project through to completion. Many spiritual aspirants have a strong

capacity to adore God, but far fewer have the capacity to manage spiritual projects and undertakings successfully here on earth. One of the reasons for this inadequacy is the alarming emphasis placed on passivity and withdrawal from an active life by so many religious and spiritual traditions. As a result, in the effort to shift polarity from earthly success to spiritual achievement, many people make the mistake of rejecting all of the signs—and skills—of personal accomplishment. In most cases, however, these skills do not need to be rejected; they merely need to be redirected to serve spiritual goals.

The 7 of Pentacles is an image of a bright young person with a pet duck. The decorations on his chin strap indicate creative connections with archetypal patterns. The duck represents well-trained skills and an ability to act in the physical plane. In the background, there is an amorphous gray blob which may be the outline of a grove of trees. Scattered throughout the gray blob, almost like ornaments on a Christmas tree, are the seven pentacles. The gray blob represents the loosely organized substructure of any group, nation, race, or culture; the seven pentacles represent points of opportunity within the substructure. The challenge of achievement on the physical plane lies in being able to take the inspiration of a good idea and then call forth those elements on the physical plane that can be used to achieve success. When the 7 of Pentacles appears, it tends to indicate that the project or issue at hand has excellent potential for success; we simply need to harness and follow through with the hard work needed to attain it. It can also mean:

- Your own fears and worries, or the low opinions of others, may sabotage your efforts.
- Your feeling of being overwhelmed by the odds against you is not based in reality. Rely on the strength of your inspiration.
- You have a very small margin of error. Make no assumptions; leave no part of the project unattended.

The 7 of Cups presents a different facet of the same lesson. There are seven cups arranged in space, each with a different object rising out of it: a hand with a rod of power, a head, a bowl of fruit with a butterfly, a cobra, a rainbow, a flower that looks a lot like an atom, and a diving helmet. It is almost like the Tarot version of "Let's Make a Deal"—should we choose what's behind door one, door two, or door three? Actually, the answer is "none of the above." These seven objects represent the glamorous ways the world views success and achievement—the sirens of popular fads and fashion. Part of the lesson of spiritual achievement is learning to remain unaffected by the standards of heroism, achievement, and stardom of popular culture. We cannot let our wish life or our personal ambition color our vision and displace the sure hand of spiritual guidance. When the 7 of Cups appears in a layout, it suggests that we are basing our actions on false assumptions. Far from achieving our goals, we are in danger of cutting off our contact with spirit. It can also mean:

- You are behaving like a child in a candy shop. It is time to grow up.
- You are looking for a miracle to catapult you to success.
- You are trying to find a short cut to enlightenment. There are none.

The 7 of Rods is a striking contrast to the flashiness of the 7 of

Cups. It suggests that while the temptation to ride the waves of popular fads and fashions may be great, true achievement comes through patient, well-conceived growth. It is the image of a farmer or husbandman grasping a horizontal rod and using it almost magnetically to draw up the six other rods beneath it. He has even assumed the nature of the rods—note the wooden appearance of his cloak. He has identified so closely with his work that he almost breathes it and eats it. It is this kind of responsibility and commitment that leads to true achievement—the capacity to nurture the work at hand with a deep, abiding love and wisdom. When the 7 of Rods appears in a layout, it suggests that unless we are willing to devote ourselves entirely to the work at hand, we cannot expect it to be a success. It can also imply:

• You are being too inflexible in the way you look at a problem.

• You are diverting too much of the energy of a project to your own personal ends for it to be able to succeed.

• It is important to delegate responsibility to those prepared to handle it.

• You are abusing your authority and responsibility. It is possible to nurture growth without resorting to harsh criticism and stern strictures.

The 7 of Swords completes the Tarot's statement on the lesson of achievement. It is the image of a man turning inward, with a bundle of five swords slung over his shoulder; the other two are by his right side. The dominant part of this portrayal is the obvious symbolism of conflict emblazoned on his back. This individual has such a clear understanding of the spiritual meaning of success that he does not mind taking on the appearance of failure or even humiliation, if it lets him reach his spiritual goal. He has selected the spiritual forces he needs for his work and has directed them forcefully into the work at hand. The fact that he has stirred up conflict or opposition, perhaps strong enough to overpower him,

180

is of little importance. The long-term impact of his work will produce the changes in human consciousness that he seeks. When this
card appears in a layout, it indicates a need for clearly defining
what the higher self would view as achievement or success in this
endeavor—and then proceeding as the higher self would have us
proceed. It can also indicate:

• You must rely on your intuition for a true understanding of
what needs to be done.

• You have trouble generating self esteem and self-approval.

• There is a tendency to be overwhelmed by the burdens of life.
Do not allow yourself to slip into self-pity or depression.

The Four Eights

One of the most misunderstood of all spiritual concepts is that
of sacrifice. It is generally supposed to involve the renunciation of
all pleasure and personal satisfactions in life, in exchange for a pure
life in spirit. The resulting image that most people form of the
spiritual life is so dull and lifeless that it frightens away many good
people. Of course, this concept of sacrifice is just false advertising
conjured up by the type of vandals who throw bricks through
church windows. The true meaning of "sacrifice" is that it is the
work of making life sacred. As we grow in spiritual devotion and
commitment, our dedication to making life sacred deepens. Eventually, there do come times when we have to make choices. There
may, for instance, be an opportunity to help a friend—or a chance
to go to the beach. Which do we choose? If we have learned the
lesson of sacrifice, we would choose helping our friend, because it
helps us fulfill the ideal of making life sacred, whereas going to the
beach would merely be pleasurable. But it must be clearly understood that we are not renouncing trips to the beach. We are only
exercising the higher of two priorities. We decide to go to the beach
some other day.

  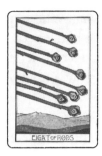 

The 8 of Pentacles represents the lesson of sacrifice on the physical plane, primarily in terms of our work or service. It is a card of a carpenter—allusions to Jesus are not coincidental—who is working in an "upper story." The window is open to spiritual influence. The hat indicates full intuitive contact with spiritual energies. The three nails in the breast pocket suggest complete control of the personality. It is possible to look right through the floor and see the cloud pattern through it. The physical duties of the work at hand are not important, in other words. We sacrifice the work we do to a larger plan—we see our work as an opportunity to make life sacred, through our attitudes, our behavior, and the services we perform. This does not mean that we should quit our present jobs and enlist in missionary work. That would be a stupid renunciation in most cases. Instead, it means that we renounce the personal focus of our work and find ways to make the work we already do a part of our spiritual practice. After all, why should we not be able to express spiritual love, wisdom, joy, and strength through whatever work we perform? When this card appears, it suggests that there is a conflict between some major facet of our physical needs and our spiritual direction. It could be a conflict between our views on money and spirit, or our attitude toward work and spirit. We need to review this problem and rearrange our priorities so that we serve spirit first, our personal needs second. It can also suggest:

• There is a window of opportunity for progress. Seize it!

• The challenge is to reveal the presence of God through all that you do.

• The service you are performing is not in harmony with the divine plan.

Sacrifice, of course, often becomes an emotional issue. Even though spirit sees the gains to be made, the emotions tend to focus on what is being given up—especially since it so often seems to be something we cherish! In the 8 of Cups, the need to reconcile the emotions with sacrifice is addressed. A person stands facing a wide river or lake. His path has led him to this point, and he knows he must cross over and continue his journey on the other side. But he will be unable to take with him the eight cups behind him, with which he is very much identified, as we can tell from the fact that his cloak spreads out behind him and embraces the cups. A waxing moon is in the sky, indicating that the potential for loss is actually more imaginary than real. The opportunity for gain lies ahead. All the person needs to do is realize that he can never lose anything of value—any element of spirit. If he has truly built up his treasures in heaven, and not on earth, then leaving the cups behind will be no more traumatic than leaving behind excess baggage. When this card appears, it suggests that the emotions are rebelling against a proposed course of action or some facet of our destiny and work. They need to be taught to like it, for as Alexander Pope put it, "Whatever is, is right." The 8 of Cups can also mean:

• You need to bridge the gap between the conscious and unconscious mind.

• You are carrying harmful attitudes and ideas with you. You need to eliminate these residues.

• Your attitudes have brought you to the brink of loss and disaster.

The 8 of Rods is one of the starkest in the whole Tarot. It is eight parallel rods angling through space, with a barren landscape below them. This image suggests the abstract nature of the mind, and in specific, the nature of archetypal thought. Archetypes are divine forces which are alive, active, and moving. They are full of fire and light and, when contacted, will illumine the mind. To work with them, we must rise above the visualizations and images we have been so used to and learn to think abstractly, with pure thought. This is the way we make the mind sacred, by nourishing it only with the highest, noblest type of thought. When this card appears, it suggests that we need to invoke the ideal plan of the higher self, along with the power to implement this ideal plan, to help us deal with the situation at hand. It can also mean:

• The force of your destiny has brought you to this state. You need to accept it and learn to like it.

• You are second guessing the higher self. This is a silly endeavor.

• You need to sacrifice your personal opinion in deference to the wisdom of someone who knows much more than you.

• You are using truth cruelly; learn to blend it with compassion.

The teaching on sacrifice is completed in the 8 of Swords, in which the spiritual aspirant is blindfolded and tied to a post. Four swords stand vertically on either side. There is a tan amorphous blob in the background and a gray one in the foreground. The base of the aspirant's clothes form a stand of ancient residue of evil, which is undoubtedly the foundation of the restriction. This creates an image of being trapped by the swords, but once again, the true meaning of this card is considerably different. The aspirant has allowed himself to be limited and restricted by form in order to pursue spiritual work. He is not paying heed at all to the fear and pessimism in the surrounding environment; he is completely focused in the inner dimension of being. By allowing himself to be "captured" by materialism, the force of spirit within him is able to build in strength and eventually break the bonds of materialism. In this way, the work of the swords is completed. When this card appears in a layout, it implies that we must define our sense of restriction or limitation in terms of the plan of the higher self, not in terms of our own desires. Milton's blindness may have been a limitation, after all, but he never would have written *Paradise Lost* if he had been able to see. The 8 of Swords can also suggest:

• You have blinded yourself to those who would help you.

• The confinement you feel is only temporary. Identify with spirit, which has no sense of restriction.

• The restrictions you sense are self-imposed. Seek out their roots and change them.

The Four Nines

The ninth lesson of spiritual development, as taught us by the Tarot, is inclusiveness. Through the first eight lessons of the path, we reach the point where we realize that our true humanity lies in the higher self, not the personality. The challenge of physical life is to develop the personality to the point where it can personify or embody without significant distortion the divine qualities of love, wisdom, joy, and peace. This process of bringing heaven to earth in such a way that we truly reveal the presence of God is called "individualization." We prove our individuality, in other words, by being able to individualize these divine energies in our life. But through this long period of perfecting individualization, we nonetheless remain focused within a finite body and personality. Our habits, attitudes, aspirations, and self-definition all revolve around our finiteness. The spiritual energies we individualize, however, are not in any way finite. They are abstract, universal, and infinite. To express them in their true nature, therefore, we must learn the spiritual lesson of inclusiveness—the ability to reach beyond ourselves and our finite existence and embrace the multidimensional

nature of spiritual forces, the brotherhood of mankind, and the divine plan of God.

In the 9 of Pentacles, the first challenge of inclusiveness is stated. A woman, representing the higher self, is holding a white cockatoo or exotic bird in a loving way. Three pentacles adorn the white feathers of the bird; the other six are scattered in the gray cloak of the woman. In the background is a grape arbor and a tree. The suggestion here is the aspirant is nearing the stage of individuality, but still has one major obstacle to hurdle: himself. The skills and brilliance of the personality, represented by the exotic bird, are a bit too highly valued; moreover, the higher self is still viewed as passive to the active, dynamic personality. This polarity must be shifted before true individuality can be attained—the higher self must become active and dominant to the compliant and receptive personality. To do this, however, the personality must detach from the pressures and conditionings of mass consciousness, even in the most subtle ways, as indicated by the pentacles on the gray cloak. In addition, he must begin to learn the lesson of inclusiveness, as attested to by the grape arbor, which suggests the words of the Christ: "I am the vine, you are the branches; whoever remains in me, with me in him, bears fruit in plenty." The tree in the far background symbolizes the evolutionary progress of all humanity, which becomes more and more our major concern. When the 9 of Pentacles

186

appears in a spread, it tends to indicate that we need to revise our thinking so that we look at the situation from the perspective of the higher self, not our personal needs and wants. It can also mean:

- The job being offered you has excellent potential for advancement and self-fulfillment.
- You need to express a deeper level of thankfulness for the blessings of your life.
- You may be running the risk of sounding arrogant and "know-it-all."
- You are ignoring the excellent guidance you have been receiving.

In the 9 of Cups, the emotions learn the lessons of inclusiveness. This is an image of a competent, talented worker in the fields of life, who knows his status and achievements. The pink dot at the throat indicates a very strong creative ability; the badge on his hat and the cups, which are arranged almost like trophies, testify to the acclamation his work has received. The patterns on his sleeves indicate that he is no stranger to conflict; he is either controversial or busily involved in resolving conflict and establishing peace. But note the V-shaped pattern that divides the man from the cups. This is the same pattern that indicated the transcendent nature of God when it appeared in the major arcana. The implication is that this very confident man must now define his place in the world entirely in terms of the universal presence of God, not himself. These are not his cups—they are God's cups. Each is filled with a different spiritual energy. But the man does not require these cups for his own fulfillment. He acquires them so that he can play his part in fulfilling their purpose. He does not seek to own these cups, but rather use them according to their divine design. When the 9 of Cups appears in a layout, it suggests that we need to weigh our motives and expectations. Are we still being driven by personal needs and goals? Or have we taught the emotions to be inclusive—to embrace divine purpose and make it our own? It can also mean:

• Take care not to become too smug. Others can do the same work you do. No one is more important than the service they render.

• You fit into humanity like a square peg in a round hole. Revise your self-centered attitudes.

• You are performing your work well. Look for ways to increase the helpfulness of your contribution.

The 9 of Rods emphasizes the growing inclusiveness of the individual. It is a simple image of the spiritual aspirant, all of his connections fully awake, surrounded by nine vertical rods. These represent the spiritual opportunities available to him, as well as the spiritual forces ready to help him as he proceeds with his work. The great challenge to him is to choose those projects that will a) be in harmony with the divine plan, and b) attract support from a wide range of spiritual forces. The more he can identify with the plan of humanity, and understand how his talents and skills can serve this plan, the more successful he will be. When this card arises in a spread, it suggests that we need to choose between a number of possible options, all of which seem equally favorable. The key to choosing wisely is to select the option that best fills the purpose of the higher self. This card can also imply:

• You are being indecisive. You can see so many options you have paralyzed your decision making capacity. Simplify!

• You need to respect and cherish the contributions of others, not be envious or jealous of them. Reform!

• There is great power behind your plan. When the time is right, act confidently.

The story of inclusiveness is completed in the 9 of Swords. In this image, a woman sits by a casket, her hands covering her eyes in apparent grief. She has set down the jug she was carrying beside her. Large boulders or mountains of the ancient residue of evil loom

188

behind her. Nine parallel swords cross the sky horizontally. The odd thing about this image is that by the time an aspirant reaches this level of development, death is not viewed as a horrible thing. It is just a transition from a cramped level of consciousness to a more expanded one. What troubles the woman, who now represents the personality, is that she must face these mountains of ancient residue, and she is not quite sure she yet has the full support of the higher self. She has been momentarily caught up in the infectious doubt, pessimism, and cynicism of mass consciousness. This has caused her to set down the jug of her service; she is on the brink of despair. But what she has forgotten is that spirit is just as present as it ever was. She still has contact with the nine swords above her; it is only her inner conflict and turmoil that have caused this momentary lapse. When this card appears, it indicates that we are facing an issue we do not have to deal with alone. This is an issue the whole of humanity must face; it is not a personal assault on us. We should therefore identify with the strength and power of the divine plan, and let it help us meet this challenge. We may feel all alone at times, but we need to remember that one person plus God constitutes a triumphant force. The 9 of Swords can also mean:

• Your grief for your losses is understandable, but it is crippling you. It is time to restore health and move onward.

• Do not dwell on the failures of the past. They have brought you to the present with its many opportunities for success. Dwell on them.

• The higher self has not abandoned you. Reach out and summon its help—and then get ready to act on it!

The Four Tens

In many ways, the tenth card in each suit is a restatement of the ace. The difference is that the ace represents the ideal of each level of energy in its pure, abstract nature, whereas the ten repre-

sents the ideal in full and glorious expression, through the vehicle of the enlightened agent of God. As such, the lesson of this position is service, the process of bringing a portion of these qualities to those who are unable to tap them for themselves. When the Christ admonishes us to feed the hungry, give drink to the thirsty, take in strangers, clothe the naked, visit the sick, and comfort those in prison, He is not just referring to the literal meanings of these acts. He is speaking primarily of the spiritually hungry and thirsty—those who crave wisdom and understanding; of the spiritually bereft and naked—those who feel abandoned by life; and the spiritually ill and imprisoned—those who are trapped in self-deceit and materialism. To these people, we need to bring light, love, joy, and hope; if we fail to do so, we harm ourselves, the whole of humanity, and the Christ. This is the essence of true service—bringing a new measure of light, love, joy, and hope into the world. It has little to do with what humanity normally labels "service" and absolutely nothing to do with spreading dogma and religious biases.

The 10 of Pentacles is a glorious scene. It depicts a man and a woman—our spiritual purpose and our spiritual talents—standing under an arch and looking at a castle in the distance. The castle represents their true spiritual home. Their little child, representing the enlightened personality, peeps behind the cloak of his parents and looks back at the physical plane, symbolizing the fact that while we draw our inspiration from within, our work nonetheless is still in the physical plane, serving the needs of humanity. It can also imply that we must control the child within us, lest it sabotage our spiritual maturity. When this card arises in a layout, it implies a need to strengthen our contacts with our spiritual sources on a daily basis, but not to the point of forgetting why we are here on earth. There is much to be done, and we have our role in doing it. The 10 of Pentacles can also suggest:

• Your understanding of the ideal is admirable, but you must learn to deal with the conditions of life with greater detachment.

• Your view of the spiritual life is mostly just a fantasy of your own; it is not based on genuine insight or experience.

• The "communications" you are receiving from inner sources are just cliches and truisms coming out of your own subconscious.

The 10 of Cups presents an image that leads many interpreters of the Tarot to talk in glowing terms of happiness, true love, and the like. The true meaning of this card, as it exists in the Real Tarot, is far more substantial. It indicates that the dual nature within us has finally been harmonized and the goals and purposes of the higher self and the personality are one and the same. As a result, we are able to penetrate to the heart of every issue and serve from a position of authority. The cups form an outline that suggests a heart; the full spectrum of energy seems to flow from the center of the heart in the form of a rainbow. When this card appears, it indicates that true service lies in helping others resolve the inconsistencies and confusions within their consciousness, thereby achieving integration. It does not involve gratifying their wishes or giving them what they want; it involves giving them what they need. As we serve, we must learn to work always from the benevolent heart of the divine purpose. The 10 of Cups can also mean:

• The issue at hand has great potential for your advancement and growth.

191

• You have put too much importance on a single issue or re-lationship. If you become dissatisfied with it, what will you rely on for strength?

• You are being blinded by your wish life. Be more realistic.

The 10 of Rods demonstrates the integrative nature of spiritual service. It suggests that as our work of serving others becomes more and more dominant in our lives, it gives a focal point for all of our inspirations, values, beliefs, and expectations. In this way, we become more and more completely integrated into the inner life from which we draw our guidance. The man in the 10 of Rods is turned inward, away from the physical plane, and is carrying a sheaf of 10 rods, all of them forming a focal point in the area of his hands, which symbolize service. When this card appears, it reminds us that spirit does not exist to serve us; we exist to serve spirit, by implementing its goal and projects. The 10 of Rods can also mean:

• You are focusing too intently on some activity. As a result, you are running the risk of becoming unbalanced. Restore equilib-rium.

• Even though all the facts indicate otherwise, you are unwilling to give up a prejudice or emotional bias that is distorting your thinking.

• There is a flaw in your basic assumptions about life that will eventually leave you with great doubt and uncertainty.

The final word on service is presented by the 10 of Swords. This is the image of a man lying face down on the desert floor, with 10 swords stuck in his back as though he were a pincushion. His arm bears the insignia of conflict and his lower back is adorned with the pattern of ancient evil. Mountains loom in the background. It cer-tainly appears to be a desperate situation, but nothing could be farther from the truth. As was the case in the 6 of Swords, these swords indicate connections with powerful divine forces; the image of lying face down on the desert merely reinforces the fact that in serving the plan of God we must be blind to worldly wisdom. True service, in fact, seldom takes us to the Garden of Eden, instead, it leads us into the most barren stretch of desert or the most wicked city on earth, so that we can redeem evil. The purpose of service is not to deliver pompous sermons against evil, but rather to transform it, cleanse it, and help redirect it so that it becomes receptive to spirit. Esoterically, this is the card of greatest activity, wakefulness, and livingness in the whole Tarot. When it appears in a spread, it suggests that we need to die to the ways of the world before we can truly serve the inner dimensions of life. It can also mean:

• You are being tempted to betray your most cherished values and beliefs.

• You have done yourself great harm by maintaining such a low self-image. Recognize yourself as a child of God!

• The seeds of spiritual service lie in the issue at hand. What are these seeds and what is your responsibility for planting and tending them?

These are the ten spiritual lessons of the Tarot. If you make these ideas and principles the core of your interpretation of the minor arcana, it will form a coherent, stable structure in your associative mechanism. Your interpretations should not be limited to these ideas and insights, of course; any card will have dozens of potential meanings, depending upon the question asked and its position in the map. But if these ideas form the base of your associations, they will help protect you against "off the wall" kinds of interpretations—and guide you ever more surely in the direction of personal and spiritual growth.

These lessons are a foundation that you can build on for many years to come.

CHAPTER ELEVEN

Weaving the Tapestry

In interpreting the cards of the Tarot, always keep in mind that these are multidimensional forces, not static symbols. It is not possible to make definitive interpretations of any of these cards, as one might describe an orange or an automobile. Just when you think you have fully understood a card, it shows up in an entirely new context. This is why it is not feasible to try to memorize a bunch of meanings for each card, then crank out the best one as the card arises in response to a question. Each time you use the Tarot to explore the inner dimensions and meanings of life, it is important to approach it as though you were using it for the first time. Look for new meanings, in other words—never rely on what a card has meant before. This is not to imply that you should ignore what a card has meant before—it is important to build a strong basis of associations for each card. But do not let associations become dogma, lest you close the door on fresh inspiration.

If possible, think of each card as a prism, rather than a flat, two-dimensional card. A prism has many surfaces. You can look at it from many different ways. But the true purpose of a prism has little to do with its surfaces. To understand a prism, you have to penetrate to its interior. There, it will fragment pure light into the colors of the spectrum—or bend light so that it can be seen at new angles. To understand the archetypal forces of the Tarot, you must regard each card as a prism that refracts the light of each archetype in such a way that you can comprehend the message that answers your question. A week later, the same card may arise in response to a totally different question. But now you are looking through a different face of the prism, and the message of the archetypal force is completely new, completely fresh. It is the same light, but a different color.

In the beginning, you will look at the card and see just the card. But as your skill in interpreting grows, and the base of your associations widens, you will begin to realize that the Tarot is taking shape as much in your mind as it exists in the deck. The cards serve as starting points for your interpretation, but the real process of interpretation occurs in your mind. It is therefore of great importance to train your mind to work with the Tarot carefully. Especially in the beginning stages, do not rush or hurry through any Tarot consultation.

For this reason, once you have formulated a question, shuffled the cards, and laid out the ten cards of your map, take some time to reflect on the entire layout. Do not just launch into interpreting the cards in order, from starting point to fulfillment. Look for repeated patterns among the cards—repeated numbers, repeated artistic themes, and so on. How many cards from the major arcana are included in this map? Are any of them from similar positions in their respective septenates? Do any of them have repeated artistic themes? How many cards are there from each suit—swords, rods, cups, and pentacles? Does any one spiritual lesson or face show up more than once? Do any of these cards have repeated artistic themes?

The idea is to try to discern the dominant archetypal forces at work in this situation. In most cases, there will only be one or two primary forces. If you can understand these, then you can make real progress with answering your question. After all, these one or two forces are portrayed by ten cards. The Tarot will therefore tend to repeat itself, unless the question is so complex that it must use one card for every archetypal force. In most cases, three or four of the cards will probably deal with one of the archetypal forces; three or four others will reveal the second. The others will hint at methods to use in harnessing them or problems that have to be solved. But the Tarot is not actually repeating itself. The prismatic nature of the Tarot is showing you three or four different facets of the multidimensional nature of each force. It is helping you view this spiritual, dynamic force from several different perspectives, so that your chances of harnessing it increase.

Perhaps you are trying to improve a relationship with a friend. This friend has done something that offends you, and you are finding it difficult to forgive him. You wish you could, because you care deeply for this person, but your emotions are unable to get past the hurdle of deep hurt. So you ask the Tarot, "How can I learn to forgive this person?" The answer, inevitably, will be that you need to learn to love more fully and completely. But love, as an archetypal force, is multidimensional in nature. It is not the shallow, one-dimensional energy we usually call love. That is just a feeling of attraction, limited to the emotions and no more enduring than happiness. The true force of divine love is far more complex; it can be expressed through the emotions as mature caring, but it will also be expressed through the mind as a deep level of empathy and through our spiritual level as a strong commitment to the welfare of others. As Paul put it, "Love is always patient and kind; it is never jealous; love is never boastful or conceited; it is never rude or selfish; it does not take offense, and is not resentful....Love does not come to an end." In other words, true love would not be offended by what your friend did; it cannot be broken by a mere disagreement or injury.

Having to get this message through to you, how would the Tarot proceed? It would pick a card that would indicate that love is based on understanding as well as affection. It would similarly pick

197

a card that would remind you that you value friendship as a spiritual quality and should not be so hasty to judge. It might also select one that would encourage you to look at this problem from the perspective of your friend, and try to determine why he acted as he did. The Tarot might also throw in a card to warn you of the consequences of holding onto grudges and resentments—one of those cards with stones and boulders of the ancient residue of evil prominently displayed on it. In these ways, the Tarot would be leading you to an understanding that forgiveness is a way of cleansing your attitudes and feelings; it lets you get on with life. You do not have to demand an apology from your friend in order to forgive him; you forgive him for your own sake, so that you do not carry this burden with you. Moreover, as you forgive, it releases the emotional blockage of your sense of being hurt. This in turn frees up the mind to look at the situation much more clearly. In many cases, you may see that you have contributed to the problem by exaggerating the extent of the offense; you may need to offer an apology for your own behavior.

The Tarot, in other words, weaves a tapestry of symbolism, based on the associations already in your associative mechanism, that will lead you to the best understanding of this situation you are capable of. The art of reading a Tarot map is to view it as this kind of tapestry, and try to determine how the threads of each card interweave to form a coherent answer. When you do this properly, the resulting map is every bit as much a thing of beauty as a work of art hanging in a museum. It reveals divine intelligence and benevolence.

Two different people asking the same question will get two different maps because the content of their associative mechanisms will be different. The images on the Tarot cards will suggest different meanings to each of them. But the archetypal message will be the same in both cases. After all, love and goodwill are the keys to forgiveness regardless of who you are. So even though the outer tapestry of images will vary, the inner tapestry of ideas and divine guidance will be the same.

The key to discerning this tapestry in your mind lies in The Fool. We have seen that The Fool summarizes the forces of the major arcana and synthesizes them; he likewise acts as a bridge between the major and minor arcanas. In a figurative sense, it is The Fool—the emerging spiritual nature within you—that asks the questions, at least the truly significant ones. The Fool represents that element within the personality which knows enough to know you do not know enough, and has the humility to ask a higher source for guidance and help.

The Fool is therefore an excellent role model to imitate as you try to interpret any given answer. Do not begin the process of interpretation with a fixed idea as to what the answer will be; approach this as a journey into understanding. To the degree that you are willing to learn something new about yourself and life, you will; to the degree that you want to hear exactly what you already believe, you will. Whether or not the Tarot will be a tool of revelation or a tool of self-deception is entirely up to you. It can be used in either way.

As you reflect on the ten cards in a layout, try to discern what the inner message is. If the cards for the creative challenge, purpose, and fulfillment are all swords, for instance, this may be a major clue that the issue at hand is of some importance to you spiritually. If the cards of destiny and the real question are both sixes, this is a big hint that you need to exercise greater self-discipline.

As I survey a spread, I try to discern which card or cards are the most important to understanding the inner message. This will vary with every question. In one layout, it might be the 2 of Cups in the position of the spiritual ideal, advising me that the major issue is one of commitment and betrayal. In another spread, it might be the 8 of Rods in the position of the endowment, suggesting that the problem at hand has been caused by the highly argumentative and self-righteous style of the person asking the question. In some cases, it may be two or three cards, forming a duality or a triangle, that give me my first real clue.

Once I have determined the most significant card, I frequently begin my interpretation right there—in the fifth or ninth spot on the map. I will see what other cards are related symbolically to this card and proceed in whatever order seems most sensible. I will eventually interpret all ten positions in the map, but it will probably not be in sequential order, from one to ten. I have no compunction about jumping all over the map, in whatever order strikes me as proper intuitively. There is just one rule to remember in this regard. You are asking the Tarot to answer your question. Once you have formulated your question and laid out the ten cards, the die is cast. Now it is up to the Tarot to answer you. So let it answer! Do not impose your expectations or some set of rules on the Tarot. Respect its intelligence and insight. If it seems appropriate to interpret one particular question in a completely different manner than you have ever used before, do so! Let the Tarot—and your higher self—guide you.

Once I have discerned the major theme of the inner message, I then proceed with filling in the details that create the whole tapestry. But I am never in a hurry. I do not look for simplistic answers from the Tarot, and try hard to return the favor by avoiding simplistic interpretations. I may spend ten or fifteen minutes examining the spread as a whole, looking for clues to insight just like Sherlock Holmes would look for clues at a murder scene, before I begin interpreting any single card. I may also spend as much as thirty minutes exploring the inner meanings of just one card. With other cards in the same spread, I may spend only two or three minutes, especially if their role is to reinforce the statement of the primary cards. But on the whole, I devote an average of eight to ten minutes to interpreting each card.

As a beginner therefore, do not be afraid to spend even longer in trying to interpret the inner message to your questions. The work of a beginner is to build up proper associations with each card in the subconscious; this process is actually far more important than interpreting the answers correctly. If you zip through a Tarot spread in ten minutes, you are defeating the purpose of using the Tarot. If you are looking for quick answers, use the I Ching, which tends to be much faster. If you are looking for simplistic answers, read the astrology column in your newspaper. Use the Tarot only if you want a thorough understanding of the forces and conditions, spiritual or otherwise. Give it a full opportunity to live up to its full, creative potential.

If, after working patiently to understand the cards in a map, you are still unsure of the inner message, do not become discouraged. If eight of the cards in the spread make sense to you, but two of them are still enigmatic, ask the Tarot for help in understanding the role of these two cards in this spread. Focusing on one of the two cards, shuffle the remaining cards in the deck. Ask that you pick a card that will clarify the meaning of this card to you. Then repeat the process with the second card, if necessary.

Keep in mind that while you are still in the beginning stages of learning to interpret the Tarot, you may have to research some of the difficult cards. If The High Priestess appears in a spread, and you cannot figure out what it means to you, it may be helpful to research the descriptions of the Temple of Solomon in general, and the twin pillars of discipleship in particular. As you check out some of these symbolic references, it may well trigger the insight you need to complete your interpretation.

In this regard, it is also helpful to remember that you do not have to come up with the full answer within some specific time frame, as though you were playing a basketball game. If you hit a dead end in interpreting a particular message, set it aside for a day or two. "Put it on the shelf" of your subconscious, where the unconscious portions of your mind can work at deciphering it for you. Then return to it after a few days. You will be surprised what new insights suddenly well up in your mind as you look at the spread again.

As you get more experienced intuitively, it may only be necessary to take a short break of a few hours or even a few minutes to let the unconscious decipher a message that stumps you. In fact, you can often accelerate the process by specifically invoking help from your higher intelligence. When I am stumped, I will take a break to get something cold to drink—or perhaps make a telephone call. But before I stop, I silently invoke the guidance and insight I need to understand the spread. When I return, suddenly the insight I had been struggling to grasp is there before my eyes, so clear and sharp that I am left wondering how I possibly could have missed it in the first place!

In a very real sense, every time you use the Tarot, you are recreating it. You are not just getting an answer to your question, but you are also building a stronger foundation of insight that will serve you well in future uses of the Tarot. The more you use the Tarot properly and wisely, the greater your ability to use this tool grows. In fact, if you work intelligently with it for long enough, you will find that the symbolism of the Tarot becomes a permanent part of your thinking process. You become the Tarot.

This is the challenge of correct interpretation. The Tarot is not a pack of playing cards; it is a living system of divine intelligence. Each of these cards can be like seeds that you plant in your own awareness. Then, by nurturing these seeds with constant practice and repeated use of the Tarot, you can cause them to grow in your own subconscious. As this happens, it will add structure and purpose to your own thought processes. This is why it is important to approach interpretation in the manner described in this book— seeing the minor arcana, for instance, as a series of ten lessons in spiritual development. It guarantees that the interpretations you place in your subconscious will be healthy and helpful ones—ideas that will help you grow.

There are no limits to what can be done with the Tarot. What *you* do with it, of course, is entirely up to you. It is a gift of The Fool to you. If you use it wisely, it will serve you well.

CHAPTER TWELVE

A Word of Warning

As is true with any effective tool, the use of the Tarot can expose us to certain dangers, if we are careless or foolish. It is important to know what these dangers are, so we can avoid them. At the same time, however, we must take care not to magnify these dangers out of proportion. Any intelligent, sane person can use the Tarot without worry or fear. Properly used, the Tarot is safer than a kitchen toaster or popcorn maker.

Indeed, one danger typically associated with the Tarot does not even exist. This is the claim made by religious bigots and fanatics that the Tarot is the mischievous invention of the devil, and using the Tarot will cause us to succumb to satanic influences. It is true that one of the cards in the major arcana is "The Devil," but it is equally true that the same word appears frequently in the Bible. In point of fact, the Bible and the Tarot have a good deal in common. They both can trace some of their roots to the esoteric tradition of the Kabalah; they both can be used as guides to the inner dimensions of life. What annoys the average religious bigot about the Tarot is that it is a tool which enables the intelligent human being to make direct intuitive contact with the higher self and divine intelligence, thereby eliminating the necessity for a clerical middle man—be it priest, pastor, or rabbi. In evaluating the rabid claims of religious bigots about the Tarot or any other tool of divination, it should be remembered that for more than fifteen hundred years the church discouraged its followers from reading the Bible, lest they discover more about contacting God than was deemed desirable by the clergy!

The true dangers associated with the Tarot lie in the psychic dimensions. In order to tap the full power and potential of the Tarot, it must be used intuitively. It is not necessary to have intuitive faculties when you first start working with the Tarot, but as your skill in using it develops, these abilities should unfold, at least to some degree. As already mentioned, the correct use of the Tarot will encourage these skills to unfold properly.

Unfortunately, most people who have developed some measure of psychic ability have a very poor understanding of these skills. This is to be expected, of course, since we do not have accredited schools or colleges for the training of intuition. As a result, the average psychic is capable of occasionally producing some startling observations, but lacks reliability, consistency, and discrimination.

It is the lack of discrimination—the ability to separate the wheat from the chaff—that is most troubling in working with the Tarot. Because the Tarot has a long history and tradition, it has been polluted by careless and foolish usage as much as it has been enriched by intelligent usage. As described in chapter one, there are many different levels of the Tarot, ranging from the gypsy fortune telling level to the archetypal forces of the Real Tarot. Each of these levels has a psychic reality that is almost entirely independent of the other levels. So it is quite possible for one person using the Tarot to tune in to the fortune telling level, a second to plug in to the intellectual level, and a third to attune to the archetypal forces of the Real Tarot. Obviously, the results and quality will be vastly different in each case, even though they may be using the same deck and investigating the same question.

This is not a hit or miss proposition. A person who lacks discrimination and falls back on his or her feelings will always tune in to the lowest, crudest level of manifestation. In the case of the

Tarot, this is the fortune telling level. An esoteric student who has learned the basic lesson of discrimination but has yet to learn to focus at archetypal levels will automatically tune in to the intellectual Tarot. Only the person who is accustomed to working with archetypes will discover the Real Tarot—and even then, he or she must be careful not to drop to a lower octave accidentally.

The danger is that anyone who tunes in to the fortune telling Tarot will never suspect that he is dealing only with leftover thought-forms of unintelligent people. The associations he makes, and the insights he gains, will seem to be solid, real, and genuine. Moreover, they will often be confirmed by others—perhaps even discarnates—to be amazingly accurate. Such a person will therefore reject out of hand the notion that he is being heavily swayed by the fortune telling Tarot. And so he will continue to operate as before, blissfully accepting his self-deception as a marvelous intuitive ability.

Even though these insights are accurate, in a strictly literal sense, they are not worth anything. The knowledge that you are going to meet the proverbial "tall, dark handsome man at 3 p.m. next Thursday at the deli next to the corned beef" may be fascinating, but it could also be harmful. This tall, dark handsome man may turn out to be nothing but trouble. The advice satisfies our craving for cheap thrills, but it does nothing to prepare us for mature, responsible living. In fact, it heightens our irresponsibility.

This type of fortune telling is really a form of clairvoyeurism. It does not educate us; it simply appeals to our basest drives and instincts. As such, it can lead to serious imbalances in our perspectives on life and our values, if indulged in excessively. Over a long period of time, a constant emphasis on cheap thrills and tawdry titillation will impoverish our character and warp our priorities. It may even lead to serious problems with sadness, depression, and grief.

The problem is even greater with people who are inexperienced in using the Tarot. These people are totally unaware of how easily psychic distortions can occur. But the lack of knowledge seldom inhibits them. Americans in particular operate on the assumption that ignorance *is* bliss, and will often presume a level of competence where absolutely none exists. This type of person will pick up the Tarot, practice with it a few times, and then consider themselves an expert. They must be a "natural," they assume, because the interpretations flow into their mind so easily. But the insights they are getting are probably just the residue of the fortune telling Tarot.

In most cases, of course, the antidote for ignorance is knowledge. Unfortunately, this is not true in the case of the Tarot, because much of the written knowledge available on the subject is also polluted by the fortune telling influence. As a result, anyone who uses one of the instruction booklets that accompanies most Tarot decks, or even one of the standard books on the Tarot, is almost certainly sealing his or her fate. These instructional booklets put the reader instantly in touch with the fortune telling Tarot. If you build your base of associations for interpreting the Tarot on this foundation, you may never be able to escape the abyss of the fortune telling Tarot.

The fortune telling Tarot assumes that the questioner is seeking a superficial answer to one of life's problems. Instead of wanting to know how to become a more kind and loving person, the questioner will want to know if and when romance will enter his or her life. Instead of wanting to know how to make a better contribution at work, he or she will want to know if a promotion is forthcoming. And so the patterns of the fortune telling Tarot are designed to cater to this level of trivial pursuit and vanity. There is no depth to it; it may accurately foretell the death of a loved one or associate, but it gives no clue as to how to deal with this event or what its meaning is. It thrives on superstition and cheap thrills and reinforces them at every turn.

The danger of tuning in to this level of the Tarot in interpreting it is a simple one: as we have seen, you actually build a system of symbolism and thought in your own character as you work with the Tarot. If you are plugged into the fortune telling Tarot, the system you build will be superficial and fatalistic. It will make you vulnerable to superstitions, fears, and threats. It will sentimentalize your emotions and blur the lucidity of your thinking. You will be polluting your awareness and not even know that you are doing it.

In addition to the instruction booklets that come packed in the decks of cards, most of the commentaries on the Tarot in book form are also marred by heavy fortune telling influences. The simple tradition of ascribing a positive meaning to an upright card and a negative meaning to a reversed card is an example of this fortune telling tradition at work, and how insidiously it creeps into even the best commentaries. Even worse is the tendency of many commentators to construe some cards as favorable, other cards as unfavorable. One book, for instance, boldly states: "The 9 of Cups is by far the most favorable card in the minor arcana. It denotes perfect harmony in love and friendship." But the same text encourages us to rue the appearance of the 9 of Swords: "The 9 of Swords is a card of suffering, grief, and passivity in the face of adversity. It is ruled by Mars, planet of war. Here we penetrate the world of unconscious conflicts, deep-seated neuroses, and madness. Blood and poison are associated with this card." The commentary on this card concludes: "This card is the most ill omened in the minor arcana."

It is exactly this kind of nonsense that gives the Tarot a bad name—and illustrates the immense danger of tuning in to the fortune telling Tarot. The author quoted above would undoubtedly reject the notion that she was influenced by the fortune telling Tarot; she would refer to volume after volume of research that she did, and to her own intuitive experience. She would probably add

that her book is far more complete in its approach to the Tarot than mine. But in using the Tarot, completeness is not necessarily a virtue, since the bulk of everything written on the Tarot succumbs to its fortune telling influence. Discrimination is a far greater virtue.

The relevant point is that no card in the Tarot is inherently favorable or unfavorable; it depends upon the question, the card, and its position in the spread. Each card represents an archetypal force. In the abstract, the 9 of Cups represents the emotional satisfaction and fulfillment that comes from a job well done. But these cards never appear in the abstract; they always appear in response to a question. If the questioner wants to know why he is not getting a promotion, and this card appears, it may imply that he is too proud and vain to see his weaknesses on the job. Until he replaces this vanity with a genuine sense of making a valuable contribution to his work, he will continue to stagnate. On the other hand, if the questioner wants to know why he is being asked to take on new responsibilities, the card probably is suggesting that his past performance has earned him the right to new and expanded duties. In either case, the archetypal force represented by the card is the same. Whether the card appears to be favorable or unfavorable depends entirely on whether the questioner is cooperating with the energy—or resisting it.

The same can be stated for the 9 of Swords. At first glance, this card does appear to be a frightening omen. But as you begin to explore the dynamics of this card, you begin to see it in an entirely different light. There is a woman who is covering her eyes with her hands. She has encountered a closed casket and set down the jug she was carrying. Massive mountains of grief or depression loom behind her. In the sky, nine swords cross the picture from left to right, in parallel. Superficially, this card is suggestive of death, mourning, and grief. But at deeper levels, it bespeaks of the inner courage to face the difficult challenges of life without neglecting our duties. The 9 of Swords represents a tremendous level of support from the spiritual dimensions of our being. In its fullest esoteric sense, this card is a summons to the spiritual aspirant to leave behind the things of the earth and enter into a full communion with the spiritual elements of life. In many ways, it is reminiscent of the Christ's statements in Luke 9:

> Another to whom He said, "Follow me," replied, "Let me go and bury my father first." But He answered, "Leave the dead to bury their dead; your duty is to go and spread the news of the kingdom of God."
> Another said, "I will follow you, sir, but first let me go and say good-by to my people at home." Jesus said to him, "Once the hand is laid on the plow, no one who looks back is fit for the kingdom of God."

In this sense, the 9 of Swords can represent the need to establish correct spiritual priorities, giving service to God a higher priority than the duties of physical life. It should be easy to see, therefore, that the 9 of Swords is not by any stretch of the imagination "the most ill omened card in the minor arcana." Its significance depends entirely on the question and position of the card in the spread.

It may seem harmless to utilize a reference book or other text in developing your ability to interpret the Tarot—but it is a risk fraught with great danger. The influences of the fortune telling Tarot are just too strong. They seep into virtually everything written on the subject. It is therefore wisest and most sensible to shun the written texts and develop your own foundation of associations and interpretations. This is the approach I have encouraged in this book.

Just ignoring most of the written interpretations of the Tarot is not enough, however, since fortune telling interpretations are easily tapped into psychically. The way to steer clear of these cheapening influences is much the same psychically as it is physically. If it is our intent to contact the archetypal forces behind the images and to seek in-depth answers to meaningful questions, we will automatically tend to rise above the fortune telling Tarot and work at more substantial levels. We exclude the lower-level interpretations by our "altitude" of mind.

In addition, we should systematically exclude from our motives and intent any hint of gossip, clairvoyeurism, snoopiness, escapism, or fantasy. Each of these represents an open door to the fortune telling level. In fact, it is a good idea to purge any tendency toward pettiness, childishness, fatalism, or a strong wish life as well. Each of these will tend to cheapen our use of the Tarot and keep us from using this wonderful tool to its capacity. There are different reasons why for each of these problems:

Pettiness is a problem because it traps us in the sphere of our personality and makes it difficult to sense the larger picture of how the archetypal forces are affecting us. The petty person will tend to use the Tarot as a substitute for his own thinking, not as a stimulator of it. Every time he hiccups, he will ask the Tarot why. Such pettiness is an abuse of a tool like the Tarot, which is meant to open up profound understanding of the important issues of life. The more petty we are, the less likely it is that we are dealing with archetypal forces.

Childishness is a problem of our modern culture. It has become so popular to celebrate the "child within" that we sometimes forget that the purpose of childhood is to produce mature adults. As a result, many people have presumed a kind of license to be immature. This type of attitude can be disastrous in dealing with tools of divination, especially the Tarot. Since the Tarot is presented in the form of a deck of cards, it is difficult for some people to view it as anything other than a game. But it is not a game and should never be treated as one. It is a tool to be used in exploring the inner dimensions of our psychology, in understanding the meaning of our experiences, and in discovering the influences of divine archetypes in our life.

The childishness of our modern age has led to all kinds of new imitations or spinoffs of the Tarot, all presented as games. One attempts to blend the patterns of karma and astrological influences with the Tarot; another transforms the Tarot into a board game. These games are produced with enough glitz and glamour to make Milton Bradley envious, but they are, in the final analysis, just games. They can connect the user to fortune telling patterns of the astral plane, but they fall far short of connecting with archetypal forces. They serve no function in either personal or spiritual growth.

One of the key steps in developing a sense of mental discrimination is the ability to discern between an idea of substance and one of superficiality. It does not matter how much you believe in a system or trust in it; if it is not designed to link you with the mind of God, it will not. It is therefore of great importance to assess the basic design of each of these systems before using them. It is just as prudent to weigh the level of inspiration of a Tarot deck, as described in Chapter One, before using it, and to evaluate the validity of any book on the subject before relying on it. This is what it means to be an adult.

Fatalism is a problem that can creep into the use of any tool of divination. It produces a paralysis of individuality that thwarts growth and wisdom. This problem is often seen in the use of astrology, where practitioners sometimes become so fatalistic that they will not take any action without consulting their horoscope, and will refuse to act if the signs are "unfavorable." Of course, no signs are unfavorable—they simply point to a set of circumstances we tend to fear. Just so, we must never let our use of the Tarot stifle our individuality or stunt our initiative. If the Tarot indicates that a certain proposal may be fraught with difficulty, it is silly to conclude that we should abandon our idea. If the idea is a sensible one, we should use the Tarot to discover how we can meet the problems and difficulties intelligently, putting them to work for us.

Each of us does have a destiny, at least in the sense that our own higher self has created a plan for our life and directs us accordingly. What we do with this plan is largely up to us, however; the plan may be predetermined but our response to it and implementation of it is not. We should never allow ourself to feel cramped or restricted by this plan; it is designed to help us grow and expand. Fatalism twists our perceptions of life and robs us of much of our character.

A strong wish life is a danger in using the Tarot because it can so easily distort our interpretation of the cards. If you are inquiring what the outcome of a project will be, and you have a strong desire that it be favorable, there is not much the Tarot can do to withstand the ferocious bias with which you will interpret whatever cards arise. This distortion can occur even when you are not consciously aware it is happening—indeed, it is much more likely to happen under such conditions.

The only antidote to a strong wish life is careful training in objectivity and detachment. We must be alert to the ever-present possibility of self-deception and seek guidance from the Tarot itself, whenever possible. In addition, it is helpful to recognize tendencies to escape reality and to hide behind pretenses in our

214

thinking, if they exist, and work to remove them.

It may seem as though this is a lot to remember. How can we keep in mind all of the problems to avoid, as well as all the meanings of seventy eight cards, while trying to make sense of the question we have asked? The answer is that we are not expected to. The Tarot is not a mental food processor, where we dump the ingredients in one chute and guacamole comes out the other. It is the substance of our values and intent that protects us. If we are trying to use the Tarot as a means of building our mind and refining our intuition, we will fare all right. If we should happen to stray into self-deception, the Tarot will try to warn us. This is part of its basic design: to protect not only its own integrity but also the integrity of anyone who tries to use it with sincerity and humility. But if we are secretly enchanted by the possibility of getting the inside scoop on a friend or associate, our clairvoyeurism will sabotage our efforts and expose us to lower influences.

It should now be clear why a firm understanding of divine archetypes and a dedication to the examined life are so important in learning to use the Tarot. If true insight into life is your motive for using the Tarot, you should have no trouble developing a mature, productive ability to use it. But if you are more interested in cheap thrills, in hanging out a shingle as a psychic or "reader," or in indulging in wish life oneupmanship with your friends, you are a candidate for instant self-deception.

Whatever path you choose, the Tarot will oblige, so choose wisely.

The Next to the Last Word

NINE OF CUPS

"Well!" a voice thundered out from nowhere. "You certainly shot down the fortune telling Tarot!"

I looked around but saw nothing. Then, slowly, a wisp of what looked like white smoke began to take shape in the center of the room. It became more solid and began to take on colors. Nine cups formed near the ceiling, a kind of arch. Underneath them appeared the image of the man from the 9 of Cups, his hands on his hips. It looked as if he owned the world.

"May it rest in peace," I replied.

"Well, some of us characters from the Tarot were fond of the fortune telling Tarot," the 9 continued. "We kind of hate to see it buried so forcefully."

"You're kidding!"

"Yes, actually I am," the 9 admitted. "But in every jest there is a grain of truth. Whenever we felt like slumming for a while, we would slip into the fortune telling versions of ourselves and go have some mischief."

"That sounds cruel," I protested.

"Well, it's not like we ever took advantage of anyone who didn't deserve it," the little fellow said jovially. "We just played a few tricks on people who were hell bent on deceiving themselves anyhow. We simply made the deception a little more effective. Kind of like a cosmic practical joke—a pie in the face. That sort of thing. Nothing to actually harm anyone."

"Oh, go on," I said. "I don't believe you."

"Yeah, I can see," the 9 of Cups protested drily. "Well, don't worry yourself—I was only joking. You know the Tarot wouldn't allow such a thing. It protects the guilty as well as the innocent."

"I thought so."

"We're just trying to have a little fun—pull your leg. Using the Tarot should be fun. Don't let this book get too dreary. Lift people up, don't put them down, I always say."

"What would you suggest?"

"I could give you my impression of the Tarot," the 9 said.

"I'm not sure I want it," I said.

"Just shuffle the deck and pull out a card—any card."

I did as directed. The 6 of Swords popped up.

"The 6 of Swords!" the 9 chortled. "The patron saint of leaking boats, we call him. Next time you need a ferry across the River Styx, be sure to call on him. You'll never make it in that boat, and heaven will have to take you in. Besides which, what is that thing on his hat—a moose? Couldn't he get into the Elks?"

"What is this, anyway," I asked—"The Don Rickles version of the Tarot?"

"More likely the Rodney Dangerfield version," the 9 responded. "Here, fill one of my cups with some beer and pick another card."

I drew the 3 of Pentacles.

"Oh, goody," the 9 chuckled. "You've had some real fine things to say about this lad. Of course, what you've never understood is that he got caught sniffing some crazy glue, and in his haste to hide the evidence, he managed to permanently bond his hands to that pillar. He's stuck like that for eternity."

"I'm not sure these interpretations are a real contribution to the Tarot," I suggested.

"Of course they are," the 9 suggested. "You know as well as I do that the Tarot often gets it messages through by using puns and inside jokes. Draw another one."

"It was the 9 of Pentacles. "Ah-ha—one of my cousins," the 9 of Cups said. "She carries that bird with her everywhere she goes. For a long time I thought she was a ventriloquist."

I chuckled politely.

"You wanna know a secret?" the 9 asked.

"What?"

"She's not the ventriloquist—the bird is!"

"Which still leaves open the question of who is the dummy," I added.

"Say, that's not too bad," said the 9, "You looking for work as a straight man? We could make a good team."

"No thanks," I replied. "I'm a good deal straighter than I ever wanted to be as it is."

The 9 laughed. "I knew you had a chuckle or two in you. Draw another."

It was the 10 of Cups.

"Oh, rapture," the 9 swooned. "I think I am going to overdose on cuteness. How did they let this card into the deck, anyway?"

"There are many proper meanings to this card," I said.

"Yeah, but I'm more interested in the improper ones," the 9 said, winking.

I laughed. "I am beginning to see that. I thought you showed up for a serious purpose, but I was mistaken. You're just a repressed stand-up comedian."

"Not really," the 9 of Cups said, "although I do love my work. I just wanted you—and your readers—to see that you should have no preconceived ideas about the Tarot. To build the kind of associative mechanism you described, you must be open to all possible interpretations, even slightly scandalous ones. You must be willing to joke with the Tarot, as well as listen seriously to it. After all, if you fail to see the twinkle in my eye, what else about me are you missing?"

"A point well taken."

"A good sense of humor helps you look at life from a higher, more detached perspective. It makes you more inclusive. And if you can't laugh at yourself, you are heading straight for a lot of self-deception."

"So, you had a serious purpose after all. Behind all that guff, there is actually some substance."

"Shhh," the 9 scolded me. "Don't let anyone hear you talk like that. I have an image to maintain. It's not much of an image, but at least it's all mine."

"Okay. Are there any other cards in the deck you wish to interpret for us?"

"Oh, what the heck. Pick one more. It will be my swan song."

I picked the 4 of Rods.

The 9 of Cups began humming the theme from *The Twilight Zone.* "The fourth dimension is calling me," he announced. "See those four rods? They look like four sticks stuck in the ground, don't they? Don't kid yourself. This is a doorway into the fourth dimension. Anytime you want to come visit us, just walk through that archway, and we'll be waiting for you. But now I must depart."

He stepped through the portal and disappeared. His nine cups went with him, one of them still half filled with beer. I was left with only a memory—and a secret doorway to the inner side of life.

CHAPTER THIRTEEN

The Real Tarot

The Tarot is much more than a deck of seventy-eight cards. It is a proven system for interacting with the archetypal forces of the mind of God. It is a tool that permits us to explore the inner dimensions of life, once we have mastered it. It is a method for training the mind to think more powerfully.

Over the years, trivial uses of the Tarot have tarnished its image. As a result, many people carry with them silly impressions of the Tarot. Some condemn it as the work of the devil; others decry it as a plaything of superstition. Both of these conclusions are based on prejudice and misinformation, but they will not change until the people who use the Tarot stop using it in trivial ways and start using it in important, spiritual ways. We each have a responsibility to use the Tarot in the noblest, most inspired way.

The most common question asked by people who know nothing about the Tarot is, of course, how does it work? These are the same people who will ask, "How can you be sure that God is real?" Whenever I am asked this question, I am tempted to answer, "How can God be sure that you are for real?" But I am a polite and courteous person, so I ask the question only in my imagination. Nevertheless, I am left wondering, "Has this person ever spent five minutes walking through the woods? How can any reasonably intelligent person spend more than five minutes in the beauty, harmony, and grandeur of nature and question the existence of divine benevolence and intelligence?" It might be possible to lose track of God in the middle of a city, but in the heart of nature, every bird and leaf and stone is an advertisement for the presence of God. It can only be that these people have never been taught how to use their eyes and ears. Perhaps their eyes and ears are, after all, just sense organs, which have never been connected to their minds and hearts and innermost spirit.

I draw the same conclusions when people ask, "How is it possible that the Tarot can actually answer my questions?" The question continually flabbergasts me, because the answer is so obvious. I am tempted to respond, "How could it possibly fail to answer your question?" But I know that would sound arrogant, and I really do not need one more black eye. So I patiently explain that all of life is filled with divine intelligence. How does a salmon know to swim upstream and return to his place of birth to spawn? Divine intelligence. The salmon does not even need a Tarot reading to guide him. How do the seeds of flowers know to germinate in the spring? Divine intelligence. And they do not need to hear the word from their local horticulturist to do it, either. How do we happen to fall in love and marry the one person on earth who can teach us the lessons in living we most desperately need—even though we may resent it? Divine intelligence. It is only too bad that most marriage counselors do not possess the same measure of divine intelligence. Everywhere you care to look, life is permeated with divine intelligence. This is what it means to say that God is omniscient. Life is designed to give us the answers we need to make our way in life. Not just us humans, but all life forms. How does a cat know to find shelter before a tornado or hurricane comes sweeping through? Nature tells him. How can we find out what we should be learning in the lessons of our life? Nature will try to tell us, but we often refuse to listen. We are not as sensible as dogs and cats. We need an extra tool, like the Tarot, to help us.

Human life is not the mystery or enigma that most people

assume it is. The answers to all of our questions are always close at hand. We merely need to develop the eyes to see and the ears to hear what is perfectly obvious. We need to realize what a marvelous tool the human mind can be, if we train and nourish it properly. We have come to recognize the importance of training the mind to think intellectually. As of yet, however, we have not grasped the importance of training the mind to work intuitively. As a result, the concept of plugging into divine intelligence is a strange and foreign one to many people. It even threatens some. But we must remember not to mistake ignorance for wisdom. If we are un-informed about some subject, our judgments on it cannot possibly be wise.

Divine intelligence has an answer to every question you can pos-sibly formulate. We have been designed to formulate these questions and ask them. Inquisitiveness is a hallmark of the mentally alert person. There is no reason to settle for ignorance or uncertainty. As the Christ admonished us, "Ask, and you shall receive!"

So get in the habit of asking. The Tarot is not the only tool that can provide the answers, of course. The I Ching, the Runes, and astrology are also excellent sources of guidance. Even nature itself is constantly giving us omens that can guide and direct us, if only we would pay attention to them and interpret them wisely. It is relatively difficult to learn to interpret the many omens of nature, however. This is why initiates have developed systems such as the Tarot. Their virtue is their finiteness—we only have to deal with seventy-eight cards. But if we remember that these cards are just the outer symbols of inner realities—the Real Tarot—then the finite-ness of the Tarot is not a limitation. Through the use of the finite system of the Tarot, we can discover and open the door which leads to the infinite nature of wisdom and love.

As you work with the Tarot, therefore, always keep in mind the purpose behind the asking of questions. The true objective of using the Tarot, or any other system of divination, is to train the mind to work with the archetypal forces which are the Real Tarot. The cards are the door, but each of us must learn to walk through the door and discover the reality within.

The Real Tarot of the minor arcana consists of the ten spiritual lessons we must master in harnessing the energies of each suit. The Real Tarot of the face cards is the measure of skill we ought to have in working with these forces. The Real Tarot of the major arcana is actually the various spiritual forces the Divine Personas embody, the spiritual principles the Divine Attributes represent, and the spiritual realms the Divine Spheres embrace. The master of ceremonies for the whole show is The Fool.

At first, these descriptions may seem almost too pat, too cute. But as you explore the inner dimensions of the Tarot, the scenery and customs will become more and more familiar to you. You will discover that there is real power associated with the essence of each of these forces; as you identify with a card such as the 9 of Cups, this power rubs off on you. You begin to experience the power of joy behind the irrepressible joviality, and you begin to understand that there was a spiritual purpose behind the seemingly flippant remarks made in the last interlude. There is also a definite power that led you to a deeper understanding.

As you gain confidence in working with the Tarot, it makes sense to create a purposeful program for using it. My recommendation is to devise a program for self-examination, as suggested in Chapter Three. Take an area of your life that needs transformation and refinement. If you are not sure where to begin, ask the Tarot for guidance. Formulate a question such as: "What is the best place to begin the work of transforming my character into something better able to embody the love and wisdom of the higher self?" See what the Tarot says. Then adopt its recommendations for your work of self-examination.

Work on this one project as your major use of the Tarot for several months, or longer. As other questions arise, especially questions involving practical issues of daily life, feel free to direct them at the Tarot. But always keep coming back to your major work, your major theme. Eventually, you will begin to notice signs of integration occurring. Even the practical issues which at first seemed to intrude on this project now seem somehow to be incorporated into it. The tapestry you are trying to weave in each consultation of the Tarot is beginning to be woven within your own life experience and character.

The benefits of this kind of approach are many. First, it will relate your personal life to the Real Tarot. Second, it will show you the underlying patterns of intelligence that have always guided your life, even though you have failed to see them. Third, it will open you up to a direct awareness and ability to experience the archetypal forces and spiritual qualities of life.

Through the Tarot, justice no longer needs to be just an abstract principle. We can come to experience it as a living, moving force—something we can invoke when conditions are out of balance in our life or when someone threatens us unjustly. We can learn to infuse the quality of justice into our own thinking and actions, so that we become an agent of justice on earth.

Through the Tarot, joy no longer needs to be a philosophical nicety. We can come to taste joy directly as one of the qualities of life, as represented by the 9 of Cups in the minor arcana and The Star in the major arcana. We can come to understand the distinction between happiness, which is transitory, and joy, which is a permanent attribute of divine life. Happiness is drawn from our interpretation of the events of life. Joy flows into our life from our awareness of the plan of God and its archetypal expression.

Through the Tarot, we can understand what it means to build conditions of peace. In card after card, we confront the seeds of

227

conflict and are shown how to manage them. As we learn to over-come these patterns of conflict, we begin to sow the seeds of peace. Simultaneously, we comprehend that there is an inner force of peace which can nourish these seeds in the outer life and cause them to grow, just as The Emperor nourishes his flowers and draws forth their beauty.

Through the Tarot, we can come to terms with an abstract force as complex and powerful as death. We will be able to see this force in its rightful position, as a force we are meant to master and use every day, to help us leave behind the baggage of our past and move forward to seize the opportunities of the present and the future.

Through the Tarot, we are able to interact directly with the duality of life, not in a theoretical way, but in the context of our own problems and challenges. We are able to put ourself in the position of the Page of Rods and understand what it means to tread the razor-sharp edge of the Noble Middle Way. We can train the mind to work with greater discrimination and the emotions not to react to the ebb and flow of duality, but to respond instead to the greater creative purpose behind it.

As we work in this way with the Real Tarot, we gradually refine the process of thinking. In a real sense, we develop a new level of thinking. Instead of thinking in terms of static ideas, words, and concepts, we begin thinking in terms of patterns. We grasp whole patterns in a single perception. This skill emerges gradually over a long period of time, but it is one of the results of the proper use of the Tarot. It is the ability, in essence, to look at a Tarot map and comprehend the relationship of all ten cards at once, in a single glance. It also involves the capacity to look at the ten cards before you and be simultaneously aware of the relationship of each card to all the rest of the cards in the deck.

Nor is this particular skill of thinking of use only in exploring the

Tarot. It is one of the primary higher mental skills. It lets you, for example, take a new bit of information and instantly update all of your previous associations, assumptions, values, and principles in the light of this new input. It also lets you take a fragment of creative inspiration and write a whole novel from it, or develop a new course of instruction, or produce a whole series of new inventions.

We also begin thinking in terms of forces. We come to realize that ideas and patterns are filled with living, dynamic power. These forces have an identity and purpose of their own. So it is not just a question of what we want to do with Strength—it is also a question of what Strength wants to do with us. Working with the Tarot leads us to reshape our thinking so that we are able to harness the true essence of these ideas. It teaches us the lesson of The Hanged Man—the need to reverse our perceptions of life. The inner dimensions of life are not just interesting realms to explore and hunt for hidden treasure. They are our home. They are the source of our inspiration, direction, and purpose. They are the heart of our being.

In the final analysis, we are not just exploring the Tarot. Our real work is to explore these inner dimensions of creativity, spirit, beauty, joy, and wisdom and make ourselves truly at home with them. The Tarot is an excellent tool to select for this adventure, but we should not think just in the narrow terms of the Tarot. Our goal is to discover the richness of divine life, the treasures of heaven. The Tarot is a system that will lead us there and let us explore these vast regions reliably, safely, and helpfully.

Welcome to the Real Tarot. The door is open. It is now up to you to explore the vast realms beyond the open door and learn from the experience.

Sample Readings

One of the best ways to learn to use the ideas presented in this book is to sit in on an actual demonstration of answering a question. While it is not practical for you to attend a reading in person, it is possible to arrange for the next best thing. What follows in Part Two are the transcripts of five actual Tarot readings, performed live and recorded on tape. These transcripts will give you the flavor and feel for how to proceed in weaving the tapestry on your own.

A number of people participated in these sessions, and some of their questions and remarks appear in the transcriptions. I refer to them by their first names. Their true identities are: my wife Rose, Leslie Swanson, Jim and Nancy Grote, and Betsy Salt.

These transcripts have been edited for the book. The complete readings on these questions, as well as many others, are available on cassette tape from Light.

The five questions asked in these sample readings are:

What is the impact of anger on consciousness?

What are the primary responsibilities of raising children?

What can be done to reduce pessimism in world thought?

What is the esoteric purpose of having pets?

What should be the goals of the New Age?

TEN of PENTACLES

IX

I

ACE of SWORDS

EIGHT of SWORDS

SIX of SWORDS

TEN of SWORDS

MAX

VIII

STRENGTH

KNIGHT of SWORDS

CHAPTER FOURTEEN

The Impact of Anger

Carl: The question is: What is the impact of anger on con-
sciousness? The following cards have come up in response to this
question:
The starting point—The Ace of Swords, upright.
The counterpoint—The 10 of Swords, reversed.
The creative challenge—The 10 of Pentacles, upright.
The purpose—Strength, upright.
The endowment—The Magician, upright.
The destiny—The 8 of Swords, reversed.
The real question—The Knight of Swords, upright.
The unseen forces—The Moon, reversed.
The spiritual ideal—the 6 of Swords, upright.
The fulfillment—Justice, reversed.
There are four cards from the major arcana, five swords, and
one pentacle. We are clearly dealing with a subject with deep spirit-
ual implications, since nine of the ten cards are either swords or
from the major arcana. And since the sole pentacle is the 10, which
deals with the lesson of service, its connotation is spiritual as well.
Right up front, the Tarot is telling us that anger is a very serious
issue—not one to dismiss lightly.
Let's also look for points of tension. The 8 of Swords has a
definite relationship with Strength, which is the eighth card in the
major arcana. The major grouping, however, is that of the Ace of
Swords, the 10 of Swords, the 10 of Pentacles, and the Magician.

In numerology, the two digits of 10 are added together to produce the number 1. So all four of these cards are 1's.

We can start at the starting point, with the Ace of Swords. This is an image of a sword stuck in the ground between two flowers. It reminds me immediately of the scene in *Excalibur* where Arthur plants his sword between the sleeping Lancelot and Guinevere, thereby splitting the union of the land, imprisoning Merlin, and causing evil to spread over the face of the nation. The sword represents Arthur's authority, because he had extracted it from the stone. By planting it between Lancelot and Guinevere in an act of anger, he betrayed his duty as king and the authority of Excalibur. This card is telling us that whenever we plant the sword of anger between us and anyone else, we are inducing a tremendous impoverishment of our character. We may feel righteous, we may feel that we have absolutely no choice. But by expressing anger, we are betraying the inherent strength of our righteousness. We can look at the card of Strength in the position of purpose; this strength is meant to be used to guard against intimidation and temptation. But anger is an abuse of this strength—a cheap way out, as it were.

Many people, of course, feel that anger is an expression of strength. They see something imperfect and get angry at the imperfection. But this is a false expression of strength. We must learn to deal with imperfection without getting angry. You may be right, but when you let anger overtake you, you become dead right. Anger poisons us. If we indulge in it often enough, it can literally kill us. In *Excalibur*, Arthur's anger destroys everything he had worked to achieve. He spends 10 years in a daze, a coma.

Notice also how there are strings attached to the sword. Whenever you wield the sword of anger, you establish relationships you are going to regret, because all of these strands are going to have to be untied and reclaimed. So anger complicates life tremendously. This is not to say that we should become a Pollyanna, and believe

236

that everything is wonderful in this most wonderful of all worlds. It simply suggests that we need more constructive approaches to imperfection than anger.

There is another dimension to this card, too. This card reminds us that many people do not share this perspective on anger. Many people view anger as an important weapon in their arsenal of skills. To them, anger is a way of getting what you want. But if you happen to be one of these people, take a quick peek at the 10 of Swords and the 8 of Swords These are fairly accurate portrayals of what anger does to you. It blinds you, it gags you, it pins you down to the problems and people that make you so angry. You are stabbing yourself in the back—or inviting others to do it for you.

Rose: Are you also doing that to the person you are angry at?

Carl: To a degree, yes, but remember that the flow of water is always strongest at the source. So the damage anger does to your own consciousness is far greater than that done to the other person.

There is a secondary meaning to consider here, especially in light of the card of the spiritual ideal, the 6 of Swords. Human consciousness is designed to express great force. This also gives us a great responsibility not to abuse this expression of power or strength. When you talk about strength of character, many people instantly think in terms of being the meanest S.O.B. in the valley. But this is not the true meaning of human strength. The true expressions of strength by a human being are patience, courage, and integrity. It is the strength to live by your values and not change them willy-nilly to suit your convenience—or the demands of others. This is true strength. It has nothing to do with aggressiveness or anger. The 6 of Swords represents the capacity to generate a great deal of energy for our self-expression—enough to impel our ship across the waters. When we succumb to anger, however, this short-circuits the proper flow of our energy. All we can generate, as a result, is negativity. Over a period of time, the negativity of this anger will poison our system and weaken our true strength. We become unable to express the strength of our spiritual self—just the reactiveness of our negative feelings.

Moving on to the 10 of Swords, in the counterpoint position, we have to determine just what the quality of energy is that is flowing through those swords stuck in the individual's back. Are they swords that motivate us and fill us with divine love, goodwill, and joy—or are they the swords of our anger that we are sticking into ourself as though we were a pincushion? Both types of energy flow through the same system of energy distribution, but their impacts are very much different. The divine energies of love and joy enrich our self-expression. Anger attacks our system, impoverishing our consciousness and killing our body.

The next card is the 10 of Pentacles, the creative challenge. This card highlights the theme we have already mentioned of learning to deal with imperfection. It is the image of a man and a woman behold-ing the ideal—Camelot, the Garden of Eden, whatever. They have a glimpse of the inner reality of spiritual perfection. It's glorious, wonderful, and inspiring. But then there is their little kid. He's looking back at the physical plane and saying, "Yes, but look at all the imper-fection in creation." The adults represent the maturity within us that responds to the ideal; the kid represents the immaturity within us that responds to the seeming imperfection of actual conditions on earth. And it is easy to list all of the problems of humanity—war in the Middle East, rebellion in China, drugs on the street, and so on—and very soon you can get all worked up and angry. But that is the immature way to approach imperfection. You lose your sense of balance. It's like going into a restaurant and being served a marvelous meal and complaining about the creases in the tablecloth! We do this all too often in our lives. We are surrounded by beauty and inspiration and benevolence, and yet we allow our imaginations to dwell on what is wrong with life, not what is right.

These are the roots of anger—it's a cheap, emotional way to express our disapproval of imperfection, rather than taking the much more demanding step of working to correct it. Whenever we are angry, we are in essence betraying our perception of the ideal, because we are giving more credence and importance to the distortion of the ideal than to its dynamic spiritual presence. We try to shout down imperfection, rather than lovingly and patiently working to change it.

There are people who will sabotage your efforts, will fight against you, and will even try to humiliate you. There are all kinds of unpleasant conditions in life. It's very tempting to respond to them with anger. But it is a mistake, because anger unleashes our immaturity. It is a sign that we have never outgrown the brat we were when we were a kid.

We have already taken a peek at Strength. This is in the position of purpose. Just as nuclear energy can be used to destroy cities or to supply them with electricity, there are likewise constructive and destructive uses of our personal energies. We are meant to channel our strength into productive, constructive activities. Anger interferes with that.

This is not to say that we should repress anger. If you bottle up anger, you may not be expressing it, but you are still angry. So the answer is neither expressing your anger nor repressing it, but learning to transform it. We need to learn to transform anger into the strength to forgive, the strength of compassion, and the strength to build toward the ideal. In this way, we transform the negativity of anger and make it productive, constructive.

Going on to the position of the endowment, we encounter The Magician. And if you also look at the position of the destiny, where we have the 8 of Swords, you can learn something fascinating about the interplay of the Tarot. The cards of the endowment and the destiny are almost always paired. This is a marvelous example, because on the one hand we have The Magician, with all of his skills and creative understanding, ready to act in life with wisdom, and on the other hand, we have a striking image of what happens to The Magician if he succumbs to the temptation of anger. He becomes trapped in the power of the energies he has invoked for creative use. He is blinded by his anger and bound by his own righteousness. The eight swords normally stand for great spiritual force to be used creatively, but here they just form a prison. And that's not all—he is surrounded by clouds of fear and confusion. This is the impact of anger on consciousness. It creates a trap within our own subconscious—and we are the prey. The contrast between The Magician, representing our potential, and the 8 of Swords, indicating what anger does to our potential, is phenomenal.

This takes us to the foot of the pillar of revelation, where we have the Knight of Swords. This represents the real question. The Knight of Swords suggests that we have a duty and obligation to serve the ideal. Anger is a highly subjective, selfish expression. It is dependent entirely upon our subjective interpretation of events. The Knight is able to look at the events of life from a high enough perspective that he is able to be compassionate, not angry. He is able to say, "Well, this person is only misbehaving because he does not understand the ideal. If he knew better, he would never have done such a stupid thing." What such a person needs is compassion and pity, not anger. Anger won't help him learn; only our compassion will. The angry person is presuming the right of judgment. "I know more than you do, so you had better listen to me." That's the angry person's perspective. It's very presumptuous and immature.

Of course, the standard question thrown at me when I say this about anger is: "Wasn't Jesus angry when he upset the tables of the moneychangers in the temple? Can't anger be used constructively?" And the answer is that the Bible does not state or even hint that Jesus was angry. It merely says He drove them out of the temple. It

240

was a forceful act, but all of His acts were forceful. There is no indication that He was angry, mad, or enraged. In fact, in the very next
sentence it says He healed the lame and the blind It would be impossible, even for the Christ, to express anger one moment and
healing love the next. The energies are incompatible. So we must
assume, if we are going to assume anything, that He tossed them
out as an act of compassion—the same compassion He then used
to heal the lame and blind. It was an exercise of His spiritual
authority, yes—but without anger or bitterness.

We need to cultivate this same kind of firm but compassionate
response to imperfection. This is the message of the Knight of
Swords. The further we tread the spiritual path, the more we will
encounter imperfection. The Knight of Swords is constantly encountering imperfection. But the moment he becomes angry, no matter
how right he may be, he drops the sword of service. He forfeits his
spiritual authority and renders himself useless. It becomes a personal vendetta; selfishness creeps in and service ends. The purpose
of spiritual service is to bring new measures of divine love and
wisdom into the earth. You can't do that if you are getting angry all
the time.

The eighth position, the unseen forces, is occupied by The
Moon. This is a card of mass consciousness and ancient patterns of
cultural or racial anger. These are the unseen forces. When we get
angry, we can lose control very fast, because there are all kinds of
free floating patterns of anger around that will rush right in and feed
our rage. Becoming angry is like opening a Pandora's box we cannot control. In fact, if our anger is strident enough, or repeated
often enough, it can weaken our individuality to the point where a
certain kind of possession can occur. Unpleasant beings that thrive
on anger will come in and attach themselves to you. That may
sound fantastic, but it is true. I have seen it happen.

The other facet of this phenomenon is that anger is a negative, destructive energy. As you entertain it, it will not be content with a mild outburst. A weakness toward anger will therefore expose you also to fear, depression, grief, jealousy, and resentment. This can quickly become a downward spiral.

There are no spiritual expressions of anger. That is the point I want to make very clear.

The card in the position of the spiritual ideal is the 6 of Swords. This card tells us something quite profound. A very powerful individual is using spiritual force to impel his boat across the waters. The waters, of course, stand for the emotions, but far from being roiled with anger, they are as calm as glass. He is steering his boat toward its destination, the mountains in the distance. So the spiritual ideal is to have complete and full control over the emotions, so there is absolutely no chance of succumbing to anger. Anger would sink the boat. At the very least, it would stir up the waters. But this very wise person is sailing smoothly along, because he is in full and perfect control. He has not repressed anything; he is simply at the helm and able to direct all energies properly.

This brings us to the fulfillment and the card of Justice. This is basically a statement that every outburst of anger has to be corrected. The laws of life cannot be mocked. The lack of emotional maturity brings its own consequences. This is especially relevant for people on the spiritual path. If you are going to be an agent of justice, you cannot indulge in anger. If you are going to act with authority, you cannot afford fits of anger. Anger locks you into the problem and separates you from the solution. It estranges you from the vision and sense of purpose toward which you should be leading your followers.

I am open to questions and comments about this layout.

Betsy: Is criticism a form of anger?

Carl: The word *criticism*, of course, has two distinct meanings. It is important to have a critical mind that is capable of discriminating between the real and the unreal aspects of life. We must also be able to critique our own efforts and sometimes those of others—in order to help them. But when criticism becomes destructive and immature, then it tears apart and destroys. It is no longer helpful. And yes, this type of criticism can be linked with anger, although it is not actually one and the same thing. Anger is primarily an emotional reaction to imperfection, whereas harsh criticism is a mental reaction. They are often found together, but not always. The impact on consciousness is very destructive in both cases, however.

Rose: Is vengeance an aspect of anger?

Carl: Sure. It's a specialized form of anger.

Rose: I'm thinking of vengeance in the sense that you get angry and then cannot forget the offense. You have to see it avenged.

Carl: The individual feels there is no possible way the situation can be corrected unless he personally exacts the pound of flesh. Vengeance is even more immature than ordinary anger. It suggests that you need the actual taste of blood in your mouth before you will be satisfied. It's a total perversion of the concept of justice, and a complete nose-dive into selfishness. Justice is a universal force. We have our parts to play from time to time as agents of justice, but this does not include personalizing justice and making ourself policeman, judge, and executioner.

Rose: How does the angry person come to the conclusion that anger and vengeance are self-destructive?

Carl: It can take several lifetimes of pursuing pointless cases of vengeance before they realize they are trapped in their own anger— trapped in the 8 of Swords.

Betsy: Is anger just an individual phenomenon or can you see it at a group level?

Carl: Sure—the Moon card indicates that. Anger is highly contagious and can sweep through racial and national groups extremely fast. It does not take much to inflame a mob to anger.

In certain world hot spots, such as Ireland, the Middle East, and Iran and Iraq, we are dealing with thousands of years of accumulated anger. And yet we are trying to solve it as though we were a bunch of schoolgirls playing jacks. First of all, it is stupid to make a world issue out of a neighborhood brawl, which is what these problems are. Second, we have to understand that these people must get tired of being angry before any real peace can be established. As long as their anger exists, so will the fighting. It's time we grew up and understood the dynamics of world peace. It's not nuclear bombs that threaten peace. It's anger.

CHAPTER FIFTEEN

Raising Children

Carl: The question is: What are the primary responsibilities of raising children? These are the cards that will provide the answer:

The starting point—The 7 of Rods, reversed.

The counterpoint—The 7 of Cups, upright.

The creative challenge—The 3 of Swords, reversed.

The purpose—The 9 of Rods, upright.

The endowment—The 6 of Pentacles, upright.

The destiny—The 10 of Swords, reversed.

The real question—The Chariot, reversed.

The unseen forces—The 4 of Rods, reversed.

The spiritual ideal—The Hanged Man, reversed.

The fulfillment—The Moon, reversed.

There are three cards from the major arcana, all in the pillar of revelation. To me, this indicates that the esoteric responsibilities of raising children are far more significant than what is realized by society. There are two swords, three rods, one cup, and one pentacle. Three cards are numbered 7—the 7 of Rods, the 7 of Cups, and The Chariot. This emphasizes the spiritual lesson of achievement and forms a triangle of relevance between these three cards. The 3 of Swords is linked in the same way to The Hanged Man, since the two digits in 12 add up to 3. And we have the same kind of parallel between the 9 of Rods and The Moon.

I want to make a few general observations first. The 7 of Rods is an ideal card for the starting point, because it is a card of respon-

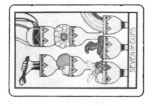

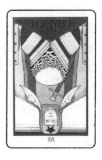

246

sibility. It is basically echoing the question and confirming that there are, indeed, great responsibilities in raising children. It is also by implication making a distinction between having children and raising children. This card is stating that while it is possible to have children irresponsibly, it is not possible to raise them except within the scope of responsibility. If you are not a responsible parent, then you are not raising your children. They may end up raising themselves, but you shouldn't be given any credit for it.

Probably the most significant card in the map is The Hanged Man in the position of the spiritual ideal. This is a card that encourages a reversal of attitudes and priorities from a primarily physical perspective to a primarily esoteric one. This card—plus the three 7's—implies that one of the most basic responsibilities of raising children is to produce mature adults. Now, no one would overtly disagree with that, but if you evaluate how they actually interact with their children, you would find that this concept is very much different than what most people would believe. Most parents want children because children are cute, and in many, many cases, they raise them to stay children. They aren't raising them to be adults. They are raising them to stay children. That's why so many parents have so much trouble adjusting to their children as adults once they are over 21.

The only way to assess the success of raising children is to evaluate how well prepared they are for adulthood when they turn 21. Are they able to be self-sufficient? Are they mature emotionally? Do they have a strong capacity to think? Can they act on their own—do they have a mature sense of individuality? Are they aware of their higher self and able to contact it for guidance?

So much for the overview. Let's go back to the 7 of Rods. The man is a farmer, what the English might call a husbandman. He is holding the one rod horizontally, above the other rods; it is almost as though he is magically drawing the other rods upward, evoking their growth. And look at the nature of his cloak—it is almost as if it were made of wood. This symbolizes a close identification with what is being grown—and almost a communion with the inner spirit. To me, this implies that the first responsibility of the parent is to the inner self of the child—to help the child grow in the direction the soul indicates. Our motive should not be to teach our children to be just like us—or even to try to give them all the advantages we never had. It should be to give them the opportunities their own higher self wants for them. That's our starting point.

The 7 of Rods also suggests that it is the duty of parents to provide a strong structure of values, ethics, principles, and goals for their children. They need to provide a framework in which the child can grow—a framework of guidance, love, and self-discipline. This card is warning us not to be permissive—children need a healthy set of parameters to guide their growth.

The counterpoint is the 7 of Cups, upright. In this particular reading, the reversed cards describe the responsibilities of parenting; they are reversed to remind us of the basic theme of The Hanged Man. The upright cards will point out the problems or social conditioning that might interfere with fulfilling these responsibilities. Actually, the three upright cards are a pentacle, a cup, and a rod—the three main areas of childhood development (the physical body, the emotions, and the mind). So this amounts to a pretty strong indictment of the job society does in providing guidance and help to parents at all levels.

The 7 of Cups represents the popular fads and magazine theories about raising children. Just one example of this would be the fraud about "quality time," which is basically just a rationalization for not spending sufficient time with the kids. Most of these popular theories of child raising, the 7 of Cups is telling us, are in fact excuses for avoiding responsibility, rather than guides to fulfilling it. We need to ignore the popular beliefs and cultivate a strong sense of values about child raising on our own.

Another message of the 7 of Cups is that there is an immense range of individuality among children A lot of parents believe that they have to treat all of their children equally—"We put your older brother through hell, and he's not too neurotic, so we're going to treat you the same way. We want to be fair." [Laughter.] Now, it goes without saying that you need a certain amount of evenness in dealing with more than one child; it is never acceptable to make one child a favorite and the other children also-rans. But there needs to be a recognition that each child comes into this life with a character and an individuality already largely shaped. Character is not just something that mysteriously rises out of environment, heredity, and early childhood experiences. These things influence and shape character, of course, but the fabric of a child's character has already been largely woven in earlier lives and experiences. This is something the parent cannot control—and should not try. It is just part of the raw material the parents must learn to work with. The parents need to try to discern what this fabric of character is for each child, and give them the opportunities and help each needs—not just a blanket policy for all. And they should refrain from imposing their own choices on the child—educational, career, friends, and so on. Teach your children to make wise decisions, and then let them follow their own lights. If you have taught them well, they will do well.

This applies even to likes and dislikes, values, and ethics. Most children do adopt the patterns of their parents, at least at first. But the worst thing you can do is to encourage your children to imitate your values and ethics. Challenge them to think about them! Don't let them just fall into a religious belief—make them understand it well enough that they can defend it to you. If they end up believing what you believe, fine. But it should also be fine if they end up believing something different, so long as they have thought it through intelligently. If all they do is annex your values and ethics without understanding them, you are sending them into adulthood without adequate preparation. So teach them to think for themselves and make their own decisions.

There's a tendency for far too many parents to project their own character and lifestyle on their children. This is not healthy. There is a vast range of character among human beings, and no matter how highly you think of yourself, the world does not really need additional carbon copies of you. One is enough. Let your children be themselves. They cannot be you.

In this regard, the 7 of Cups also seems to be suggesting that it is important to teach children to dream and be imaginative. In a sense, the 7 of Cups could be considered "the fairy tale card." It reminds us that children need fantasy and wild improbabilities, in order to nurture their thirst for exploring life and satisfy their curiosity about the unknown. Curiosity and the imagination are healthy aspects of childhood; they should be nurtured, not discouraged.

The creative challenge is the 3 of Swords. This card ties in nicely to the themes we have been examining with the 7 of Cups. Parents and children choose one another for the lessons they can help each other learn. I have done many consultations for parents, and I am continually impressed how much parents and children deserve each other. [Laughter.]

Nancy: That's not fair! [More laughter.]

Carl: Parent-child relationships provide a perfect crucible for growth. When the parents are young, they tend to have a lot of fantasies about having 2.5 perfect children, or whatever the average is these days. And often they feel that the measure of a perfect parent is having perfect children. But this is unrealistic. The 3 of Swords is reminding us that growth is the major challenge of parenting, and that the growth of the child is going to intersect with the growth of both parents. And this can be painful, unless the parents anticipate it and welcome it.

You are not going to have perfect children. You can sustain the fantasy for a while, but sooner or later, the bubble will burst. If nothing else, the teenage years will do it. [Laughter.] During the teenage years, the child is busy defining his or her individuality. Self-esteem is assaulted; peer pressures are very strong. The child has to start making decisions about life—about what he's going to do with his life—and if that's not bad enough, the hormones start raging out of control. [Laughter.] They're testing the waters. They want to be treated as adults.

The parents, at the same time, are suddenly realizing their child is no longer a baby. So they go into their swoon song: "Oh, my God, I'm losing my little baby." Now, that's the last thing a teenager needs to hear. He wants to be an adult and be treated as an adult. So there is a certain amount of rejection of parental guidance and opinion. If the parents won't let go, the child must force the issue—or remain a child forever. This process of rejection or rebellion only becomes a problem if the parents stand in its way. It's natural for the child to pull away from his or her parents and assert independence. It's only a problem when the parents resist it or take offense by it.

As parents, we should expect to learn from our children. We should expect our children to reveal our inadequacies. And we should expect to overcome them. This is one of the most dramatic ways you can teach your children what it means to grow and be mature—to have the maturity to recognize your weaknesses and shortcomings and to correct them. To my mind, the real challenge of parenting is to demonstrate to your children your own active involvement in personal and spiritual growth. Your own desire to learn is the best inspiration your children can have. This is the kind of role model children need—they need to see what it means to be a mature adult. What they don't need is the example of parents in their thirties or forties going through "mid-life crises." We all have our crises, of course, and the capacity to meet them wisely and courageously conveys a wonderful message to children. But "mid-life crises" are crises of immaturity, not maturity. They are a sign that these individuals failed to learn the lessons of adolescence, and are now repeating their stupidity when they ought to know better. These are not healthy examples for children.

The bottom line is this: if you want your children to grow up to be intelligent, independent adults, you have a responsibility to act as an intelligent, independent adult. You have a responsibility to set an example of maturity and a strong interest in personal and spiritual growth.

The 3 of Swords also suggests that the creative seed of a child is its inner spirit. This may be a shock to many parents, but it is a key to understanding the esoteric principles of parenting. During childhood, the parents are meant to serve as a surrogate for the child's real self, because the child is unable to contact it directly. It is therefore the duty of the parents, esoterically, to act as agents for the child's soul—which is not a child, after all, but a mature being that has been involved in evolution for millions of years—and prepare the child so that when it becomes an adult, it will be able to contact the power, wisdom, and love of the soul on its own.

Once the child reaches adulthood, the parents must then reverse their role and let the child's soul take over as the directing, nurturing, and guiding force. If the parents have done their work properly, the child should have the self-esteem, the self-possession, and the sense of individuality it needs to make its own decisions and way in life. The child should have the full support of its parents, but the parents should allow the adult-child to establish its own lifestyle. These last few comments anticipate The Hanged Man in the ninth position.

The card of purpose is the 9 of Rods. It is almost as if these rods are measuring sticks. And this tells me that one of the great responsibilities of a parent is to nurture and protect the child's self esteem and self-approval mechanism. The most fragile element of human psychology is our self-esteem; it can be broken very easily. When a child is young, it looks to its parents for approval and esteem. But by the time it becomes an adult, it needs to have internalized the process of self-approval in order to survive. It is therefore the duty of the parents to teach the child the importance of liking itself and to help the child build a proper mechanism for self-approval.

I was fortunate in my childhood, in that my parents always supported me and encouraged me to think for myself. But I am amazed by the number of adults who were seriously damaged during childhood by the thoughtlessness—and sometimes malice—of their parents. I have run into cases where parents told their children they were not good enough to succeed, that they didn't deserve anything better than they had—even cases where the parents told their children they were stupid! This is criminal abuse, but it happens.

I am not suggesting that parents feed the egos and vanities of their children; this would be counterproductive. I am talking about the ability to reflect on a job well done and say, "That is good." I am talking about being strong enough to take criticism and not be devastated by it. I am talking about being betrayed by friends and not taking it personally—to realize that you are still a decent human being, no matter what some foolish people might think. These are not skills or capacities that children learn automatically. They have to be taught. And this is one of the primary responsibilities of parenting.

Jim: I don't see how you got all those ideas out of the 9 of Rods. How do you do that?

Carl: Well, the 9's in general are cards of individuality and inclusiveness—of learning what it means to be a human being who can stand on his or her own but also can be attuned to the higher self and the needs of others. In the 9 of Rods, the 9 upright rods strike me as the component parts of the kind of structure each child needs to build—the structure I first mentioned when we were talking about the 7 of Rods. And one of the key elements to this structure is the self-approval mechanism. In a sense, each of these nine rods represents a different facet of the structure of our character—our self-esteem, our capacity to think for ourself, our ability to handle criticism, our knowledge of right and wrong, and so on. So I tried to describe these lessons briefly in my comments.

Jim: So you didn't just make it up—it was actually in the card.

Carl: It was actually in the card.

The card of the endowment is the 6 of Pentacles. There's a double meaning as it applies to this question. First, there is the very basic statement that it is the responsibility of the parents to provide shelter, food, and the basic necessities of life for their children. But of course, this is a responsibility that has been turned into a nightmare in our modern society, where many parents have overdone the material side. They have surrounded their children with material goods far surpassing basic needs, to the point where many young adults have a warped attitude as to what is a necessity of life. And then many parents use this as a club to hold over the heads of their children. "Just look at everything we've done for you," they will say—but of course the only thing they have done is suffocate them with material possessions. The implied message of their statement is, "Why are you such an ungrateful brat when we have given you so much?" But these parents need to listen to the ingratitude of their children and try to understand why this is a relevant message.

The second statement this card is making is that it is the responsibility of parents to give each child an endowment or legacy that will carry them through adulthood. This is not an endowment

254

of money—it is an endowment of self-esteem, a thirst for learning, a willingness to work, a set of useful skills, a fundamental optimism and joy of living, and strong ethics and values such as integrity, courage, and honesty. In addition, they need an understanding that life will support them if they will cooperate with life. This is an endowment they can carry for the rest of their lives. It is the best gift parents can give their children.

Now, this endowment is not given children by lecturing them. It is given them by inspiring them to develop skills that will let them be self-sufficient, and ethics that will let them lead a balanced lifestyle of integrity and honesty.

The final card in the cross of definition is the 10 of Swords. The person in the 10 of Swords seems to be dead in the desert, but in fact he is very much alive and alert. The 10 swords stuck in his back are signs of spiritual connections. Coming in the position of destiny, immediately following our comments on the endowment, this card suggests that the best legacy a parent can give is a strong foundation on which the child can build his or her connections with the higher self and the inner planes. This is the first great challenge to the child after becoming an adult and leaving the family home— to replace the connections it had with its parents with new connections with its higher self. And whether or not this happens is going to depend a great deal on how the parents raised the child. This is one of the reasons why I always recommend that parents expose their children to church. Adults are often disappointed by the weak content of most churches, but the kind of instruction children receive in church is usually invaluable. Yet if the parents are disenchanted with church and stop going, in most cases the children will stop going to church as well. And then they are deprived of a strong ethical and devotional base which is of paramount importance.

Of course, an ethical base is never built just by sending your kids to church. It must be reinforced by the parents. The 10 of Swords is subtly encouraging you to teach your children to look for the deeper meanings and purposes in life's events. Point out the hidden workings of cause and effect. Teach them to recognize divine intelligence pervading all of life. Make it natural for them to stop and question why their playmate punched them in the nose, instead of just getting mad.

Let's go on to the pillar of revelation and the real question. Here we have The Chariot. With this particular question, The Chariot is reinforcing the idea that the higher self of the child is a mature adult far wiser than the parents, even though the personality is just a child. The real question, therefore, is: To whom are the parents responsible? And the answer is the higher self of the child, as well as the adult potential of the child. It is the plan of the higher self for the child that the parents must serve, not their own whims or hidden agenda.

There is also the suggestion here that many of the problems the child must face in the years of childhood will have roots that are much deeper than anything that happens in this life. Each child brings with it a certain residue of problems from the past; these must be worked on in childhood. It is the duty of the parents to help the child face these problems and lovingly support it as it struggles to overcome these weaknesses and flaws. It is the responsibility of the parents to accelerate growth, not to get in the way of The Chariot and get run down.

In this regard, The Chariot is also reinforcing the parental responsibility to teach their children self-control and self-discipline—to be able to harness the urges and desires of their human nature and use this power to drive the chariot. In other words, they must learn to use these energies to become self-sufficient, so that they are in fact driving the chariot, and not be driven by it.

The next card is the 4 of Rods, the unseen forces. In this case, it stands for the ideal of what family should be—the ideal family environment. The family is meant to be a place of refuge, a source of stability, continuity, and support. It is an environment in which intimacy can be developed and learned; where each person can feel free to be himself or herself without fear of criticism or being degraded. Strong families develop shared activities which nurture this sense of continuity and stability. In some families, it may be everyone sitting down and eating dinner together. In others, it will be something else. But there will be mutual activities that give the children a chance to feel comfortable, protected, and embraced. When they need help, they know to whom they can turn. It's very important to create the right kind of atmosphere, not just physically but also emotionally and mentally.

This involves, by the way, recognizing how much damage can be done by parents having arguments out in the open, for the whole family to observe—or by open feuding with aunts and uncles, that sort of thing. It also involves creating a climate where it is possible to teach children that sometimes the mature approach to living is the opposite of what everyone else is doing. Children need to be told that it's all right to be different—to go against the flow of popular opinion and peer group pressure. They need to be encouraged to think for themselves—and have the courage to act by themselves, when necessary.

We've already discussed the spiritual ideal, The Hanged Man, at great length. The Hanged Man demonstrates that he is willing to be supported by spirit even though he must hang upside down and be held only by one strand of rope. There are times in all of our lives in which we must act with this kind of faith and steadfastness in the life of spirit. If parents can demonstrate this to their children, not just in theory but as a living, vital presence, their children will be immeasurably enriched by it.

The card of fulfillment is The Moon. This has a very much different meaning here than it did in the reading about anger. In this context, it reminds us that the individual child in the individual family is ultimately a part of one large family, and that is humanity. And the individual child has psychic links to mass consciousness, as well as spiritual links to the body of mankind. Each child needs to be taught of its relation to its community, its nation, and to the whole of humanity. It needs to be taught of its role in human civilization.

The Moon is a restatement of the last theme we touched on with The Hanged Man. Have you taught your children to be individuals—or just to be faces in the crowd? To be individuals, they must learn discernment. They must learn to chart their own course, even if it seems out of step with their group—or society as a whole. They need to learn to trust in the guidance of the higher self.

As you, as a parent, teach and nurture your child, you are, in effect, teaching and nurturing a whole generation. Your child is your tiny portion of the generation, but the generation is nothing more than all these tiny portions put together. So in the broadest sense, your responsibility as a parent is not just to your child or its higher self—it is also to your child's generation and to humanity as a whole.

Let me stop on that note.

CHAPTER SIXTEEN

Pessimism

Carl: The question is: What can be done to reduce pessimism in world thought? These are the cards that came up in response:

The starting point—The 8 of Cups, reversed.
The counterpoint—The High Priestess, reversed.
The creative challenge—The 9 of Pentacles, reversed.
The purpose—The 6 of Swords, reversed.
The endowment—The Tower, reversed.
The destiny—The 10 of Swords, upright.
The real question—The 2 of Rods, upright.
The unseen forces—The 5 of Pentacles, upright.
The spiritual ideal—The 6 of Cups, upright.
The fulfillment—The World, upright.

The first remarkable feature of this spread is that the first five cards are all reversed and the last five are all upright. This suggests to me that the first five cards deal with the causes of pessimism in world thought, and the last five deal with possible solutions. It also suggests that this is a problem which must be addressed particularly by spiritual aspirants, largely because no one else is going to give a damn. There is also a hint that some of the problems of world pessimism are actually caused by spiritual aspirants, who accidentally magnify the problem instead of cleaning it up. The aspirant tends to be so much more aware of the problems of human life that it is easy to thoughtlessly succumb to pessimism.

There are three cards from the major arcana in the spread, two

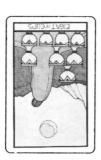

swords, one rod, two cups, and two pentacles. The 6 of Swords and the 6 of Cups form a bond that emphasizes right use of energy and self-discipline; the High Priestess, being numbered 2, and the 2 of Rods, also form a significant pair.

The starting point is the 8 of Cups. This is the image of a person looking out across a river or lake to the mountains beyond. He must cross the river but has no boat; in order to continue on his journey, he must leave the eight cups in the foreground behind. So there's a sense of loss and sorrow. He knows he has to cross the river, but he's not happy about it. He's singing the blues—"Nobody knows the trouble I've seen." Actually, everyone has seen this same kind of trouble, but it would be rude to spoil his self-pity. He's ready to launch into some really heavy complaining—bitch, bitch, bitch.

This is a simple statement that one of the major sources of pessimism in world thought is the negativity in the attitudes of individual human beings. We believe it is our God-given right to complain about life, and so we complain. We revel in negativity. People nourish themselves on fear and self-doubt; they wallow in worry and uncertainty. They focus on the pain of breaking emotional attachments, as the fellow in the 8 of Cups is doing. They look at their problems and they magnify them to immense proportions, until they become crippling, paralyzing threats.

The esoteric root of the 8 of Cups is sacrifice. At times, life calls on us to give up something so that we can get something even better. But we happen to cherish what we are asked to give up, and we are not sure the trade will be worth it. The point is, we do not train ourselves to make joyful and intentional sacrifices. We find it distasteful, and for no good reason. You can see this in our country today. You cannot preserve freedom or democracy unless the majority of citizens are willing at times to make sacrifices and forego certain rights, for the good of the country as a whole. But we've lost that spirit. All anybody can think about today is defending their rights and never, ever giving any of them up. It's an inability to make sacrifices. So when a boss comes along and asks employees to make a sacrifice, no one can handle it. That's when the grumbling and complaining begin. We have lost the ability to remain cheerful in the face of adversity, loss, or delay. All we know how to do is bitch and complain.

The moon in the 8 of Cups reminds us that mass consciousness is a controlling factor here. It is considered to be chic to be pessimistic and cynical. If you are optimistic and helpful, you are out of step with mass consciousness. So this is an enormous problem.

The counterpoint is the High Priestess. As you can see, she is sitting in front of a veil or curtain that is drawn back to reveal a vision of the inner dimensions. In other decks, like the Rider Tarot, the curtain is not drawn; it hides the inner reality. And this tells us something very important about pessimism. A lot of pessimism we must deal with is the result of religious authorities and philosophers insisting that the true understanding of life is a big mystery. Sin is a mystery. Life after death is a mystery. The meaning of the crucifixion is a mystery. For eons and eons, we've been told, "It's all a mystery. Don't even try to understand it. We will tell you what you need to know." Once upon a time, this worked. But now enough people are developing their minds that they are no longer satisfied by the lame excuse that all of life is just a mystery. And this leaves people in a mental vacuum which breeds pessimism. There is a growing intellectual doubt and confusion which is the basis for pessimism.

We have to draw back the curtain and say, "It's not a mystery at all. There's the castle, for Pete's sake: there is a vision. There is a plan. It all makes sense. We can understand poverty, famine, and warfare. They are tough problems, but we don't have to be overwhelmed by them." We need to demystify life as the first step

262

toward eliminating pessimism. There are certain groups that don't want that message to get out, of course—they are starting to protest even as we talk about it here. [Laughter.]

The High Priestess speaks directly to this problem. If you can look beyond the surface level of problems, she is telling us, you will find something much more important. And if you learn to nurture the growth of humanity with benevolent love, then you will fill your void of confusion and doubt with something better than pessimism and nihilism. You will give life meaning.

The creative challenge is the 9 of Pentacles. This is an image of a person holding a pet bird, standing in a vineyard. The tree in the background symbolizes growth; the vineyard represents the work to be done. The bird, which is pure white, represents the ideals of human life. The gray cloak, where six of the pentacles are, represents mass consciousness with all of its preconditioning and superstition. This card is telling us that we tend to forget that our mission here is to grow and transform the desert into a vineyard, figuratively speaking. We run into problems such as poverty, hunger, discrimination, competition, and conflict, and we magnify them to such epic proportions that we forget all about the impulse to grow.

Some crazy person kills 27 people in a murder spree and it makes front page news. The same day, someone achieves enlightenment in Bangor, Maine, and there's no mention of it anywhere in any newspaper on the face of the globe. There are no headlines: "Another member of humanity sees the light!" with a subhead reading: "Twenty-fifth person this year to achieve union with God." [Laughter.] We announce the failings of humanity in big type and revel in the dirt and scandal of humanity, calling it news. But the news does not report on the evolutionary progress of humanity. We thirst for information about the seedy side of life. We have a fascination with the murk and muck of humanity.

This fascination with gossip and gore is a breeding ground for pessimism. Mosquitos need a swamp in order to breed, and pessimism likewise needs the murk and muck of human suffering in order to breed. What's going to stop this? It cannot be legislated. It can only be stopped as individuals realize what is going on and set their sights higher. This is a matter of individual responsibility. As Burke said, "The only thing necessary for the spread of evil is for good people to do nothing." That could be paraphrased to state: "The only thing necessary for the spread of pessimism is for good people to allow themselves to be fascinated by the murk and muck of humanity." And this is what the 9 of Pentacles is telling us—that we have to choose between what our outer senses tell us and what our inner wisdom tells us. Our outer senses may tell us that life is hell—but our inner wisdom whispers, quietly, "Not if you turn it into heaven on earth."

Our challenge is to focus on the ideals represented by the white bird, not the seamy side of mass consciousness, found in the cloak. We *can* lift up and purify consciousness. It can be done. The six of us sitting here can't do it. Even 60 people can't do it. But if six hundred or six thousand people took it on as an individual responsibility, and taught their children to approach life with dignity, optimism, and a strong sense of the ideal, it would gradually have a startling impact. We need to focus on the potential of humanity for growth, not its potential for crime and corruption. This is an important step toward reducing pessimism.

The card of purpose is the 6 of Swords. This is a card we've seen once before. It reemphasizes what I've just been saying about the need for a stronger awareness of and dedication to the principle of growth. We do not value human growth enough. Frequently, growth experiences come to us in life, but we are so focused in our emotions that we completely fail to see the potential for growth. We view the experience entirely as a threat to our security or sanity or well-being, and react accordingly, which of course magnifies and exaggerates the hardship. And then we conclude that life is hell, and we sow the seeds of pessimism. Perhaps we flunk out of school. The personality may be humiliated by this and view it as a first class disaster. It probably says, "How could you do this to me, God?" Of course, it wasn't God who forgot to study, but God is a convenient scapegoat for all problems. This is because most people pray to God in the hopes He will prevent all disasters in our life, which is juvenile. The higher self, of course, is looking down at the personality, who is filled with humiliation and anger, and thinks, "How ungrateful! I went to a lot of trouble to make sure you would fail, because you need to learn to be more self-motivating. You've been a deadbeat for entirely too long. And this is the thanks I get!" [Laughter.]

The higher self often leads us into important opportunities for growth, just as the steersman may direct his boat into rough waters, but the personality misinterprets them and views them as disasters. This, in turn, leads to a more and more pessimistic and superstitious approach to life. The solution to this is a simple one, of course. People need to get into the habit of spending time every day counting their blessings and expressing gratitude for everything they've learned, their friends, and all of the good things that have come to them. If you spend just five mintues every day reviewing your blessings and being thankful for them, this simple exercise will neutralize any pessimism you have in a very short time. It's an exercise that reminds you that there is a helmsman guiding the barque of your personality across the turbulent waters, and so you need not be afraid.

Looking at this card of the boatman guiding his ship across the waters reminds me of how often people will make comments like, "I'm waiting for my ship to come in." And yet, what they fail to realize is that they have never sent a ship out! [Laughter.] The expression, waiting for your ship to come in, stems from a couple of hundred years ago when a merchant would invest a lot of money in a fleet of ships and send them out to bring a cargo of goods from the Orient or somewhere. He was literally waiting for his ships to come in—but he had reason to expect them to arrive. But most people today who are waiting for their ship to come in don't even own a ship, let alone have it out to sea! [More laughter.] I'm speaking figuratively, of course. But these people build up big expectations that have no justification whatsoever. They are just lusting for things they have done nothing to earn. And when they don't receive them, they blame their emptiness on life. This is how pessimism takes root. It's often just an irrational response to our own self-imposed shallowness and emptiness.

The endowment is The Tower. Waves are beating on the side of the tower; lightning has struck the top and it has caught fire. It even looks as though the vultures are beginning to circle. This is a card of crisis. Now, the sad fact of human life is that most people need a jump start in order to grow. They need some kind of shock to get them off their rear ends and make some changes. In fact, people are so lethargic that it often takes a major crisis to wake them up. But this means that many people associate growth with crises, and therefore view growth as unpleasant—something that always involves suffering. This is not an accurate conclusion, but people draw it anyway. They view crises—and by extension, growth—as something distasteful, perhaps even tragic. People often have a tremendous resistance to growth and change, and view them as threats. And this leads to a very pessimistic view of growth in mass consciousness.

Then we put our imaginations to work—we worry. Worry is the secret weapon of pessimism. Our child becomes a teenager and starts experimenting with life. And we worry and fear the worst. What happens to all that worry and fear? It doesn't just float away and fall into the ocean like volcanic ash. It stays in our subconscious and becomes the seeds of pessimism. But it's not just we who become pessimistic—we feed world pessimism at the same time. Humanity as a whole worries about its future in the same way. This is how pessimism builds and builds. In one sense, the tower is the shrine of our worries and fears.

To go back to the High Priestess, if we understood that God really does have a divine plan for evolution and that all these crises are a part of it, we could put a curb on these worries and fears, and that would cut down on the pessimism. Instead of worrying that humanity's going to blow itself up, we need to rely on the wisdom and benevolence of God's plan. We have to give God credit for being able to fulfill His own plan. It is really arrogant to assume that we could blow up the planet against God's will, if you stop and think about it. If God's will is powerful enough to generate all creation, surely it is powerful enough to keep a bunch of half-cocked humans from blowing it all up. Where's our faith? Whatever happened to the notion of cooperating with God and serving His plan? We may mouth the words, but the pessimism in world thought betrays the fact that we do not put our faith and devotion to work in our attitudes and values.

We live in a rich, wonderful time. I'm looking ahead of the 6 of Cups here. But most people take these blessings for granted, as though they deserve them. We need to stop taking life for granted. We need to start being grateful to God for the blessings all humanity enjoys—and for the crises which cause us to think and grow, too. It's all part of the package.

Pessimism and optimism are basically points of view. If we have a healthy attitude of devotion and gratitude toward life, we will be optimistic. But if we have a sour, self-centered, "woe is me" kind of attitude, we will be pessimistic.

The 10 of Swords is the card of destiny. This card is telling me that our basic value system is polluted and warped by these roots of pessimism. You may think I am exaggerating, but in looking into the past lives of various people, I have been surprised to find how many still carry seeds of pessimism picked up in lifetimes thousands of years ago. In ancient Greece, for example, there was a school of philosophy known as the Cynics. The word cynicism is derived from their beliefs. And this is what the person in the 10 of Swords is representing. He is lying face down in the dust of the desert; from his perspective the world is nothing but dry dust. "My mouth is full of dry dust; the world is full of dry dust. There is nothing worthwhile here." This is his philosophy, and it is not too far removed from many of the leading philosophies of human life. Look at existentialism. It is the philosophical equivalent of "my mouth is full of dry dust." It has no higher perspective than that of whatever we happen to experience. It has no inner vision. It has no transcendent base. It is purely materialistic. And if your whole life has been nothing but dry dust, then that becomes your world view—if you are an existentialist. It is out of this kind of philosophical blindness that cynicism and pessimism can arise and pollute human thought. And we are taught these attitudes in elementary school, high school, and college. We are even taught these things in Sunday School! The magazines we read and the news shows we watch on TV—they all reflect the limitations of a pessimistic world view.

To change this, therefore, we need to purge our value system. We need to weigh these philosophies and realize how corrupt they actually are.

If you go out tonight and get mugged, you will lose a few hundred dollars and get some bruises. In a week or so, it will be virtually a forgotten memory. But if you watch TV tonight and are mugged by a Cynic or an existentialist philosopher—mugged mentally, as it were—the damage may last thousands of years and many, many lifetimes. That's what the 10 of Swords is telling us. This poor fellow has been mugged by the existentialists and nihilists. We have to be very careful what we put into our personal value systems, and what humanity as a whole embraces and adopts for its values. Philosophy is not just a game for the idle rich; it is something that shapes the character of each and every one of us. So we had better make damn sure that any philosophical system we buy into will be good for us. We had better make sure it has an esoteric basis—an inner vision and an inner perspective based on the plan of God and divine love and wisdom. We had better make sure that it embraces the importance of growth to human beings and to the whole of civilization. And at the heart of our philosophy, we had better make sure that it encourages us to be optimistic, not pessimistic. Because intelligent people will always choose optimism over pessimism. Whenever you run into someone who is basically pessimistic, take pity on them. They are the victims of intellectual thuggery.

The 10 of Swords is also advising us to take a more active role in life. There are serious problems in the world, but crying and whining about them has never solved a single one of them. We've been put on this planet to play our part in fixing what's wrong. That's our primary spiritual duty. So get to work. Whenever you encounter imperfection, do what you can to correct it.

All right; let's look at the pillar of revelation. The real question is the 2 of Rods. And this is suggesting that pessimism is a function of the analytical nature of the mind—the tendency of the mind to break things down to their component parts and evaluate them on that basis, instead of as a whole. It's kind of like our cynical friend in the 10 of Swords visiting the White House and finding dust on some book or antique, and saying, "See, it's dust. I was right all along. Life is nothing but dust!" [Laughter.] It is very important for the mind to be well trained in analysis and deduction, but it must always operate within the context of the bigger picture. The fellow in the 2 of Rods is holding a globe to remind us that every idea and concept is first and foremost a complete picture with an inner perspective and meaning as well as an outer expression. And the globe as a whole is more important than any of its parts.

It is impossible to be pessimistic if you are truly thinking in terms of the whole. Pessimism derives from examining some of the facts, but deliberately ignoring others. So the real question is: What are we doing to develop the mind, not so that we can fill it with someone else's cynicism, but so that we can become a lucid observer of life on our own?

To put this in another way: learn to look for the *light* in the world—the light of the globe—not the darkness that still exists. Because the light casts out the darkness.

The unseen forces are represented by the 5 of Pentacles. Here are two folks heading for Mecca or Shangri-la, but all they can think of is how much their feet hurt, how long it's been since they ate, and the rigors of their journey. They are ignoring the beautiful presence of harmony over their heads and focusing exclusively on the trials of the trip. They have succumbed to grimness. And again, this is something that religion has inadvertently emphasized. We have been taught to wear our suffering on our sleeve—to be proud of the sacrifices we must make. And it has given spiritual growth a bad name. In this country especially, we are suffering from the legacy of puritanism, which advocates grimness and systematically tries to exclude fun, celebration, and joy from the spiritual life.

Let me make this as clear as I can. There is no virtue in suffering. There is virtue in triumphing over suffering, but there is no virtue in suffering. There is virtue in right sacrifice, but there is no virtue in suffering. If you decide you must help others, but do it with grimness, you are being no help at all. If you give a million dollars to charity, but regret doing it, you have given one million dollars worth of regret. To cure the problem of pessimism in world thought, we have to shatter this illusion that life is hell and that suffering is spiritual. There is no logic to it, but millions of people accept it without questioning.

If you are focused in either grimness or pessimism, you cannot possibly be in tune with spirit. These negative states are antithetical to spirit. So, one of the true antidotes to these conditions is to spend more and more of your time attuning yourself to spirit, because these problems cannot exist on that wavelength.

This is what the 6 of Cups means here in the position of the spiritual ideal. We're meant to see the beauty of life at every level, and act as though we were filled by this beauty. We are also meant to share this beauty with others. If someone else is suffering, we need to share with them our sense of beauty to whatever degree they are responsive. But most importantly, we are meant to enjoy life and every facet of life. We are meant to enjoy our relationships and our responsibilities. We are meant to enjoy the work we do. We are meant to enjoy spiritual service and growth. If we are pouring this kind of joy into our life, we make a powerful statement that shatters pessimism. It is joy and a sense of delight in living that breaks up pessimism in world thought.

Not surprisingly, the card of fulfillment is The World. This reminds us that we are supposed to be constantly expanding our awareness—and the awareness of all humanity. Pessimism, however, is a force that shrinks and contracts. None of the great breakthroughs of human living have ever been made by a pessimist or a cynic. To break new ground, you need to work with an energy which expands. Optimism expands; pessimism contracts. Joy expands; sorrow and self-pity contract. So if you want new opportunities, harness optimism. If you want to lose ground, opt for pessimism.

This is true for humanity as a whole. Societies that are fundamentally optimistic are able to expand. Societies that are basically pessimistic decline.

We may have time for a few questions or comments.

Leslie: I thought it was interesting that in the 8 of Cups the cups are empty and in the 6 of Cups they are full.

Carl: Yes.

Leslie: There's a big difference.

Rose: They must not be empty or he wouldn't leave them behind.

Carl: Well, in this spread they are obviously empty, because the card is upside down! [Laughter.] I think Leslie's point is that they represent emptiness to him, because he must give them up—or thinks he must. It is in the voids of spiritual emptiness that pessimism breeds. When the cups are full, as they are in the 6 of Cups, there is no room for pessimism.

CHAPTER SEVENTEEN

The Role of Pets

Carl: The question is: What is the esoteric purpose of having pets? The Tarot answered with the following cards:

The starting point—The 6 of Pentacles, upright.
The counterpoint—The Ace of Cups, upright.
The creative challenge—The 8 of Pentacles, reversed.
The purpose—The Knight of Pentacles, upright.
The endowment—The 4 of Swords, reversed.
The destiny—The 2 of Cups, upright.
The real question—The Fool, reversed.
The unseen forces—The Wheel of Fortune, reversed.
The spiritual ideal—The 7 of Cups, reversed.
The fulfillment—The Queen of Pentacles, reversed.

There are two cards from the major arcana, one sword, no rods—

Rose: It looks to me like The Fool is carrying a rod.

Carl: Yes, that's true. That's why we can be certain he's not really a fool. But we have to count The Fool as part of the major arcana, not as a rod.

There are three cups and four pentacles. The only parallels between cards numerologically are between the Ace of Cups and The Wheel of Fortune. But both The Wheel of Fortune and The Fool exhibit a downward flow of divine energy at the top of the card which always suggests to me a facet of the transcendent nature of God. There are four upright cards and six reversed ones.

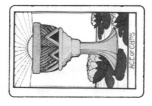

274

Have I covered everything?

Leslie: What do the upright and reversed cards mean?

Carl: The distinction is not too important in this spread, but the upright cards deal with the conventional aspects of our relationship with pets and the reversed cards deal with the inner relationship—the hidden potential to use pets as a doorway into inner levels of consciousness.

Betsy: So the meaning of upright and reversed cards will be different with each question you ask?

Carl: That is correct.

Betsy: I've been noticing that you are not using a significator for these questions. In some of the tapes you did years ago, you used a significator. Why have you changed?

Carl: There's no reason to limit yourself to 77 cards when you could be using all 78. When I first started working with the Tarot, I thought a significator was helpful, because it encouraged people to think through the meaning of their question. I never chose a significator in the way that is standard in the fortune telling uses of the Tarot—where one of the face cards is used to represent the person asking the question. I always chose the card that best seemed to embody the question. And this helped people formulate their questions intelligently. But now that I have written my book, and spent a whole chapter explaining how to form intelligent questions, I don't think this crutch is necessary. So I have stopped using the significator.

Actually, I personally stopped using it about five years ago.

I think we'd better begin. Let's jump for a minute to the last card, The Queen of Pentacles. This card certainly emphasizes that we are meant to care for our pets; it emphasizes all the themes of stewardship, responsibility, and kinship with all life. But far more importantly, to me, it also suggests that working with pets is one of the key ways we can open the door to the inner dimensions of life.

Anyone with a little bit of awareness who has a dog or cat will begin to notice the rich inner bond that develops between a pet and a human being. Dogs and cats are naturally psychic, so if you interact with a pet at anything other than a superficial level, you will begin to become aware of this psychic nature. And of course, our ability to communicate with pets with English is limited, so we are forced to learn to communicate at more abstract levels—through our love and affection, our joy, and so on.

But I am getting ahead of myself. Let's go back to the starting point, where we have the 6 of Pentacles. We saw this card before, in the question on raising children. But in this spread I am going to interpret it in an entirely different way—in fact, in a way that I have never interpreted it before. I am drawing a clue here from the fact that The Wheel of Fortune is also part of this map, in the position of unseen forces. So I am inspired to interpret the 6 of Pentacles in terms of karma. There is, of course, the Biblical injunction that we are meant to exercise dominion over all the things of the earth. But in early times, when man was first evolving, and had not yet developed tools, we didn't have dominion over all the beasts of the earth. We didn't have the physical strength to be a match for some of the wild animals. These animals would prey on humanity. And this is one reason why mankind has been the agent for the massive killing of the buffalo and the whales and other wild animals—it is the wheel of karma come full cycle. But that represents the line of least resistance in karmic balancing. At least some elements of humanity have advanced in the intervening thousands and thousands of years and choose the higher road of taking responsibility to develop a relationship with animals—especially the more intelligent ones. And so they take them as pets and train them to serve as their companions, either inside their home or outside. Obviously, you don't share your bedroom with a horse, but a horse can become an excellent companion.

It is important to observe that humanity has a wide range of relationships with animals. Many people who domesticate animals
treat them with kindness and goodwill, and become very close to
them. Sometimes they overdose on kindness and even spoil them.
Other people treat their pets as something to dominate or enslave.
Or they train dogs to be ferocious and to serve as attack animals.
But a lot of our attitudes toward animals in general and pets in
particular are still being shaped by ancient patterns of karma. We
are drawn into some of these relationships as a means of developing more correct relationships with the animal kingdom. So there is
a definite responsibility to owning pets. They are teaching us as
much about life and love as we are teaching them.

The 6 of Pentacles also reminds us that pets are earthbound,
meaning that they are totally stuck in their physical bodies and
senses. By their associations with humans, this earthbound focus
can be broken.

The Ace of Cups is a true counterpoint to what we've just been
talking about. Even though we have a karmic responsibility to care
for the advanced animals and help them develop, we are meant to
respond to this challenge with the highest qualities of care—with
the purest forms of goodwill, affection, and kindness we are capable
of. This is a card which tells us we need to shift our sights to a
higher, more noble level. We are not meant to focus on the roots of
the lilies extending below the surface of the water into the muck at
the bottom, but rather to rise with the cup to the glorious light
radiating at the top. We are meant to learn to act with goodwill,
compassion, and tenderness. And pets are one of the primary ways
that many humans learn to express these qualities. It's often very
difficult for some humans to learn to express goodwill and compassion toward other human beings, because they get involved in such
intense conflicts with them. But almost anyone can take pity on a
stray cat or a puppy dog. Many people who have cut themselves

off from humanity are able to rediscover goodwill and tenderness by having pets.

The ideal represented by the Ace of Cups in this case is kinship for all life, or what Schweitzer called reverence for all life. We are meant to pour the light of love into the life of our pets.

Our third card, the creative challenge, is the 8 of Pentacles. And it is a very real challenge. The challenge is to establish more constructive relationships with the advanced animals. There is a suggestion here that one of the disadvantages of all our technological advances is that we are no longer dependent upon domesticated animals for help in the work we perform. Shepherds are no longer dependent on dogs for herding the sheep. We don't even need to rely on our cats to catch mice. And there is another side to this. So many people in this modern day are no longer exposed to the experience of growing up in a rural environment where they have to take care of animals and learn the ways of animals. Being around animals as a child is an invaluable way to learn a lot of the lessons of life. But modern technology has taken this aspect of life away from many, many people. Now, I am not complaining about this, because I see it as just another turn of the spiral of human development. But we need to look to a higher turn of the spiral and speculate on what it will mean to establish new and better productive relationships with the higher animals, especially our pets.

Humanity is not alone on the planet. We share it with the animals, plants, and minerals. And we are meant to incorporate all of these life forms in our work of building the City of God on earth. Sometimes in our zeal we abuse these life forms as we try to harness them, but on the whole, we are responding well to the plan. Right now, humanity seems more focused on incorporating the mineral kingdom into its work than the animal kingdom, and that is fine. But the animal kingdom has always been extremely important to us in terms of sharing our work and we need to study the animal kingdom creatively from the standpoint of how we can further expand our interaction with the advanced animals.

It can be something as simple as beekeeping. [Laughter] You smile when I say that, but there is a simple example of man and animal working together. From an esoteric point of view, it is a shared labor, a shared work. And the 8 of Pentacles, with its open window to the inner planes, strongly suggests there are many far more advanced and enlightened ways we can share our labors and joys with the animal kingdom that are as yet undiscovered. This is our challenge.

The card of purpose is the Knight of Pentacles. To me, this card reminds us that we need to share our life with our pets with respect and affection. They are meant to be our companions, as in the case of a rider and a horse. We should respect the divine life within them and their capacity for growth. We are meant to serve as their conscience, their guides, and their intelligence. This is one of the roles of stewardship we are expected to play. And as we do, we come to understand the life within our pets and respect them. They are not just "dumb animals." They don't have the language skills that we do, or the ability to read or write, but they can certainly communicate with each other—and they could communicate with us if we weren't so exclusive and narrowminded.

The notion that animals are noncommunicative is something that is perpetuated only by people who do not have very much experience with animals. We have a herd of llamas. And one of our mama llamas, Dawn, just gave birth to a son, Julio. As soon as she gave birth to him, Dawn began talking incessantly to Julio. After a few days, she slacked off, but for the first two or three days, she talked to him almost incessantly. She was teaching him how to respond to her.

After a week, we opened the pen and let Julio explore. And the moment he got to the imaginary line where the gate had been up to a few minutes before, Dawn started calling to Julio: "That's far enough—don't go any further than that unless I am with you." And so he would come back to her. Eventually, they both went out to explore, but she kept calling him back to her if he started to stray further than she deemed safe. At one point, he discovered his legs and started to bolt on the run. He ran about fifty feet until Dawn looked up and shrieked, "Stop that!" And he stopped and came back to her.

She wasn't speaking English, of course—she was communicating in llama language. But it was clear what her message was—and it was clear to Julio, too.

I don't mean to overemphasize this issue of communicating with animals. It is just one example of the need for a greater respect for the life within our pets. These are beings with some level of consciousness. They may not be able to perform algebraic computations, but we are able to communicate with them. So one of the purposes of having pets is to learn what it means to master and train and guide the animals in our care and take responsibility for them. And this is a very important lesson for us humans. To some degree, the relationship we have to pets is something like the relationship of our own higher self to us. The obstacles are much the same, in any event—how do we overcome the enormous gap in consciousness and learn to bridge it so that we can become companions?

We serve the divine plan by having pets—if we treat them wisely and compassionately—because these animals are enriched by the lessons of intelligence and individuality they can learn from us. We're enriched in return as they share in our work and productivity and as we learn to expand our consciousness to understand their needs.

The card of endowment is the 4 of Swords. The key to interpreting this card in this situation is the sword at the bottom of the picture—at subconscious levels, as it were. And this suggests to me that animals are very responsive to us and are imprinted by our own character, even more so than our children. Our children grow up and become teenagers and rebel against us, but our pets do not rebel, unless we abuse them seriously. They are shaped by our own nature to an extent that is far greater than most people imagine. If we are kind and loving and helpful, they will respond directly to that. If we are mean and vicious and selfish, they will begin to reflect these characteristics in their own behavior. Naturally, part of this phenomenon involves the principle that like attracts like. If we are a vicious person, we will tend to choose a vicious pet. But this is only one piece of the puzzle. Pets do have their own personalities. They can be highly individualistic, with one cat being very much different from the next cat. But they are also highly susceptible to imprinting from the humans around them. So we have a tremendous responsibility to imprint our pets wisely. If we teach a dog to attack other people and tear them limb from limb, we are slowing its evolution, not accelerating it. Now, I am not suggesting that it is not legitimate to train dogs for police work and similar assignments. There's a difference between training a German shepherd to be an effective police dog, where the training is accompanied by a great deal of love and companionship, and training a dog to be mean and vicious.

A recent use we have developed for dogs is to serve as guides for the blind. This is a marvelous way to harness the potential of this pet. These are the kinds of creative uses for these companions we need to explore.

We need to realize that having a pet involves a great deal of responsibility. You can't abuse that responsibility. It's not a difficult responsibility, but it does extend beyond just feeding them every day and protecting them. It involves making sure that the imprint we are making on their character is a good one. And it involves making sure the relationship is a two-way street. We should not just have a dog or a cat because we are lonely—we should be giving as much as we receive.

This is illustrated in the card of destiny, the 2 of Cups. Look at the top of the cups—they form the symbol for infinity. The duality involved here is giving and receiving, and through this relationship, we open up the inner potential of having pets. What is this inner potential? Well, for one thing, there is a tremendous amount of goodwill that can be tapped. Our pets are not intellectual companions or our equals—but they are meant to be our companions along the way. They are evolving and developing, just as we are, but at a different level. So we can enrich their development and we can learn many lessons by interacting with them.

Look at the strands flowing from the girl's cap on the right side of the picture. These tend to indicate relationships. And so, this card is confirming that our ties with our pets are valid relationships. We are meant to have these extra relationships. They are healthy for us. We can enrich the animal kingdom and they can enrich us.

This takes us to the pillar of revelation and the real question, which is occupied by The Fool. The Fool is a symbol for human individuality and the process of individualization. In this position in the map, it is therefore clearly indicating that the esoteric purpose of having pets is to help them prepare for individualization through our association with them. Animals have group souls, as compared to humans, who have an individual soul. The advanced animals that become our pets are approaching individuality, but have not yet reached it. By identifying more closely with humans, they learn many of the attributes that give them more character and more of a sense of personality. So their evolution can be tremendously accelerated by this association. Having pets is one of the primary ways that we human beings perform our service to God—usually without even realizing what we are doing! Of course, the nobler our own expression of individuality is, the stronger and more useful our imprint on our pets will be. This is symbolized by the white flower of The Fool. And the rod he carries suggests that we need to act intelligently in executing our responsibilities toward pets. We are strengthening the astral body and helping to germinate the mental body that is beginning to form in the animal.

The card of unseen forces is The Wheel of Fortune. This is almost a companion to The Fool in this particular map. It reminds us that the animal kingdom has an evolutionary plan of its own. It intersects with ours, but has a movement and a cycle that is unique to it. Humans can serve a strong role in helping animals advance, but this card in this position again reminds us of the need to practice great humility and respect as we fulfill our responsibilities. It is not our right to have pets—it is our privilege. And we need therefore to be as responsive to their needs and their development as we can be. It would be hard for any individual to tune in and discern what the evolutionary needs of the animal kingdom are. But we must not arrogantly assume that we can do anything we want, without consequences. We need to respect and love the basic integrity of the divine life within these animals. If we can maintain a proper level of respect for the evolution of these beings, then we will be guided in most cases to do the correct and proper thing.

The spiritual ideal is portrayed by the 7 of Cups. This is another card that appeared in the question about raising children. But it will have a completely different meaning here. In this instance, it reminds us that there is a rich diversity of life. Sometimes, people fall into ruts and become stagnant. Often, having a pet will help lift you out of some of these ruts. And if you are reasonably intelligent, a pet can also help you start looking at certain situations from a new perspective. Let's say you have a cat, and the cat comes up to your door and purrs and purrs. You open the door and there's a live mouse in his mouth. Many people thoughtlessly impose their own values and reactions on the cat and make it clear that he has done something that offends them. But that is really narrowminded. The cat has just been doing his work. He's been out there earning his keep and pay. He has brought this mouse to you as a gift. To scold him or criticize him immediately limits your relationship. You need to look at it through the cat's eyes, and praise and reward him for his intent and his skill. You can give a cat an inferiority complex in a hurry if you act thoughtlessly at these times.

Now this is not to say that you cannot put some restrictions on these situations. We have trained our cats that they are not to bring their prey into the house. We have also patiently encouraged them to understand that they don't actually have to eat them—the food we give them is much better for them. Sometimes they listen, sometimes they don't. But eventually, they can learn to modify and enlighten some very basic instincts. We just have to be patient and not apply our standards and values to a life form that has millions of years of evolution in making it a good hunter. We need to treat pets with a sense of humility and piety that will lead to a genuine reverence for the divine life within them.

We tend to be fooled a lot by the assumptions we make based on outer appearances. We think of animals as dumb creatures. But whether it is an animal or a plant, a tree or a boulder somewhere, there is divine life within it and we need to learn to relate to this divine life without all the silly assumptions we are prone to make. To be truly in touch with our own higher self, we must also be able to recognize the higher, spiritual elements within animals, plants, and the mineral kingdom. So pets can provide us with a tremendous learning experience. Having pets encourages us to develop an inner rapport with the spiritual essence of animals. In fact, someone who has learned to care for pets and treat them compassionately, and has extended this capacity to the way they treat other people, is often much more in tune with their higher self than people who have great esoteric knowledge of spirit but still lack love.

Now, you may be wondering—how did I get all that out of the 7 of Cups? Well, I pulled the example of the cat and the mouse out of my own experience. But it illustrates the basic point of the 7 of Cups, which is that having pets challenges us to look at life through their perspectives. It challenges us to understand their motivations, desires, and basic design. We are not meant to rewrite this basic design—that would be an affront to God. We are meant instead to see how we can work with this basic design to help our pets evolve more quickly. And that's a real challenge to us.

The fulfillment is the Queen of Pentacles, which we have already touched on briefly. And this is a restatement that we are meant to go beyond just the form level of companionship and discover, through our pets, what it means to have a relationship with the inner dimensions of life. The physical is meant to reveal the inner, the spiritual. And the higher animals reveal a whole level of inner contacts that we would not be able to tap in any other way. Some of these contacts involve angelic forces, some do not. But they are part of the rich inner life of divine creation.

Okay. I'm ready for questions and comments.

Rose: Going back to the 8 of Pentacles, one of the constructive uses they have found is that pets can be very healthy companions. They can lower your blood pressure, for example. And studies have shown that older people who have pets tend to live longer.

Carl: Llamas are good for calming you down, too.

Rose: Yes, but you can't take a llama into your house. [Laughter.] I'm talking about the calming effect a cat can have.

Carl: Sure. They come to you and make you take a break from your work. "It's time for a kitty break," they say. "So stop what you're doing and pay some attention to me." That can be a very healthy influence on people who tend to work too hard and too intensely.

CHAPTER EIGHTEEN

Goals of the New Age

Carl: The question is: What are the central goals of the New Age? And the answer consists of the following cards:

The starting point—The Queen of Pentacles, reversed.
The counterpoint—The Knight of Swords, reversed.
The creative challenge—The World, upright.
The purpose—The Hanged Man, upright.
The endowment—The Magician, upright.
The destiny—The 8 of Swords, upright.
The real question—The 8 of Pentacles, reversed.
The unseen forces—The Ace of Swords, reversed.
The spiritual ideal—The 2 of Rods, reversed.
The fulfillment—The 4 of Swords, upright.

There are three cards from the major arcana, four swords, one rod, no cups, and two pentacles. Note that both the starting point and the real question, which is a sort of starting point for the pillar of revelation, are both pentacles. This emphasizes the importance of physical involvement in the New Age. In the New Age, the life of spirit is something that will have to be demonstrated outwardly, in the physical plane; it is not something to hide behind monastery or convent walls. Also note that the one rod is in the position of the spiritual ideal and is the 2 of Rods. The chap in the card holds a globe in his hand, reminding us that wholeness is going to be a major theme of this coming time—and that we are meant to *carry* the light, not just proclaim it. The two rods suggest the duality of right and wrong, with its heavy emphasis on moralistic thinking. This duality has characterized the era from which we are emerging. Now the emphasis will gradually shift to an awareness of wholeness.

We can see this theme emerging in world affairs. It is no longer a question of which side is right, whether we are talking about Ireland, Israel, Iran, or China. It is now a question of how does this affect the world as a whole? More and more, we are going to be looking for holistic answers to the problems of life.

There are five upright and five reversed cards. The upright cards point to elements of the New Age that are already partially revealed. The reversed ones indicate elements which are more obscure and will be emerging as the period develops.

It is interesting that the card of creative challenge is The World and the card of endowment is The Magician. We are jumping all around here and taking the cards out of order, but sometimes that's the best way to proceed. These cards are telling me that very little of the New Age is actually new. Look at the Tarot. The Tarot is considered to be a New Age phenomenon. But it has been around for at least 500 years, and the evidence suggests it is at least three or four thousand years old. So far in the New Age, just about the only thing that has happened has been to dredge up a lot of very old traditions and rehabilitate them. But it's going to take more than that to make a New Age. There is going to have to be a new revelation. We have to break through our limitations and explore new ground. This is what I am trying to do with the Tarot. We have to reinvent the Tarot, so that it is suitable for the New Age.

The Magician represents all these old traditions, some of which are as old as Atlantis. There is great validity in these traditions, but it is not enough just to exhume them. We must bring them up to date and make them suitable for the twenty-first century. This is the work portrayed by The World. The World is depicted as a ring. Esoterically, this is what is known as the "ring-pass-not"—the outer limits of our knowledge. Not only do we have to reactivate all these old traditions, but far more importantly we have to give them new life. This is what will actually usher in the New Age.

So much for an overview. Let's go back to the starting point and the Queen of Pentacles. She was the card of fulfillment in our question on pets; here she is again, but as the starting point. This is a fabulous looking lady with an expensive ermine cloak. She cradles the pentacle as though she is nourishing and protecting it. This card is telling us that in the New Age, we need to discover and demonstrate the interface between the physical plane and spirit. Form is meant to reveal the presence of spirit. We are not meant to reject form, but to embrace it and spiritualize it. The physical plane is not something to leave behind as fast as we can—to get off the wheel of rebirth and keep on flying, as it were. On the contrary— the physical plane may be imperfect, but it is the ideal stage for demonstrating the redeeming power of spirit. We are meant to bring the life of spirit into the physical plane and use it to spiritualize the material world. So we have this capacity to act in the physical plane while retaining our spiritual identity.

I am not just talking in terms of personal and spiritual growth, either. Anyone who thinks of the New Age just in spiritual terms is limiting it tremendously. If there is to be a New Age that means anything, it will have to produce a New Age in science, a New Age in technology, a New Age in business, a New Age in education, and a New Age in the whole of human life. We should therefore be looking for a rejuvenation and renewal of love and intelligence in all of these fields. One of the ways the presence of spirit is revealed on the physical plane is through technology and science, as we learn to work more skillfully and intelligently with the natural resources of our planet.

This applies to the individual as well as the whole of society. We should not be afraid to make our own life a revelation of the presence of spirit, by enriching our self-expression with a stronger presence of beauty, grace, abundance, poise, goodwill, and wisdom. I can hear everybody volunteering, "I'm willing to express more abundance!" [Laughter.] It's not quite that easy. The point I'm making is that there will have to be substantial reversals of attitude.

Let me give you one example. Over the last one hundred years in this country, our respect and admiration for people with talent, skill, and genius has gone downhill rapidly. It has been replaced by envy, jealousy, and scorn. When this country was founded two hundred years ago, a person who achieved success was highly respected and looked to for leadership. Now the climate has been completely reversed, to the point where if someone achieves success, it is assumed that he or she did so through criminal activity. Our attitudes have been polluted by envy, and this has made it very difficult for genius and hardworking effort to thrive, flourish, and develop. Have you seen the movie *Tucker?* It is a movie that should be shown to everybody. And if you don't understand it, the meaning should be explained to you. If the New Age is going to have any vitality and dynamism, it must start by cultivating a new respect for genius—a new respect for accomplishment and achievement. We have got to get to the point where it is no longer a black mark to be a success.

Part of the blame for this must be laid at the door of the so-called spiritually minded. They think they must reject the material life and everything in it, wear a hairshirt, and suffer as much as possible. But this is not spiritual. Spirit is constantly taking delight in life, enjoying it, and celebrating it. What did the father do when the prodigal son returned home? He threw a party! He celebrated life. Therefore, if you are going to be in harmony with spirit, the most basic sign of it should be the ability to enjoy life on the physical plane, regardless of what might be happening. You don't have to hide in the closet and come out of it only on Christmas and New

Year's. The Queen of Pentacles wears an ermine cloak. She is living life. We should too.

The counterpoint is the Knight of Swords. The key here is this little feather or knob on the top of his helmet. I guess that's an eye on top of it.

Rose: He's got his third eye in the wrong place. [Laughter.]

Carl: Very good. This represents the ability to operate intuitively at inner levels. In general, knights represent service. And since this is the Knight of Swords, we are clearly talking about spiritual service. So spiritual service is a very important key to the New Age. In the New Age, it is no longer enough just to be self-sufficient; we will be recognizing more and more our obligation to help all human beings and serve the divine plan.

The card of challenge is The World. And the part of the image I want to call your attention to is the woman in the center of the card. She is fully clothed. But in other Tarot decks, she is nude. Esoterically, a nude woman represents Truth. But in this case, the truth is veiled—veiled, indeed, by the fashions and ways of the world. This reminds us that we often do not have a full understanding of divine purpose in everything we do. We often take a very human perspective on issues and become very righteous about them, yet fail to see how much our thinking is colored by our time and age. And sometimes, we are just flat out wrong, when you compare human thinking to the divine plan.

A good example of this is our attitude toward nuclear energy. Most of the people in this country who consider themselves as progressive thinkers have come to the conclusion that nuclear energy is a very bad thing. This is largely because of the threat of nuclear devastation. Yet nuclear energy is something that mankind is meant to develop—this is part of the divine plan. It is not part of the divine plan that we should blow ourselves up, but it is part of the plan that we should develop and learn to use responsible applications of nuclear energy. So to take actions which seriously thwart this development is to oppose the divine plan. I am not criticizing anyone when I say this, because this is an emotionally-charged issue. Many good and sincere people have let their emotions on this issue color their mental and spiritual perceptions. It happens easily. My purpose is not to criticize, but just to demonstrate how easily the divine plan can be distorted in our thinking.

The lady of truth is naked. If we have the eyes to see, we can see her. But whenever we plug into the consensus of world opinion, we immediately start to put clothes on her. We end up thinking in terms of the current fashions and trends, not with wisdom and lucidity. If the New Age is going to be any different than all the other old ages, we will have to learn to do better. We must constantly push back the frontiers of our knowledge and broaden our understanding of life. We cannot afford to become provincial or parochial in our thinking.

One of the major goals of the New Age, therefore, is to become more planetary in our thinking—but from a divine, not a human, perspective. We must learn to think in terms of the role we are playing on behalf of all mankind. What does it mean to be a citizen of the universe? How does a citizen of the universe act? What does it mean to respect the other members of humanity? In other words, if you are leading a crusade for peace, is it all right to get publicity for your cause by stirring up the fear and guilt of the public? Or do you respect their individuality enough that you will refrain from adding to the burden of fear and guilt they already carry? These are the issues of the New Age.

The card of purpose is The Hanged Man. This card makes it pretty clear that one of the central goals of the New Age is to induce a total reversal of attitude, at least among thinking people, so that instead of believing that life derives from the physical plane and has developed by chance, we come to realize that the physical plane is

292

actually just the creative tip of divine life. And this reversal of understanding will bring many new perspectives on life. We will learn to draw our resources from the inner planes and to be guided, directed, motivated, and supported by the inner life. This is not just an eloquent statement to make and then forget. It is a principle that needs to be translated into a vivid, demonstrable fact of life.

One way this might happen is in our quest for alternate energy sources. Up until now, we have drawn our energy exclusively from physical sources. At some point in time, scientists will learn how to draw energy from the subtle dimensions of life. This will force a dramatic reversal of perspectives on life—a total upheaval of our way of thinking. This could happen in a few years—or may require hundreds or thousands of years. But once science learns to harness energy from the inner levels of life, it's going to be hard to pretend that there are no inner dimensions of life.

What I am suggesting is that we need to see spirit and the inner dimensions of life as a practical source of motivation and support. It's not just something to talk about in church groups or spiritual circles. It has a practical role to play in business, in government, in science, in technology, and in education. One of the primary goals of the New Age will be to reveal the actual presence of spirit in life and prove it.

The card of endowment is The Magician. The New Age has recognized the magic of ancient traditions and has brought them back to life. What we need now is an overhaul of these old traditions, so that we can begin to see science as a magician, education as a magician, and service as a magical transformation of life. We need to go beyond the superficial levels of magic and tap its real spiritual potential. There is also the thought here that humanity has been given the tools it needs to exercise spiritual dominion over the worlds of form. But we are not taking our mission here seriously. We are too busy seeking personal fulfillment and solving personal problems to perceive the reality of our potential as a magician—as an inspired agent of God. We must therefore learn to cultivate the impersonal life and pay more attention to our duties and obligations than we have.

The card of destiny is the 8 of Swords. In this context, this card is advising us that the average human being is not much of an individual at this stage of evolution. He is still very definitely ruled by fear and the confusion of mass consciousness. He is tied and blinded by society. For the New Age to flourish, each individual must be helped to discover the full potential of his individuality. The relevance of the individual in society is going to become more important. This is why I have stressed the theme of greater respect for genius and accomplishment. These are the hallmarks of individuality, and the true flowering of individuality will be one of the goals of the New Age.

It is interesting to note that these two cards—The Magician and the 8 of Swords—appeared in exactly the same positions in the spread on anger. But their meanings are entirely different in each layout. This is because the questions are fundamentally different. Much insight into the art of interpreting the Tarot can be gleaned by carefully studying the role these two cards play in each reading.

The real question is another eight—the 8 of Pentacles. This chap has his hammer and nails and he is building something. Constructive, productive activity is going to be one of the golden precepts of the New Age. Building new structures and new systems will be of great importance. But the open window to the inner planes reminds us that the new things we build need to be inspired by the divine plan. They need to express the life of spirit through their function.

The open window also powerfully suggests that the New Age will be a time for the externalization of the inner dimensions of humanity—what Alice Bailey refers to as the externalization of the

Hierarchy. The magician—the tested agent of God—will be focusing his or her efforts on bringing the inner principles of life into manifestation on the earth plane, in whatever field of endeavor he or she may be laboring. The real question, therefore, may well be: How do we externalize the good within us so that it becomes visible on the earth plane?

There's an interesting contrast between the 8 of Swords and the 8 of Pentacles. In the 8 of Swords, the person is blinded and gagged by fear and confusion, while in the 8 of Pentacles, he is expressing his creative potential under the guidance and inspiration of higher intelligence. Both of these contrasting themes will characterize the New Age.

The card of unseen forces is the Ace of Swords. This card re-emphasizes what we said in interpreting the Knight of Swords. We bring into the New Age thousands and thousands of years of ancient residue—the residue of selfishness, cruelty, and possessiveness. This is the ancient evil that humanity has not yet redeemed, and it is portrayed by the black and white boulder-like designs at the bottom of the card. These ancient patterns will shape the kinds of events and opportunities we will experience in the New Age. But they also strongly state that we will have to face them with more enlightenment, courage, and goodwill than we have in the past. This is our obligation to the New Age.

The card of the spiritual ideal is the 2 of Rods. This is a card of discernment—the ability to see the larger picture that unites the opposite extremes of any duality or issue. It implies that we must develop the mind to the point where we can understand this larger picture and think holistically. We also have to learn to work with new ideas in such a way that we do not fragment them or diminish the power of their impact.

The card of fulfillment is the 4 of Swords, which also appeared in our last question on pets. In this spread, it is emphasizing the fact that much of the New Age will simply be a revival of many themes and opportunities from humanity's past. These are issues we failed to deal with effectively before, but now we should be able to act with more awareness and spiritual guidance.

There will be new revelations—new revelations about the relationship between spirit and form, new revelations about life after death, and new revelations about tapping spiritual power and patterns. But these new revelations will not magically change our lives. We have an obligation to respond to these new revelations with a new and greater capacity for understanding and action.

There is an ongoing continuity in life. The New Age is not really all that dissimilar from the old age. It's an ongoing continuum. And we should be paying more attention to the continuity than to any sudden disruption that might abruptly change the nature of human life. Most of the old ways of doing things are not wrong; they are just incomplete. We very much need a new revelation and a new sense of direction—but at the same time, we should not overlook the possibility that the old revelations and the old sense of direction were not so far off the mark. It may well be that we are the ones who strayed off the mark, by not understanding the revelations that have been given us.

In other words, we will miss the new revelation just as we missed the old ones—or misinterpret it—unless we are ready and prepared to embrace it. Being ready is the great challenge of the New Age.

I will entertain questions and comments.

Jim: A number of the unknown goals seem to involve service.

Carl: A point I should make is that we have a strong tradition of service already established in the "old age." But we still have a long way to go before the traditions of service, philanthropy, and generosity are widely accepted as something normal and ordinary. They are still highly suspect, and generally distorted.

Rose: This looks like a badge or something on the shoulder of the person in the 2 of Rods.

Carl: Sure. Developing the mind so that it can distinguish one rod from the other one is not a major step forward. But if we develop the mind so that it is able to serve the needs for growth, that is significant. This badge is an emblem of growth, represented by the flowers.

Rose: When you were talking about updating old traditions, I should think that *Forces of the Zodiac* would be a good example of that.

Carl: I would like to think we were doing something valuable, yes.

Rose: Well, you didn't mention it.

Carl: I guess we can always use the plug. [Laughter.] I would like to think that *Active Meditation* represents an updating of the ancient traditions of meditation—and I hope *Exploring the Tarot* will do the same for the Tarot.

Nancy: It should. Each of these readings was so different, yet they all made sense.

Carl: I hope so! [Laughter.]

ABOUT THE AUTHOR

Carl Japikse is one of the leading authorities on the Tarot and archetypal forces in the United States today. He has been conducting classes on the development of the mind, meditation, intuition, and divination for more than ten years. With Dr. Robert R. Leichtman, he is one of the founders and principal officers of Light, a nonprofit charitable organization dedicated to promoting the right use of the mind and human creativity.

A graduate of Dartmouth College, Mr. Japikse worked for a number of newspapers, including *The Wall Street Journal,* before deciding to devote his full time to teaching and writing. His other books include *The Light Within Us, The Tao of Meow,* and *The Hour Glass,* as well as, in collaboration with Dr. Leichtman, *Active Meditation, Forces of the Zodiac, I Ching On Line, The Art of Living,* and *The Life of Spirit.*

Mr. Japikse is also the developer of the *Enlightened Management Seminar* and the *Enlightened Classeoom.*

ABOUT THE TAROT

Additional copies of *Exploring the Tarot* can be purchased at your favorite bookstore or ordered from Ariel Press, 14230 Phillips Circle, Alpharetta, GA 30201. Copies of the Aquarian Tarot deck can be purchased for $13. Tarot work sheets can be purchased in pads of 100 for $3 apiece. *The Tarot Tool Kit*— which contains the book, the Aquarian deck, and one pad of worksheets—can be bought for $27, postpaid. To order by telephone, dial toll free 1-800-336-7769. Prices are subject to change.

In Georgia, add 6% sales tax.